WORDS
FOR TODAY 1998

Notes for daily Bible reading

INTERNATIONAL BIBLE READING ASSOCIATION

Cover photograph – Delegate at the Women's Methodist
World Conference in Rio de Janeiro – Sarah Bruce
Editor – Maureen Edwards

Published by:
The International Bible Reading Association
1020 Bristol Road
Selly Oak
Birmingham
B29 6LB

Charity No 211542

ISBN 0-7197-0895-8
ISSN 0140-8275

Typeset by Avonset, Bath
Printed and bound in Great Britain by
Caledonian International Book Manufacturing Co.

CONTENTS

		Page
	Editorial	5
	Morning Prayers	7
	Evening Prayers	8
1.	**The Open Book**	
	Celebrate the stories – *Pauline Webb*	9
	Celebrate the poetry – *Clare Amos*	17
	Celebrate history – *Alec Gilmore*	24
	Celebrate God's love – *Gerard Hughes*	29
2.	Jesus – Man of mystery – **Mark 1-9** – *Brian Haymes*	36
3.	**LENT** – True fasting – *John Hastings*	50
4.	Christ our High Priest – **Hebrews** – *Burchel Taylor*	56
5.	Turning to the living God – *Bernard Thorogood*	66
6.	**PASSIONTIDE**	
	The Servant Lord – *Emmette Weir*	76
	The Son of Man is lifted up – *Penny Fowler*	82
7.	**EASTER** – He is risen indeed!	
	Seeing and believing – *Bao Jia yuan*	87
	Exploring truth – *Luis V Veagra*	93
	Responding to challenge – *Jil Brown*	98
8.	**Quality of life**	
	From here to eternity – *Ralph Lee*	103
	For all the world – *Hyacinth Sweeney*	109
	Becoming one in Christ – *Cindy O'Shea*	114
9.	**PENTECOST** –	
	Filled by the Holy Spirit – *Melvyn Matthews*	119
10.	**Personalities of the Bible**	
	Jeremiah – *Jonathan Magonet*	130
	Elijah **(1 Kings 17-21)** – *Albert Friedlander*	140
	Peter – *Eileen Jacob*	146
	Some other personalities – *Ebere Nze*	151
11.	Called to lead – *Donald Hilton*	157
12.	The power of prayer – *Sheila Cassidy*	167
13.	The Kingdom is for children – *Rosemary Wass*	179
14.	Making sense of life – **Proverbs** – *Joseph G Donders*	190
15.	Examine me, O God – *Philip Barker*	200
16.	Blessed are the poor? – *Magali do Nascimento Cunha*	211
17.	Human Rights – *Keith Johnson*	224

18. **God's Shalom**
    Healing minds and bodies – *Helen Richmond*   230
    Healing communities – *Stewart Morris*   235
    Healing nations – *Marcella Althaus-Reid*   240

19. Oneness in Christ – **Ephesians** – *Salvador Martinez*   247

20. Christ comes in the flesh – **1,2,3 John** – *Jan S Pickard*   257

21. **ADVENT and CHRISTMAS – When Christ comes**
    Awake! – *Edmund Banyard*   268
    What will endure? – *Desmond Gilliland*   274
    The way of obedience – *Jane Montenegro*   279
    Christ comes to save – *Peter Millar*   285

Acknowledgments and abbreviations

We are grateful for permission to quote from the following versions of the Bible:

AV   Extracts from the *Authorized Version* of the Bible *(The King James Bible)*, the rights in which are vested in the Crown, are reproduced by permission of the Crown's Patentee, Cambridge University Press.

GNB   *Good News Bible* (The Bible Societies/Collins Publishers) – Old Testament © American Bible Society 1976; New Testament © American Bible Society 1966, 1971, 1976

NEB   *New English Bible* © Oxford University and Cambridge University Presses 1961, 1970

NIV   Scripture quotations taken from *The Holy Bible, New International Version* © 1973, 1978, 1984 by International Bible Society. Used by permission of Hodder & Stoughton Limited. All rights reserved. 'NIV' is a registered trademark of International Bible Society. UK trademark number 1448790.

NJB   Taken from the *New Jerusalem Bible*, published and copyright 1985 by Darton, Longman and Todd Ltd and Doubleday & Co Inc, and used by permission of the publishers

NRSV *New Revised Standard Version* © 1989, Division of Christian Education of the National Council of Churches of Christ in the United States of America

REB   *Revised English Bible* © Oxford University and Cambridge University Presses 1989

*J   Readings from the Joint Liturgical Lectionary (JLG2)

*C   Readings from the Revised Common Lectionary

The Open Book

This year in England, Churches are getting together to encourage more people to read and study the Bible. This movement from *Churches Together* – called 'The Open Book' – is partly a response to the Pope's challenge to all Christians to prepare for the Millennium. Fully aware of our partnership with Churches in other parts of the world, it seeks 'to make the Bible culturally relevant to the different cultures in England'. The fact is that Churches in England, which have been strong missionary Churches in the last two or three centuries, are now sadly in need of mission here. It is not just that our membership is declining, but many of our members rarely read the Bible. What a contrast to those Chinese Christians who with tears of spiritual emotion received their first copies of the Bible (page 90) after the long years of the Cultural Revolution! And what a difference from 'prisoners of conscience' who tell us how, deprived of all books, they were sustained through long periods of solitary confinement by words of Prophets and Gospels which are deeply rooted in their memories, and which no one can take away from them!

How then can we begin to encourage more people to open the Bible and begin to enjoy it, and to discover words from the living God which speak directly to them? This is our challenge for 1998. All of us who are involved with IBRA believe that we have a significant role to play here, and hope that readers in other parts of the world will pray for us and also want to share the Bible with others. We offer the following suggestions.

Start a group

Latin American Basic Christian Communities show us how Christians and many on the fringe of the Church gather in small groups to reflect together on a story from the Bible, and then to discover from it how God is directing them to serve one another and act for justice in their local community. Could you start such a group? Or is there someone you know who might be encouraged to do so? The books of the Bible were first written for communities of Jews and Christians, and are probably best understood when we read them together in community.

Provide the right help

Not everyone is helped by the same Bible reading notes. IBRA offers four books:

Light for our Path (which includes a printed Bible passage for each day) is carefully designed for the young in faith, those who are reading English as a second language, and those who need a clear, straightforward approach.

Words for Today is more provocative, for the enquiring reader who wants to explore contemporary issues and questions of belief in the light of God's word.

Finding our Way Together, for leaders of house groups, offers a variety of ways to explore the themes used in *Light for our Path* and *Words for Today*. It can also be used in an undated way by groups who are not committed to our daily Bible reading scheme.

Sample material on **The Open Book** can be found on pages 297 – 304. You can use it at any time of the year with your own group.

Preachers' Handbook helps preachers to integrate in worship the themes and readings their congregation will have studied and reflected upon during the week.

What is special about IBRA?

We are international. We are refreshed and enriched when writers reflect the culture, theology and experience of their people. The Bible comes alive in new and exciting ways.

We use the Lectionaries. This year some themes are based on the Joint Liturgical Lectionary (JLG2), and others on the Revised Common Lectionary which is more widely used. This means that IBRA can be seen as an integral part of the Church's teaching and worship.

We explore both themes and books of the Bible. We believe there is still a value in making a systematic study of books – to look in greater depth at the text, the background, how they came to be written and their place in Holy Scripture.

We use different approaches to Bible study. We are, after all, different people approaching the Bible from our own background of culture, experience and education. Our needs are different. I hope that there is something here for everybody. Some writers begin with their own experience and then lead us into the text. Others begin with the text and then relate it to life. Some write more of contemporary events and experiences, while others concentrate on unravelling the text. There is much to learn from all of them as we prepare to enter the 21st century.

James Edwards

MORNING PRAYERS

O sweet and loving God,
When I stay asleep too long,
Oblivious to all your many blessings,
Then, please, wake me up,
And sing to me your joyful song.
It is a song without noise or notes.
It is a song of love beyond words,
Of faith beyond the power of human telling.
I can hear it in my soul,
When you awaken me to your presence.

Mechthild of Magdeburg (c.1210-c.1280)

Set aflame our hearts with love to thee, O Christ our God, that in that flame we may love thee with all our heart, with all our mind, with all our soul, and with all our strength, and our neighbours as ourselves, so that, keeping thy commandments, we may glorify thee, the giver of every good gift.

Orthodox Kontakion for love

Lord, your love encircles the world,
Embracing all creation and each of us.
May we in turn reach out in ever-increasing circles
Of loving prayer for those known and dear to us,
For those whose needs we know,
And for the countless millions who suffer today,
Their names and faces unknown to us,
But each known within the circle of your love.

Margaret James (UK)
From More Living Prayers for Today (IBRA)

Lord, whatever this day may bring,
Thy name be praised.

Dietrich Bonhoeffer, Germany
(Written while awaiting execution in a Nazi prison, 1944)

EVENING PRAYERS

O Lord, our palm trees can no longer
hide us from the world. Strengthen our hearts
that we may look with confidence to the future.

Prayer from Tahiti

O Jesus, King of the poor,
shield this night
those who are imprisoned without charge,
those who have 'disappeared'.
Cast a halo of your presence around those
who groan in sorrow or pain.

Protect those whose livelihoods are threatened.
Encourage those forbidden to worship.
Encompass your little ones
gone hungry to sleep,
cold and fitfully waking.
Guide your witnesses for peace.
Safeguard your workers for justice.

Encircle us with your power,
compass us with your grace,
embrace your dying ones,
support your weary ones,
calm your frightened ones –

and as the sun scatters the mist on the hills,
bring us to a new dawn,
when all shall freely
sit at table in your kingdom,
rejoicing in a God who saves them.

Kate McIlhagga (UK)

Lord, protect me from the perils of the night.
Keep me from thinking of the past day's troubles
and from worrying about what the future holds.
Let my mind not be unquiet, nor my tired body unrelaxed.
May my thoughts be for those whom I love
and if sleep does not come easily to me,
let me remember, however hard life seems,
that I am blessed. Amen

Nicola Lindsay, Ireland

THE OPEN BOOK –
Celebrate the stories

Notes based on the Revised English Bible by
Pauline Webb

Pauline Webb, a Methodist local preacher, is a broadcaster and writer on religious affairs. She chairs the Advisory Commission on Communication for the World Council of Churches, and locally is a member of a large, multi-racial church at Harlesden in North London, where she leads Bible study and trains lay preachers.

Story-telling has always been one of the most effective means of communication. St Paul, writing to the Christians in Corinth, uses a beautiful Greek word to describe one of the purposes of preaching. In 1 Corinthians 14.3, the word that is translated 'encourage' (RSV), or 'comfort' (AV) is *paramuthian*, which literally means telling a story. In classical Greek it is used to describe the way in which a parent comforts a child by telling a bedtime story. Fairy stories, myths, legends, tales of long ago are found in all cultures as a way of passing on important truths and traditions. The question to ask about a myth or a legend is not, 'Is it factually true?', but rather, 'What does it mean? What truth does it convey?' The Bible is full of stories, some historical, some legendary, some mythical, but all conveying profound truth about life.

Thursday January 1   *Genesis 2.4b-25*
'It begins with the tale of a garden'
This ancient, naïve story of the beginning of human life, much older than the priestly poem which celebrates Creation in Genesis 1, has come out of profound reflection upon human experience. The questions it addresses are not scientific or historical. They are questions about the nature of humanity and of divinity. As human beings we experience a sense of lost innocence and alienation from God. The story assures us that it was not ever thus. We inherited from our Creator a Paradise, where human beings are meant to live in harmony with the animal world and where men and women were created for partnership with one another. In such a state of innocence, there need be no

sense of guilt or shame. But what was so dangerous about that tree, which would give human beings the knowledge that properly belongs to God?

Reflect: Celebrate those experiences of life which are reflected in this story and which still seem to bring us glimpses of a lost Paradise: the astounding beauty and harmony of nature, the affinity we feel with the animal world, the ecstasy of sexual love, the joy of human relationships, the sense of God's presence in the early morning and the quiet of the evening.

✻ *Lord, you have made a beautiful world.*
 Forgive us for all that we do to spoil it. Amen

Friday January 2   *Genesis 12.1-9*
Leaving home

Moving house, it is said, is one of the greatest stress points in life. The story of Abram's journey from his settled home in Harran out into the desert towards Canaan prefigures the later journeys of Jacob and then Joshua. Each of their stories reminds us that the life of faith is never a static one. God continually calls us into new situations and new places. He has plans for our future that affect not only us, but all whose lives come into contact with ours. Every decision we make, about where we live, what work we do, which partner we choose, will have far-reaching effects. Wherever we go, our lives can bring blessing or curse to others, both now and for many generations to come. As we progress through the various stages of our lives, we too, like Abram need to make a time and a place for the worship of God.

✻ *Lord, we pray for all who this year*
 will be undertaking new journeys,
 moving to new homes,
 taking on new responsibilities.
 Give them your blessing
 so that they in their turn may be a blessing to others,
 and, wherever they go,
 may be aware of your presence with them. Amen

Saturday January 3   *Exodus 2.1-10*
The baby in the bulrushes

Like many early Hebrew stories, this one has parallels in the traditions of other cultures. A Mesopotamian legend told of how, after his secret birth, the monarch Sargon I was hidden by his mother in a little basket made of reeds, and cast out upon the river Euphrates. There he was found and adopted by a peasant and finally by the goddess Ishtar who made him a great and powerful king. There is a similar story in Egyptian legend of how the god Horus, son of the mother goddess Isis, was hidden as a baby among the reeds by the Nile and protected by his nurse from the wrath of his uncle Seth, god of famine and drought.

What is markedly different in the Hebrew story of Moses is the absence of any miraculous element. Here all the characters in the story are human beings. Notice that Moses owes his life to the compassion and cunning of women – his mother, his sister, the Egyptian slave girl and the princess. The agents of God's providence are often simple people who follow the dictates of their heart rather than the cold logic of the law.

✳ *Lord, we thank you for all women whose hearts*
have been moved with compassion to care for children
who have been abandoned,
abused or in any way endangered.
May they know that in receiving your little ones
they are serving your providential purpose. Amen

1st Sunday after Christmas, January 4   *2 Samuel 12.1-14*

You are the man!

This story comes from one of the oldest written records in the Bible. The so-called Court History of David was probably a contemporary record and, rather like modern journalistic accounts, does not shrink from exposing scandal in high places. The prophet Nathan uses the Hebrew tradition of telling a parable in order to force the king to pass judgement on his own adulterous relationship with Bathsheba, whose husband David has caused to be killed in battle. David's anger against the thief who has stolen a lamb is easily aroused. But the crunch comes with that ringing accusation, 'You are the man!' So often we can feel anger over stories we hear about others' wrongdoing, and are quick to condemn those whose scandalous behaviour hits the headlines, but how often is our anger a reflection of a sense of guilt for our own hidden sins?

✳ *Search me, O God, and know my heart; try me, and know*
my thoughts: and see if there be any wicked way in me,
and lead me in the way everlasting. Amen

Psalm 139.23 (AV)

The loyalty of love

We have become used in these days to what is sometimes described as 'faction', a dramatic story based on historical fact. Often such stories concern the lives of great figures of the past. They may not be strictly accurate in every detail but they illustrate aspects of a person's life which have come to have great significance. The story of Ruth would seem to be that kind of literature. It is in itself a dramatic tale, with complications of plot, intrigue, suspense and a happy ending. But the ending is the most important part historically, because it is a reminder that King David himself came from a lineage of mixed blood, with an ancestress who was renowned for her loyalty. The expression of Ruth's love for Naomi must be one of the most beautiful passages in Hebrew literature, bridging as it does the gulf between youth and age, and uniting two people of a different race and creed. Read again verses 16 and 17, and ponder in your mind to whom among your friends and companions you could say these words, and offer a special prayer for them.

✳ *Lord, I pray for all those to whom I am bound*
  by ties of kinship. Help me to remain faithful
  in my care for them even when times are hard
  and they grow old, and I am weary.

The visit of the magi

It is a pity that Matthew's account of the magi coming to pay homage to the infant Jesus has come to be regarded merely as a picturesque story for children to enact, rather than as the theological statement it was meant to be. It was a Jewish tradition to meditate on the Scriptures and then write stories about the present in terms borrowed from the past. Matthew, through the story of the magi, makes contemporary Isaiah's vision of the coming of the Gentiles and of foreign kings to pay homage to the Messiah (Isaiah 60.3). Matthew is concerned not simply to tell us where and when Jesus was born, but to point up the significance of his birth by describing events surrounding it in the light of the Hebrew Scriptures. Here is, as Hubert Richards puts it (in *The First Christmas*, published by Fontana, 1973), 'an evangelist asserting his faith, not writing a diary'. For Matthew, Jesus is indisputably 'king of the Jews', a royal title emphasized in the magis' question to King Herod, and acknowledged in the gifts offered to the infant, like those the Queen of Sheba had offered to King Solomon (1 Kings 10.10).

✳ *Lord, give me the eyes of faith that,*
clothed in the humility of a child,
I might see your majesty,
and grant me the wisdom to lay my best gifts at your feet,
in homage, worship and adoration. Amen

Wednesday January 7   *John 4.7-15*

Jesus crosses the boundary

At the end of John's Gospel, the evangelist writes that there were so many stories of Jesus to be told, that the whole world could not contain the books needed to record them. So the selection made by the Gospel writers must have been significant in the fullest sense of the word. John's Gospel stories always contain signs that point to the fuller meaning of Christ's coming. This story of Jesus' encounter with a Samaritan woman may well have been one of the treasured stories of the Samaritan community. The Gospel writer lays great emphasis on the traditional hostility between Jews and Samaritans. So it is all the more wonderful to note how Jesus deliberately crosses the boundary and seeks the woman's help. His approach to her is not patronizing nor self-conscious. He genuinely wants to engage her in dialogue. Try reading the dialogue as though it were between you and Jesus, beginning with his asking your help.

✳ *Lord, what could I ever possibly do for you?*
Help me to acknowledge my need of you,
and to learn from you a love that transcends
the barriers of culture and tradition,
as I share with others in the search
for the fullness of life you intend us all to enjoy.

Thursday January 8   *John 4.16-26*

Man and woman in conversation

There was an ancient tradition among the sages of Israel that said, 'He that talks much with womankind brings evil upon himself and neglects the study of the law and at the last will inherit Gehenna' (quoted by Kenneth Grayston in *Epworth Commentary on the Gospel of John*, 1990). Jesus here defies convention and talks pastorally with this woman, not only about her personal situation but about the weightier matters of theology, and the importance of understanding the true nature of worship. Again, he speaks without condescension, but with a sincere concern to communicate across the divide between the genders as well as between the races. To this woman he entrusts the revelation of his true being. I AM the one who shall come. In John's Gospel, three of the great revelations of Christ are made to women. To Martha he says, 'I am the Resurrection and the Life'. To Mary he grants his first resurrection appearance. And here, to a foreign woman, he reveals his Messianic vocation.

This year marks the end of an ecumenical decade which has stressed the importance of the community of women and men in the Church. It is only in a community which takes the insights and intuitions of both sexes with equal seriousness that we shall arrive at the fullness of God's truth.

✷ *God our Creator,*
 in whose image both male and female are made,
 teach us as men and women a mutual respect
 and a shared reverence, that our worship may reflect
 the wholeness of our lives together, through Christ
 our Lord.

Friday January 9   *John 4.27-42*

The ready harvest

John interrupts the story of the Samaritan woman in order to record a conversation between Jesus and his disciples which points up the significance of what has just taken place. Like many of us, the disciples are full of excuses for what would appear to be the failure of their mission. Like them we are tempted to say, 'The time is not ripe', or, 'There are too many other influences at work.' But Jesus, reflecting on his encounter with the foreigner, assures them that God is acting among people in more ways than they realize. When they faithfully do their work as his disciples, they will find a response in the most unlikely places.

The Samaritan woman herself becomes one of the most eager apostles of the gospel. Her testimony and the presence of Jesus among them convince all her neighbours that this man's coming has significance, not only for Jews but for the whole world. The title 'Saviour of the world' was one adopted by Roman emperors, but the Samaritans here claim it for Jesus himself.

✳ *Forgive me, Lord, when I become disheartened*
by what seems like a lack of response
to the ministry and mission of your Church.
Help me to look for signs of your presence in unlikely
*   places.*
Make me aware of the hunger for recognition,
for respect and for reverence among all people,
and help me to respond to that need,
through Jesus Christ our Lord. Amen

Saturday January 10   *Luke 10.25-37*

Pause for thought

As one who regularly has to write a radio script lasting not more than ninety seconds, I am lost in admiration of the story-telling gifts of Jesus. This, probably the best known of all parables, takes just one minute to tell. Yet it is full of character cameos, set against a scenic background, with dramatic incident. What is more, it packs its punch in the pay-off line! What a brilliant broadcaster Jesus would have made! The strength of such a parable is that it can be read from many points of view. Jesus begins by focusing our attention on the man in the ditch. In that way, our sympathy is immediately aroused. Then we see the priest and lawyer through that victim's eyes, not as law-abiding citizens conscientiously carrying out their duties, but as men failing to hear a cry of distress. We see the Samaritan not primarily as a foreigner but as a friend in need. The lawyer who asked Jesus the question that prompted this story wanted to know where the limits to the law of loving should be set. Jesus refuses to set any limits at all. Only when we can see the world through the eyes of its victims shall we fully understand what the 'undistinguishing' love of God means. Then those of us who hurry along life's high roads, bent on our appointed tasks, may well be given pause for thought.

✳ *Lord, help me to see in the man bleeding by the roadside*
the Christ whose blood was shed
so that we might all realize our common humanity.
Save me from setting limits to my loving,
and help me to look on life
through the eyes of victims of violence
whose suffering is too often ignored.
For Christ's sake. Amen

For further reflection or group discussion

● 'It's only a story.' Would such a comment about any of the passages you have read in this section devalue or enhance their significance in your eyes?

● What was your favourite 'Fairy tale' as a child? Why do you think it appealed to you so much?

● Why do you think Jesus chose the story-telling method so often? What skills do his parables reveal? What can we learn from them about good communication?

FOR ACTION

Take time to watch a play, film or soap-opera this week and ponder on the message it is communicating. Can you discern any 'gospel' in it? Try your own hand at telling a one-minute story that would give people 'pause for thought'.

THE OPEN BOOK –
Celebrate the poetry

Notes based on the Revised Standard Version by
Clare Amos

Clare Amos is editor of Partners in Learning, an educational programme for all age-groups in the Church.

Many, perhaps most, best-loved passages of the Bible, especially of the Old Testament, are poetry. Some may have been written 3000 years ago, but they touch us today with an assurance that enables us to make them our own.

As well as the Book of Psalms, much of the prophetic books and others, such as the Book of Job, are also poetry. That does not mean that the passages concerned 'rhyme' or have a fixed metre, though they use Hebrew sounds and word-play to help convey meaning – to an extent that can only be hinted at in our translations. The most noticeable feature of biblical poetry is the device known as 'parallelism' in which the second half of a verse, or a couplet, responds to the first half, either by emphasizing the first half, or by stating its consequence, or even expressing the opposite. It is an extraordinarily powerful and challenging form of speech, and one which subtly suggests that this present world and existence are not the only world and existence there are.

The American Old Testament scholar Walter Brueggemann in *Finally Comes the Poet: Daring Speech for Proclamation* has suggested that tyrants often find poetry 'dangerous' and seek where possible to silence the poet. But true poets refuse to be silenced and their powerful words echoing down the centuries will never connive with the *status quo*. We celebrate poetry not least because it makes a difference to human life and human society.

1st Sunday in Epiphany, January 11 · *Psalm 23*

The Lord is my shepherd

This best-loved Psalm, with its sense of calm and complete assurance in God's love, is cherished by many, especially by those whose acquaintance with organized religion is restricted to weddings and funerals. And this is a strength – not a criticism.

The specific context of the psalm, a pastoral scene of a shepherd and sheep on the steep hillsides and among the narrow valleys of Palestine, may be far removed from the world in which most of us live, but it speaks to the universal human desire for harmony, mercy, sufficiency and consolation, when faced with our mortality. And, in ways beyond our understanding, this psalm can lead 'sheep' who have wandered far away back nearer to the shepherd who was prepared to 'lay down his life' for the sheep. The psalm spins a web that somehow includes both Testaments and today within the beauty of its threads.

There is one final point: Psalm 23 comes directly after Psalm 22. That is probably no accident. Psalm 22 (spoken by Jesus on the cross) is one of the most anguished and powerful laments in the Old Testament. It begins in almost pitch darkness and desolation and marvellously works its way through to a vision of triumph and celebration. Perhaps it is only when we have truly prayed Psalm 22, and made it our own, that we can fully appreciate the awesome sense of trust that pervades the whole of the short psalm that follows it.

✳ *Be our strength in hours of weakness,*
    In our wanderings be our guide;
Through endeavour, failure, danger,
    Father, be thou at our side.

Love Maria Willis (1824-1908)

Monday January 12   Psalm 46

God is my refuge

Psalm 46 seems to be set in the midst of Jerusalem ('the city of God' verse 4), a Jerusalem that knows trouble and strife, as it has done through so many centuries. There are a number of links between Psalm 46 and the first part of the book of Isaiah. The original context of this psalm may well have been in those dark days when enemies besieged Jerusalem, and when Isaiah promised God's help and protection for the city against all odds. The liquidly, lovely reference (verse 4) to 'the river whose streams make glad the city of God' reminds us of Isaiah's demand that the people of Jerusalem should trust in 'the waters of Shiloah that flow softly' (Isaiah 8.6). In both texts the reference seems to be to the small spring (the Gihon) on which the water-supply and life of Jerusalem depended. Psalmist and prophet remind the people that the future of the city lay not in the elaborate water-systems that the kings of the day were anxious to construct, but rather in the miracle of God's love for, and abiding protection of his people and city. This link with Isaiah is reinforced by the refrain in Psalm 46.7 and 11. 'The Lord of hosts is with us'. The Hebrew word *Immanu* here, is strongly reminiscent of the figure of *Immanuel* ('God with us') promised in Isaiah 7.10-17.

As with Psalm 23, this psalm seems effortlessly to span both Testaments. Set in the context of a historical city and an actual time, it sets our eyes on the 'Jerusalem that is above' where God will dwell with his people (Revelation 21.3). It reminds us too that though we may not be sons and daughters of Jacob by race, we have become God's people and, if we are still and listen to his voice, we too have the promise of his protection.

✷ *Stay with us, O Lord, when we are swamped*
by weariness and seeming impossibilities.
Turn our faces gently towards you,
keep our hearts loving and our wills determined
to fight on to the end.   Mother Janet Stuart (1857-1914)

Tuesday January 13   *Psalm 103*

Psalm of praise

The glory of many of the psalms is in the multiplicity of layers which are interwoven. Psalm 103 is a good example. It moves back and forth between celebrating God as Creator of the heaven and earth, God as particular Protector of the whole people of Israel and God as Guardian and Father of each individual. Each facet of our relationship with God depends on the others. Because God is ruler of the heavens, we can be sure that he has the power to 'remove our transgressions from us' (verse 12). And though our days may be few in number, and we may feel a sense of insignificance within the infinite eternity and the cosmos, yet God's love and concern for us as individuals is witnessed to by his ongoing care and concern for his covenant relationship with the people of Israel. The psalm begins and ends with the individual – with you and me – our soul, our life is called upon to 'bless the Lord.' It seems to be saying that we are the climax of God's care and creation, more significant even than angels, hosts and works (verses 20-22).

Again, it is worth looking at the preceding psalm, Psalm 102, if you have time. The image of 'grass' – in the Middle East so short-lived – is found in both psalms, and helps to link them (see Psalm 103. 15). Yet Psalm 103 has moved on from Psalm 102 where the psalmist is uncertain as to what the future holds. Now he or she has been renewed and is finally able to see the pinprick of human life within the tapestry of eternity.

✳ *Because of our many sins,*
where shall we hide, O Lord?
In the heavens?
There resides your majesty and your glory!
In the bottom of the earth?
There your hand is all-powerful!
Even in the caves of the earth
your presence is all-pervading.
We rather come to you, O merciful Lord,
and hide in the palm of your hand,
for your love is immeasurable
and your tenderness without limit.

From the Byzantine Liturgy

Wednesday January 14   *Song of Solomon 2.3-15*

Song of love

This exuberant portrayal of the beauty and passion of human love stands out alongside the rigorous moral codes of the Old Testament, or the world-denying feel of parts of the New. It may only have made it into the 'canon' because someone, whether rabbis or Church Fathers, regarded it as an allegory of either God's relationship with the people of Israel or Christ's relationship with his Church. But it is here, and it serves to remind us that the love of another human being is not a hindrance to the love of God, but a sacramental means enabling us to love God better.

There is a lot of nonsense written about the Greek words for 'love' by some theologians. So often a sharp distinction is made between *eros* (secular human love, or erotic passion) and *agape* (Christian self-denying love). Such a distinction is simply wrong – and ultimately unhealthy. In the very ancient Greek translation of the Song of Songs – made well before the time of Jesus – the word used again and again for the lovers' emotion here is *agape* not *eros* (see e.g. 2.4). The desires and passions of human beings can be the gateway to the love of God.

In Christian history a link has sometimes been made between the Song of Songs and Mary Magdalene who met Jesus in a garden. The garden of the Song of Songs is a reminder that the history of God's dealings with human beings is indeed a love story. In one garden the love story went awry (Genesis 3) and in another it was repaired (John 20). The Song of Songs helps to remind us that it is by love that death is undone (see 8.6-7).

✳ *I tread on the grass where the dew lies deep*
While the air is clear and the world's asleep;
I tramp on the verge of an endless dawn –
for I am the Lord of the Morning,
Morning!
Darkness now has gone
And I am the Lord of the Morning.

From Enemy of Apathy – Wild Goose Songs Vol 2
Wild Goose Publications, 1988

Thursday January 15   *Job 19.21-27*

A shout of suffering

The problem of suffering, and particularly the suffering of innocent people, is an issue to which there is no easy answer. It is a challenge to faith that understandably defeats many. It is a mistake to say that the book of Job provides an answer to the problem of suffering. It doesn't. It provides three answers (one given by each of Job's 'friends'), but then knocks down each of the answers in turn as inadequate. The book never gives a complete 'answer' (can there be one?). Instead it leaves us with Job's questions, and herein lies its power and integrity. Instead of an answer, it offers us a relationship.

In today's reading, Job has virtually reached the *nadir* of his suffering. Both God and his 'friends' have become his enemies. It is almost worse than the feeling of being totally abandoned by God, expressed so powerfully by the author of Psalm 22.

It is difficult to read this passage without remembering the cadences of Handel's *Messiah*, and the Hebrew itself is difficult and ambiguous. In verses 25-26 we cannot be sure that Job is pledging faith in a life after death when wrongs will be righted and sufferings undone (indeed most Old Testament scholars deny this possibility). But we glimpse Job's sense that he will not be alone, whatever befalls him. There will be someone alongside him. The Hebrew *Go-el* is hard to translate, but 'Advocate' or 'Redeemer' gives some sense of what it may mean. Christians have traditionally understood this figure to be incarnated in the person of Christ. That may be so, but the book of Job itself tells us something important. After Job has continued to suffer and complain more, God responds to him 'out of the whirlwind' (chapter 38). The words of God there are not an answer, but emphasize the difference between God and human beings, and the limitations of human knowledge. They make clear that God hears human beings and enters into dialogue with them. God is not hidden or distant. The road to the Redeemer is begun.

✳ *Sing, my soul, when light seems darkest,*
Sing when night refuses rest,
Sing though death should mock the future:
What's to come by God is blessed.

> *From Enemy of Apathy – Wild Goose Songs Vol 2*
> *by John L. Bell and Graham Maule*
> *(Wild Goose Publications, 1988'*

Magnificat

We stake our lives on poems such as this. For whatever else the Magnificat may be, it is surely a song of revolution, a poem of a world transformed, of rich become poor, of down become up. This is a poem where the force of Hebrew parallelism, of opposites flung jaggedly together, can be powerfully felt.

Those who feel the need of liberation, whether they live in Africa, South America, or a British council flat, have long owned this poem and wanted to make it their own. Somebody has said that in the Bible the connection between God and economics is a bold and persistent one, because the Bible knows that economics is one of the two spheres in which we live our lives. So it is appropriate, as Mary sings of God identifying with humanity in the flesh of her baby, that material even more than spiritual realities form the substance of her song. And it is not an accident that Mary – and we – need poetry to help us in this task. For though we can be sure that God's way must be an alternative one to the fashion in which life is lived at the moment, we do not know enough to offer a detailed blue-print. The metaphors and images of poetry must provide our way forward.

✳ *(God) calls us to revolt and fight*
with him for what is just and right,
to live and sing Magnificat
in crowded street and council flat.

> *Fred Kaan From The Hymn Texts of Fred Kaan*
> © *Stainer & Bell*

Beatitudes

Jesus often delivered his teaching in words of poetry and rhythm: the Lord's Prayer has a dynamic poetic form to it in the original Aramaic. So also with the Beatitudes: when we read them, we feel they are for declamation, not for silent reading; they are a set piece, not in an artificial sense, but rather a proclamation of the values of the Kingdom in a way that is already changing the world through the intense purpose, the glory, of the one who is bearing the message. For this reason, the Beatitudes are often sung before other lessons from Scripture in the worship of Eastern Orthodox Churches, for to sing the Beatitudes is to 'sing in the Kingdom ...' The Beatitudes hold before our eyes a vision which seems almost impossible to live up to, and yet a vision upon which we instinctively know the health and salvation of the world depends.

Let their familiarity not cast a veil over our minds; they are, like the Magnificat, nothing less than a turning upside down of the way human society likes to organize itself. Without these words, we would not have had a Francis of Assisi, nor the monastic movement – but neither yet the challenge in our own hearts at the beginning of each day to live the Kingdom with all the passion of which we are capable.

✳ *O Thou who camest from above*
     the pure celestial fire to impart,
  kindle a flame of sacred love
     on the mean altar of my heart!

Charles Wesley (1707-88)

For further reflection or group discussion

Apparently the Magnificat (Luke 1.46-55) was banned by the dictator Pinochet when he was in power in Chile. It was regarded as subversive literature. Can you work out why Pinochet feared these words? What other parts of our Bible do you think dictators might like to ban?

FOR ACTION

Make a list of five things that you would like to change in your society in the place where you live. Start working out how to go about changing one of these.

THE OPEN BOOK –
Celebrate history

Notes based on the New Revised Standard Version by
Alec Gilmore

Alec Gilmore is a Baptist minister with 20 years' experience in pastorates in Northampton and West Worthing followed by a literature ministry as Director of Feed the Minds. He is a freelance writer and the ideas and approach similar to those in these notes are more fully developed in his recent book, Preaching as Theatre (SCM). He also lectures on the Old Testament in the Universities of Sussex and Brighton.

After watching Arthur Miller's *Death of a Salesman*, David Mamet told Miller he felt as if he had been watching his own story – 'that you had written the story of my father and me – don't you think that strange?' Miller said not at all. He had heard it too many times before. Audiences in China said the same. 'That was our story and we did not know until we heard it.' Similarly, we best celebrate history in the *Open Book*, not by trying to learn or understand and then copy, but simply by discovering that 'this is our story'. That is what we will try to do in these readings.

2nd Sunday in Epiphany, January 18   *Exodus 14.10-31*

Between a rock and a hard place

On the surface it was mad! And the reaction of Moses (verse 14) insensitive. These people had never had an easy life. Slavery is no joke whether you are on a galley-ship, a dog's body where you work, the 'victim' in an unsatisfactory relationship or a member of a group with no social standing. This is the story of too many people. When the enemy is taking a beating (as with the plagues) there is a glimmer of hope. But too often change is not even on the horizon. Then it comes. The break. They are free ... until the enemy changes his mind and comes after them! And there they are – in the wilderness, with the sea in front and the enemy behind. No escape. So it was all a dream!

If this is your story, 'sit tight' says Moses and wait for God to open a way. He may not, of course; he never had before. But this time could be different. And at least it gives hope and it is better than doing something stupid.

✳ *Dear Lord, when this is my story,*
help me to sense your presence and wait your time.
And when you tell me to 'go for it'
give me courage and strength.

Monday January 19   *2 Samuel 5.1-12*

Image and reality

We have moved on nearly 400 years since yesterday. Wanderings in the wilderness are over. Sometimes God has divided seas and opened doors. Sometimes he has left them 'sitting tight'. But these slaves have become 'a people ... a community.' They are now in a position to achieve change more gradually but two tensions remain.

First, the leader. They all know it is Saul. They also know that David is actually running the show. Saul epitomizes a world that no longer exists. Some of them never even knew it. David symbolizes a world they know and want. Time to stop playing games and live in the real world.

Second, the place. Hebron is all right but it is too tied to the past. A new leader needs a new home, a new capital, a new place on the ground. It isn't easy. Jerusalem resists it no less than Hebron, but vision, determination and persistence pay off. And fortunately David is big enough to admit that none of it was his achievement nor for his benefit (verse 12).

✳ *Father, when the opening comes and the new day dawns,*
may I always give glory to you and then receive your gift
as something for the benefit of others.

Tuesday January 20   *1 Kings 6.1-14*

Reality or sham?

Living contentedly in a house which had taken 13 years to build, no wonder Solomon felt a twinge of inherited guilt about the 'house' for the Ark of the Covenant (2 Samuel 7.2), and perhaps also because both he and his father seem only to have got round to thinking about it when they had nothing else to do (2 Samuel 7.1; 1 Kings 5.4). A more charitable explanation is that they could hardly undertake such projects and fight off their enemies at the same time, and at least when the opportunity came, Solomon seized it with both hands. This temple was to be his flagship. Raw materials only of the best, and the inside no less impressive than the outside. But there is no dodging the question as to why Solomon did it and whether it was appropriate. And the rub comes in verse 12. All very fine! But what Yahweh wants is not landmarks with plaques, presents gift-wrapped, or luxury cards at Christmas or on birthdays. He first wants us to be quietly faithful to his will, every day.

✴ *Father, when I am tempted to do the big thing,*
  check me to see why I am doing it –
  and whether the rest of my life measures up to it.

Wednesday January 21   *Isaiah 9.2-7*

Special or ordinary?

When you are in a tight corner the possibility of a surprise, a windfall, or a sudden change of circumstances can transform life. So here we have a people looking for change, but missing out at two points.

First, the agent of change is as ordinary and 'everyday' as the birth of a baby. The great moments of history are not always the dates, nor even the battles, and certainly not necessarily the victories. Too many have been won or lost as a result of a set of quite ordinary and otherwise insignificant events. In the same way some of the most important turning points in our lives often depend on something in itself quite trivial.

Second, the agent of change is not necessarily something in the future. It is just as likely a recognition of something that has happened already. Notice how the prophet points to a baby that 'has been born' (NRSV) and its significance had eluded them until the prophet drew attention to it. So often our future depends on a recognition of the source of our strength and deliverance in the present, rather than waiting and hoping for something to happen!

✴ *Lord, help me today not to miss the very simple things*
  on which all my future depends.

Thursday January 22   *Ezra 1.1 to 2.1*

A fresh start

An experience, different but similar to that of the slaves in Egypt. The slaves had never had anything and were seeking to establish themselves. These people had spent nearly 1,000 years establishing themselves – they had come from nothing, wandered in the wilderness, created a community, anointed a king, established a capital and built an army. Then, at a stroke, they lost the lot when they went into exile.

Then came the chance to begin again. The opportunity came from an unexpected quarter (Cyrus, king of Persia) and entirely independent of their own efforts. All they had was a readiness to seize the opportunity when it came, and off they went.

Then the problem. Were they to re-build everything they had lost, or did they know what to hold on to from the past and what to let go so as to build a new future? One part of Warsaw today is an incredibly accurate reconstruction of the city as it was before the Second World War; another part, the site of the Jewish ghetto, has been completely demolished and a memorial put up in its place.

✻ *Father, when I celebrate 'my story',*
   teach me what to throw away and what to keep.

Friday January 23   *John 1.1-14*

The missing link

The *Logos* (Word) was at the heart of Greek philosophy. Then one day, through increasing contact between Christians and Greeks, someone suddenly realized that the *Logos* is God, and John makes it the opening section of his Gospel. Try reading it with the Greek emphasis. Not 'the Word *was* God' but 'the Word was *God*'. It is like a person suddenly 'seeing' an ornament or picture they have 'looked at' for years – perhaps one day the sun fell on it differently, or a stranger to the house commented on it, and all at once something familiar became a means of revelation.

The presence of God is never fully real as long as it remains something out there to be grasped, but rather when we perceive it, respond to it and make it our own. For some Greek Christians it was the *Logos.* For Simeon in the Temple (Luke 2.25-35) it was the baby he had been waiting for. And for us, the incarnation may not be believing that God came in flesh but learning to recognize him and respond.

✻ *Dear Jesus, whether you be a baby, poor and weak,*
   belief, painting, picture, music, person,
   friend or neighbour –
   may I never miss you when you come into my life.

Peace and food

Imagine a people settled in a country close on 500 years, very dependent on the land, most of which is sterile. In that time many changes had taken place and some people had been more fortunate than others, but overall as some families had gone steadily up, others had gone steadily down.

Micah knew better than most the sufferings of the people, the fears they had to live with and what it was like to have no roof over your head (verse 4). He knew the price of conflict and appreciated the dreams of people who longed for things to be different. Hence his plea for 'swords into ploughshares and spears into pruning hooks'. But what is his priority? To eliminate armaments? Or to manufacture agricultural implements? Mosala, writing about Micah from South Africa, suggests it is ploughshares and pruning hooks! What makes people poor is conflict. What makes people rich is food production. Getting rid of your weapons is not enough! A sound food supply and a good economy is better, and if you have to get rid of your swords and spears to do it, so much the better.

✷ *O Lord, help me always to be so hopeful,*
imaginative and practical – and all at the same time.

For further reflection or group discussion

- Choose one or two experiences explored in these readings which seem to be 'your story' and reflect on them.
- To what extent are you living in two worlds – the 'shell' of one which has passed away and the 'embryo' of another struggling to be born? What is needed to enable you to move more fully into the present?
- Identify one or two personal experiences where great changes have turned on small events and then pursue a more specific search for events (possibly in the local church or community) which may have more significance than you realized. Use the Isaiah reading and try to identify a few 'babies'.

FOR ACTION

Choose one or two celebrations, special events, festivals in your family. Make a list of what you do to celebrate them. Separate the lists into those things which are a genuine expression of the event, those which have simply become tradition, and those which actually get in the way. Try discussing it with someone.

THE OPEN BOOK –
Celebrate God's love

Notes based on the New Jerusalem Bible by
Gerard W Hughes

Gerard W Hughes, a Jesuit priest based in Birmingham (UK), works ecumenically on spirituality, with a particular interest in people who are active in some form of justice/peace work. He is author of In Search of a Way, God of Surprises, Walk to Jerusalem and God Where Are You? (Darton Longman and Todd), and also of O God, Why (Bible Reading Fellowship).

We read the Scripture in order to recognize the reality of God's loving presence in and around us now. The God of Abraham, Isaac, Jacob, and the Father of our Lord Jesus Christ is the God who is now holding you in being as you read these words.

3rd Sunday in Epiphany, January 25   Hosea 11.1-4, 8-9
Father love

'When Israel was a child ... I was leading them ... with leading strings of love ... I am the Holy One in your midst, and I shall not come to you in anger.'

Hosea sees God as the tender father, 'I was like someone lifting an infant to his cheek' (verse 4). In the rest of his prophecy Hosea sees God as the faithful husband who never ceases to love Israel, his unfaithful wife. The most striking characteristic of God in Scripture is God's love and compassion for all creation. The book of Wisdom says of God:–

'You are merciful to all, because you are almighty,
you overlook people's sins, so that they can repent.
Yes, you love everything that exists,
and nothing that you have made disgusts you ...
No, you spare all, since all is yours, Lord, lover of life!
For your imperishable spirit is in everything!
(Wisdom 11.24-12.1)

To know God's love for us is the most precious knowledge we can have, and to let the love of God flow through us to others is the greatest happiness. It all sounds so easy and simple, so why are we not all one big happy family on this planet, free of fear of one another? The love of God remains in our heads and on our lips, but we do not allow it to travel down to our hearts and guts, for the journey is too painful and costly. We focus our attention on the cost, not on the treasure which is offered.

✳ *God, I beg you, show me your attractiveness*
so that my heart stops counting the cost of your love,
and my life becomes a channel of your goodness to me
and to all those I meet.

Monday January 26   *Isaiah 49.13-16*

Mother love

'Can a woman forget her baby at the breast,
feel no pity for the child she has borne?
Even if these were to forget,
I shall not forget you' (verses 14-15).

Isaiah sees God as cherishing mother, always faithful. 'I have engraved you on the palms of my hands', so that we are now inseparable. St Augustine described God as *intimior intimo meo*, 'closer to me than I am to myself'. To allow these words to move from our heads to our hearts we need to give them our attention. 'Be still and know that I am God'. It is difficult enough to be physically still. It is even more difficult to still our minds.

Here is a very simple exercise: sit on a chair, your back reasonably straight, but not rigid, your body relaxed. Focus all your attention on what you can feel in your body. Start with your right foot, then travel round the body slowly, feeling, not thinking. All kinds of thoughts and questions may start occurring to you. Acknowledge the presence of these thoughts or of any other distraction, but without pursuing them, and then return to feeling.

When you feel more still, listen to whatever words or phrases in this passage from Isaiah attract you. Hear the words now being spoken by God within you. Having listened, then have a conversation with God. Be as honest as you can, and don't be afraid of expressing disbelief or anger. God is big enough to take our tantrums and God is in truth.

✳ *Rid me of my fears*
and of all those certainties which make me deaf to you,
for you loved me before the foundation of the world.

Liberating love

'For God sent his Son into the world
not to judge the world,
but so that through him
the world might be saved' (verse 17).

This is the good news! Our ability to turn it into bad and threatening news is astonishing. Why is this?

Sin is not letting God be God. We all tend to create God in our own image and likeness, so that our enemies become God's enemies and our ways become God's ways. It then becomes God's will that we should condemn, oppress, and even kill those who are opposed to our interests. We build up our own securities against others, then pray to God to keep us safe within those securities, so our religion becomes a way of controlling our lives to our individual, group, or national advantage. The ancient Roman Emperors controlled their subjects by giving them bread, entertaining circuses, and then, to exercise complete control, they called themselves divine. In the desert, Jesus was tempted to turn the stones into bread, to leap down from the Temple – like a circus entertainment – and finally to take over control of all the kingdoms of the world. He rejected all these because they are contrary to God's will, and chose the way of powerlessness.

God, in Jesus, entered our world, not to control or condemn, but to save it. In Jesus God was the powerless one, the rejected one, the victim of those authorities, both religious and secular, who were struggling to retain their own security in the name of God, law and order, but he is risen again! God, in Jesus, enters our human divisions, our sinfulness, our death, not to condemn, but to save us. To begin to appreciate such gratuitous goodness we have to beg God to enable us to let go of those securities which keep us divided from one another and from our true selves.

✳ *Lord, teach me so to trust in you*
  my rock, my refuge, my strength
  that my fears no longer blind me
  and I may know the joy of your presence.

Self-giving love

'For I am certain of this: neither death nor life, nor angels, nor principalities, nothing already in existence and nothing still to come, nor any power, nor the heights nor the depths, nor any created thing whatever, will be able to come between us and the love of God, known to us in Christ Jesus our Lord' (verses 38-39).

Jesus is the image of the God we cannot see. On the night before his death, he summed up the whole meaning of his existence in a symbol. He took bread, blessed and broke it, then gave it to his disciples saying, 'This is myself given for you. Do this in my memory.' Whenever we celebrate the Eucharist, we are reminding ourselves that this is the nature of God, not just at the Eucharist, but at all times and in all places, in all our moods and feelings, in our sadness and in our joy. God's love is the heart of the universe, power of all our power. St Paul has discovered this, delights in it, and nothing can rob him of this certainty, even though he may feel troubled or worried, be persecuted, threatened or attacked, or be without food and clothing.

'Do this in my memory.' This does not simply mean 'Repeat this ritual': it means that this self-giving of God is to become the pattern of our lives, too, not protecting ourselves, our group, our nation against all-comers, but being open to them (see Matthew 5.44-45). This self-giving of God is the good news, but we need to beg God to open our minds and enlarge our hearts so that we can receive it, as St Paul did, transforming our lives from lives of self-protection to lives of self-giving.

✳ *Come, Spirit of God, hover over the chaos of my life and transform it.*
Batter down the defences of my self-constructed prison and release me into the freedom of your self-giving.

Thursday January 29   *Deuteronomy 6.4-9*
Longing for the God of love
'Listen, Israel: Yahweh our God is the one, the only Yahweh. You must love Yahweh your God with all your heart, with all your soul, with all your strength' (verses 4-5).

We cannot love on command. So how can we love God with all our heart and mind and strength? St Augustine, looking back on his life, wrote, 'Lord, you have created me for yourself, and my heart is restless until it rests in you.' We cannot be coerced into loving God, but we can be told to listen to our own heart and discover its longings.

To discover your heart's longings, here is an exercise: write your own obituary, the one which, in your wildest dreams, you would love to receive, not allowing reality to limit you in the slightest! You may find this difficult and keep wanting to change the obituary. This is a good sign, for it means you are discovering layer upon layer of desires within you. Our deepest desires are often the most hidden, even from ourselves: our more superficial desires are usually the noisiest.

Would you like to be known as a person of utterly transparent honesty, generous, compassionate, courageous, welcoming to all who come your way, capable of true friendship, tolerant, forgiving, and genuine in your love? This is your heart's longing for God, who is love. Give attention to this longing and pray that it deepens in you, so that it becomes the longing of your life, influencing every decision and every action.

✴ *Why so downcast, my soul, why do you sigh within me?*
Let me put all my hope in you, my God, my Saviour.

Friday January 30   *Mark 12.28-34*

The test of our love for God

One of the scribes asks Jesus, 'Which is the first of all the commandments?' Jesus answers by quoting yesterday's text from Deuteronomy, and then adds, 'The second is this: *You must love your neighbour as yourself*. There is no commandment greater than these' (verse 31).

How can we know whether our love of God is genuine or not? The test is in how we relate to others – any other – not just our own immediate circle, for God not only loves every human being: God has identified Godself with each one. When Jesus appeared to Paul on the road to Damascus, he did not say, 'Why do you persecute those I love?' but, 'Why do you persecute me?'

When Jesus describes the Final Judgement, he makes no explicit mention of religion. We are to be judged by the way we relate to any other. 'I was hungry, and you gave me food. I was thirsty and you gave me drink ... In truth I tell you, in so far as you did this to one of the least of these, you did it to me' (Matthew 25.31-40).

We may wish God had arranged things otherwise, allowing us to have a beautiful relationship with God, while leaving us free to deal with our impossible neighbours as our feelings dictate! The test of our love of God is in the way we deal with our most difficult

33

neighbours. What an impossible ideal! It is impossible for us, but not for God at work within us. So we have to beg God to pray and work within us. If we can do so, we shall discover that our impossible neighbour has become an invaluable gift to us.

✳ *Lord, help me to recognize that you and my neighbour
    are one,
    that my neighbour's defects are also mine,
    and that your love and forgiveness embrace us both.*

Saturday January 31   1 Corinthians 13.1-13

Let God's love flow through you

This is a most beautiful description of love, but it can throw us into the depths of despair if, in light of it, we start looking closely at our own behaviour. Do we never take offence, are we never resentful, do we always delight in the truth, even when it includes the truth of our own stupidities and defects?

Jesus said to the rich young man, who had addressed him as 'Good master', 'Why do you call me good? No one is good but God alone', and no one can love with complete selflessness but God. It is important, therefore, that we focus our attention on God's love, rather than on our own attempts to love, so that we can learn to let God love through us.

How are we to focus on God's love so that we can begin to experience it as a reality, rather than assent to it as an abstract ideal? God's love is the reality in which we live, move, and have our being. St Paul was aware of this love even when he was troubled, worried, being persecuted, without food or clothing.

Most of us cannot share this depth of awareness, but we can start to deepen our awareness by this simple exercise: at the end of each day, let the day play back to you. Do not judge yourself, approve or disapprove: just look at those moments of the day which you enjoyed. Relish them. They are gifts from God; not rewards for your virtue, but tokens of God's love for you. If you do this regularly, your perception of reality will change and, like St Paul, you will begin to know this love even in adversity.

✳ *May your love catch fire in me,
    burning away my conceit and jealousies,
    my resentments and small-mindedness,
    so that I can delight in truth,
    never condemn, but always encourage.*

For further reflection and ACTION

Find a phrase, word, or image which appeals to you from each day's reading. Hear it spoken to you now and talk to God about it, as simply and as honestly as you can. God will do the rest! For more discussion material – to use with your house group – turn to pages 297 – 304.

JESUS – MAN OF MYSTERY
Gospel of Mark 1-9

Notes based on the New Revised Standard Version by
Brian Haymes

Brian Haymes, Principal of Bristol Baptist College, is author of the 'Looking At' series published by IBRA. He is a former President of the Baptist Union of Great Britain.

There is a mystery about Jesus of Nazareth. Who is this man who performs such miracles, who teaches with obvious authority, who forgives sins, who stills storms on lakes, who casts out demons? How are we to understand him and his message of the Kingdom of God? And why does Mark seem at times to insist on secrecy about him, as if there are some things that cannot be told? Why does Jesus teach in parables whose meaning seems full of surprises? And how does he come to have such significance today?

Mark sets out to tell the 'good news of the gospel of Jesus Christ' (1.1). He also writes to help us follow this man of mystery.

4th Sunday in Epiphany, February 1   Mark 1.9-13
A means of identity

Growing up is a matter of discovering our true identity. We are our parents' child but, as we grow into teenage years, we try to discover who we are in our own right. It can be a difficult journey, for teenagers and parents alike! And it does not end, because we are always discovering who we are all through life.

Here, at his baptism, Jesus' true identity is proclaimed, not publicly but to Jesus himself. He is God's Son. Our baptism declares our identity too. We are God's children. But Jesus is special.

An Old Testament prophet once cried out for God to 'tear open the heavens and come down' (Isaiah 64.1). At Jesus' baptism the heavens are ripped open and the Spirit descends. Towards the end of Mark's Gospel he will tell us that at the death of Jesus the curtain in the Temple is also ripped apart (15.38). The centurion at the cross sees the truth. He proclaims Jesus the Son of God. So the truth becomes public but only by way of the cross. Can it

36

be that Jesus is the Son of God because of the cross and not in spite of it?

✳ *Jesus, Son of God, Saviour, have mercy upon us.*

Monday February 2   Mark 1.21-28
Authority
There is all the difference in the world between the teacher who is for ever quoting other people and the one who obviously knows what she is talking about. It is the difference between being erudite and having authority. An important task of a rabbi's disciples was to quote exactly what their teacher said. But Jesus is no one's follower and he speaks directly. We are all led to ask, where does he get this teaching from?

Genuine authority never has to pull rank and appeal to status. We recognize the real thing when we see and hear it. Authority has its own power. The outward trappings of power often disguise the fact that human beings making the claim to authority do not have it. Notice the way that dictators are so conscious of the trappings of dress and status. Jesus did not claim authority. Neither did he seek the status symbols of the powerful.

Mark presses the question on the readers. He tells of the troubled man who said Jesus was the Holy One of God. What do we say of Jesus who spoke and acted in the way he did?

✳ *Lord, may we recognize your authority*
   and experience the power of your words.

Tuesday February 3   Mark 1.29-45 *J
Angry enough to heal
The fame of Jesus grows as he heals increasing numbers of people. Jesus himself does not seem too impressed by that. He moves on, not staying to exploit his new popularity. He is not a faith healer, running his own show. He is the servant of God who has the good news of the Kingdom to tell and perform.

The story of the healing of the man with leprosy prompts two reflections. First, Jesus touched the man. By all the standards of the day this was an amazing thing to do. It broke all conventions. He touched the unlovely and discarded, but seemed to do it naturally. It was at once both daring and surprisingly lovely. God is like that.

Then, verse 41. The translations are different. Some say Jesus was moved with 'pity', others with 'anger' or 'indignation'. Are they so different? Jesus sees this man with leprosy. He is affronted by this disease that opposes the Kingdom of God. His healing is both compassionate and passionate! Why do pain and suffering move us to pity but seldom to that anger that does something about it?

✳ *Lord, awaken in us the compassion and passion of Jesus.*

Wednesday February 4   Mark 2.1-12

Forgiveness and healing

This story is a moment of transition in Mark's Gospel. Thus far we have seen Jesus healing. The following verses will describe Jesus in confrontational situations. This story is both: a healing and an argument.

The persistence of the four friends is noteworthy. They will not be put off. They will get their friend to Jesus somehow, even if they have to raise the roof.

Both healing and forgiveness are given by Jesus. The story affirms both God's power to heal and Jesus' authority to forgive sins. That authority belongs to God but here it is exercised by Jesus, and the fact that the paralyzed man gets up and walks is there for all to see. Again we find ourselves asking, who is this Jesus? No one doubts his down-to-earth humanity. And yet he does what belongs to God. His opponents protest, as we might do if anyone began to take divine airs to himself. But the paralyzed man is healed! Who has done this?

With whom do you identify in this story? The person in need of healing? The four friends? Those who are offended when their religious rules are broken? Or those who are still amazed at what Jesus does?

✳ *Lord, heal and forgive,*
and confront our limited vision with your limitless love.

Thursday February 5   Mark 2.13-17

Grace at meals

Choose your friends carefully. Bad company can lead you astray. This is the kind of good advice we give to young people. 'Bad company ruins good morals' (1 Corinthians 15.33).

It is no wonder then that religious people take care about their behaviour. The trouble is that this can lead to social snobbery and religious self-righteousness. We imagine we are so much better than these others. In fact, we may be. Our lives may have a moral quality that is superior to those who are careless about ethical standards. But what follows from this? If we are so proud about ourselves that we look down on others, then we are going to find the picture of Jesus presented in this story difficult.

There is little doubt that Jesus mixed with all comers, even those who were morally and religiously wrong. But this was not because he was careless about morals but because he was careful about God's Kingdom. Jesus' table manners, welcoming and eating with all who wanted to come, were a sign of God's Kingdom. Presence at table rested not on personal qualification but on God's invitation. What a tragedy when people exclude themselves because they do not approve of Jesus' unconditional love and those he befriends.

✳ *Lord, thank you for inviting us all to your table.*

Friday February 6   *Mark 2.23 to 3.12*

More conflicts

More conflicts for Jesus. This time the trouble is caused by those who value their religious practices above human needs. The incidents in the corn fields, and with the man with the withered hand both happen on the Sabbath.

We ought to note the sense of 'trial' that is beginning to emerge in Mark's Gospel. In the synagogue are those who watch to see what Jesus will do. They are beginning to plot against him. But he puts them at a disadvantage by asking the question about appropriate actions on the Sabbath. Ironically, those of the opposition are beginning to bear testimony to the fact that Jesus is no ordinary teacher.

Jesus does not dismiss the Law of God. He simply sees its depth. Again we have the theme of Jesus' anger, now directed at the small-minded, closed-hearted, attitude of those who put things before people. That is the opposite of what God intended. He made laws for people, not people for laws!

Jesus says that the Son of Man is Lord of the Sabbath. That implies the Son of Man determines what is the appropriate use of the Sabbath. Jesus takes authority to say how the day should be used. His actions again proclaim that God's interest is on people's well-being.

✳ *Lord, forgive our foolish ways.*
Open our lives to receive your liberty.

Saturday February 7   *Mark 4.1-9 *J*

Jesus the teacher

For the first hearers of Jesus this would have been an immediately recognizable scene. The sower goes out to sow. Mark tells us that great crowds were gathering to hear Jesus at this stage of his ministry. Were they fascinated by his teaching, his healings, his controversies? Certainly there was a popularity about his ministry at this point.

Looking forward, we can say that the parable describes the response to the gospel preaching of Jesus, the early Church and the Church in every generation. There is some response which is glorious and fruitful, some that is half-hearted, some that is instant but without depth, and some that is zero, like stony soil indeed.

For the farmer the seed is precious and not to be wasted. But the farmer in the parable distributes the seed without regard to the soil. He throws it out in hope of it being received. Certainly Jesus is very open and free in his sharing of the good news. He does not seek to control the response to his work. He scatters the precious seed in hope. That there is a harvest is a miracle.

✳ *Living God, may I have ears to hear,*
a mind to understand,
and a heart to love.

For further reflection or group discussion

● What features of Jesus, which Mark has painted so far, either attract or disturb you?
● Do you think that the Church has spoken of Jesus in ways that help us to understand the mystery of Jesus, or has it made it even harder to understand him?
● Try to talk this coming week to someone who is not a Christian and tell him or her some of these stories of Jesus. Ask how s/he responds to what Jesus said and did.

Why speak in parables?

These are difficult verses to understand. If you find them tough you are in good company. On the face of it, it looks as though Jesus teaches in parables in order that people should not get the message. That cannot be right.

To the disciples, Jesus says that they have been given the 'secret'. What secret? This could mean either that in the hearing of the parables, and acting upon them, the disciples are sharing the Kingdom present in Jesus. It is secret only in the sense that it involves listening to and obeying Jesus. It is thus an 'open' secret. Or, it could simply mean that Jesus himself is the secret, present among his disciples.

What of those on the 'outside'? Are they really told parables so that they do not perceive, understand and receive forgiveness? Sad to say, that was certainly the result of Jesus' teaching for some. Some scholars suggest that here is an illustration of an Aramaic form of speech whereby the result of something is described as its purpose. Jesus told parables to help people understand and turn to God. The result was that many did not. The sower cannot control the soil!

✳ ***Gracious God, you reveal yourself in Jesus.***
Help me to see the secret of your Kingdom.

Monday February 9   Mark 4.26-34

The Kingdom of God is like ...

The parable of the seed growing secretly is only found in Mark's Gospel. It is an encouraging thought that, although not a great deal may be seen to be happening, the Kingdom of God keeps growing.

All too easily we equate the Kingdom with the Church and we look for success in the Church in terms of outward evidence. We can grow anxious when nothing appears to be happening. But our task is to sow the seed and wait for the harvest. God will care for his Kingdom. Faith shows itself in patience rather than frantic activity.

The mustard seed parable likewise is an encouragement. From this tiny seed comes a great growth. There is hope here for small churches of every generation and place. Mustard is an annual plant. It produces seeds but they need sowing. When that happens there is harvest.

This passage ends with another reference to Jesus' teaching in parables. The parables reveal the Kingdom of God but as a mystery. There is nothing flash and obvious about God's Kingdom but it is there, and here, for those who have eyes to see and ears to hear, and a will to follow Jesus.

✳ *Lord, keep me faithful to your call.*
Help me to live in quiet trust of your coming Kingdom.

Tuesday February 10   Mark 4.35-41

Wind and wave obey him

First read Psalm 107.23-32. Here the psalmist celebrates the power of God who stills the storm to a whisper. This is utterly beyond the ability of humans. That is the testimony of experience and Scripture. So it is no wonder that when Jesus hushes the waves, the disciples ask who he is.

The sea always reminded the Jews of the great threatening waters of chaos which only God could hold back. Mark's community would also have known the storms of prejudice and fear that went with early persecution of the Church. They knew that to be a follower of Jesus did not mean a life of 'plain sailing'.

Does Jesus' question in verse 40 express surprise? After all, the disciples have begun to know the secret of the Kingdom. Are they still unbelieving? That is a hard thought, for some of the storms of life are frightening. But then this story is an assurance of the presence of Christ with us in those storms, and his Kingdom (rule) abides. The threatening chaos bows before the Lord and his name is Jesus. The fear that finally grips the hearts of the disciples is not panic but awe in the presence of one whom wind and sea obey.

✳ *Thank you Lord,*
for your presence in all the moments of our life.

Wednesday February 11   Mark 5.1-20

Demons obey him

Straight after the story of stilling the storm on the lake, Mark tells us of Jesus' power over another kind of threatening evil. Evil is a mystery. What is shown in horror films may be scary but the reality of evil is much more serious. Whether we want to personalize all this in language or not, the reality of evil in the world, destroying individuals and societies, is beyond doubt. A century that has seen two world wars can hardly believe otherwise.

The demented man must have been a frightening figure. So, notice the calmness of Jesus in this encounter and who is in control! The presence of Jesus disturbs the possessed man. The evil recognizes who is the Master, the one who must master us if we are to be made whole.

Jesus' healings are part of the proclamation of the Kingdom of God. The possessed man is made whole and immediately wants to go with Jesus to serve him. Jesus sends him to witness at home, where people will be struck by the change in his life. Jesus has power over evil. That is the possessed man's testimony.

✶ *Saving God, the evil of the world sometimes frightens us. Help us to have faith in your power. Deliver us from evil.*

Thursday February 12   Mark 5.21-34

Desperation rewarded

Let us picture this scene. Jesus is followed by a large crowd. They all want to get near him. There is pushing and touching. Then comes a woman. She is regarded as inferior because she is a woman in a male dominated culture, and her medical condition makes her unclean. Anyone she touches will become unclean. Everything in her culture says, 'Stay away, stand back, you are not allowed here, you polluted woman.' But she is desperate. She has used all her resources to receive the healing that would allow her back into society, into the company of God's people. Picture her. She does not stand on ceremony. She pushes her way into the crowd. Her desperation drives her on. She breaks all the rules, reaches out and touches Jesus.

P T Forsyth once said, the Kingdom of God is not for the well-meaning but for the desperate. There are two groups around Jesus. One group is made up of spectators. They jostle Jesus. Then there is the woman and all those others who know their need of God. She has not come to spectate. She reaches out and touches. She is healed.

✶ *Thank you, compassionate God.
You never turn the desperate away.*

Friday February 13   Mark 5.35-43

The final frontier

Jesus the man of mystery has confronted life-denying religion, illness, demonic evil, but here in this story he is faced by the last frontier, death. He confronts death in Jairus' daughter and the slaves of death in the professional mourners.

The crowd expresses a common attitude. They believe that death is the end. With our death our finitude triumphs. We are beyond human help and at an end. Paul spoke of death as the last enemy. It defeats us all for we are born to die.

But from the first, Jesus has a different response. He tells the messengers from Jairus' house not to fear but believe. They have called on Jesus and he will go with them. He does not stop to argue with those who mock him, but takes the parents to the child's bedside. With an Aramaic word of tenderness the girl lives.

Mark says that Jesus tells those present not to tell anyone what had happened but to care for the girl. How could it be kept silent? Perhaps Jesus is trying to avoid the reputation of wonder-worker? The mystery of his identity remains, except that now we have to add the overcoming of death to the story.

✳ *Word of Life, Love stronger than death,*
   Jesus Christ, we worship you.

Saturday February 14   *Mark 6.1-6*

Where Jesus could not work

Mark has been setting out the story of Jesus. One remarkable deed after another has been recounted. What people assume are impossible situations look different in the light of Jesus. But now Jesus comes home and finds, like others, that a prophet cannot rely on being honoured among his own.

Is Jesus in fact a prophet? He speaks and acts prophetically but his life and work seem to surpass Moses, Isaiah, Jeremiah and the others. So, is he more than a prophet, this man of mystery? He has healed the sick, exorcised the possessed, raised the dead. Is there nothing he cannot do?

Back home he finds those who are offended at him. Mark, with some honesty, says that Jesus could not do any miracles in his home town. He seems to be able to do anything elsewhere. But here he encounters lack of faith. This mysterious man who speaks and acts with the authority of God does not force himself on those who reject him. He will not dominate. Is it possible that in what he can and will not do we also see who he is?

✳ *Lord Jesus, help us to live your life, especially in our*
   homes.

For further reflection or group discussion

- What message do the two parables about seeds in Mark 4 have for small congregations?
- What lessons might be drawn from Mark 5.25-34 about attitudes in prayer and worship?
- Why is it so difficult sometimes to be a Christian at home?

8th Sunday before Easter, February 15　　　　　　　　*Mark 6.30-44*

A feast to satisfy all

By now great crowds are coming to Jesus, from all the towns (verse 33). His fame has spread, which is hardly surprising in the light of what he has been doing. But is this what Jesus wants?

The feeding of the five thousand is the only miracle recorded in all four Gospels. There are some particular details in Mark's account that help us grasp his perspective. For example, the reference to sheep without a shepherd may echo 1 Kings 22.17 where the reference is to a crowd without a leader, a potential army. Mark also says the grass is green (verse 39) which means Passover time, when expectations about the coming Messiah were at their highest. Have the people misunderstood and expect Jesus to be the military leader to liberate Israel? When he asks the disciples to get the crowd to sit down, it almost looks like an army formation, ranks and companies. But then the unexpected. Not a great call to arms, not manna in the wilderness, but the sharing of simple resources. The miracle meets human need. It is not designed to start an uprising. Jesus is not to be fitted into the mould of a revolutionary commander the people expect.

✳ *Thank you, Lord, for refusing the way of quick success.*
Thank you for feeding us.

Monday February 16　　　　　　　　　　　　　　*Mark 6.45-56*

The presence of God

The crowd misunderstand who Jesus is, but are the disciples any wiser? Jesus sends them away in a boat so that he can gain some space to pray. Then he comes, walking on the water. The disciples think this man of mystery is a ghost!

Jesus' reply is both comforting and illuminating. 'Take courage, don't be afraid' is his word to the anxious and fearful. But in the middle of this call is the crucial 'It is I'. It is a form of the

I AM designation found in the Old Testament when Moses asks for the identity of God (Exodus 3.14). And so in Jesus God climbs into the boat and the storm rests. Mark adds that the disciples had not understood the loaves and fishes incident. Did they think that Jesus had missed a great opportunity to seize power and lead the people in a bid for freedom? Strangely the people grasp the new opportunity to bring friends for healing, and the crowds quickly gather. Their simple faith stands in distinction to the response of the disciples. But who is this man?

✷ *Lord, when the winds and storms of life are against us, come with your presence and help us recognize your coming.*

Tuesday February 17   Mark 7.24-37
More amazing healings

It is surprising that the first Christians kept this story alive. On the face of it Jesus seems to share the prejudices of his time when this woman, a Gentile, and a member of a hated nation, is dismissed with a rather harsh word about 'dogs'. But the woman does not take offence but rather asks again in faith for her daughter. Jesus responds with alacrity. Her reply shows faith which Jesus cannot deny.

What is the meaning of 'first' in verse 27? It must mean that there is a second. The theme is a missionary one, for Jesus comes initially to his own people but then, second, to the Gentiles. This would have been important to Mark's community, mostly Gentiles themselves. So the picture we are getting again is of an extraordinary man. Jesus cares for Gentiles. His mission is not confined to his own people.

The story of the deaf and dumb man is the last in a series of healings, all of which have raised the question of Jesus' identity. Again there is the command to secrecy. We who read the Gospel know this impossible. But we realize that more than a wonder worker is here. How will that truth be known?

✷ *Thank you, Lord, for the wideness of your mercy.*

Wednesday February 18   Mark 8.11-13
Give us a sign!

As we read the story of Jesus we sense a growing tension. This extraordinary man of mystery is not going to be ignored by the authorities. One way to settle his credentials is the way Moses suggested in Deuteronomy 13.1-2, that is, by giving a sign. The Pharisees have come to test Jesus.

Are those who ask for signs really wanting a kind of proof? But what would count as proof of God? Jesus has already acted in ways which we have seen are usually only open to God. Wind and waves obey him, demons flee, the diseases that are an affront to the Kingdom are dealt with speedily. The ordinary people recognize power when they see it. But these doubting Pharisees, how can they see the truth? Their request shows how blind they are. Faith in God does not deal in signs. They will not be given what they ask for.

Yet, we shall come to see with a Centurion Jesus dying on the cross. He sees the Son of God (Mark 15.39). Is this the key to the mystery?

✳ *Gracious God, forgive my lack of trust.*
I ask not for a sign but faith in Jesus your Son, our Saviour.

Thursday February 19   *Mark 8.22-30*

You are the Christ

We are coming to a key moment in the Gospel. But first, another miracle from Jesus. Significantly, after all the misunderstandings and lack of perception by the disciples, we have a man given his sight. First the man is given partial vision. The story thus far has included disciples who have seen something of the meaning of Jesus. But this man needs more to receive full sight.

Up until this point in the Gospel people have been amazed and puzzled at the works of Jesus. But we have also been given hints that there is more. What more? Peter makes the confession, 'You are the Christ!' And we notice again the command to secrecy. Why can they not dash all over the country shouting the good news? Because people would misunderstand. On the basis of what they have already seen and heard, they might think that for Jesus to be the Christ of God would make him the miracle-worker *par excellence*. But this would be a half-truth, indeed not even half. There is more to Jesus, and the story of a wonder-worker is seriously incomplete. Even this glimpse needs a second touch for sight.

✳ *Lord, forgive us when we do not recognize our limitations and fail to see how much we need your gift of sight.*

47

The astonishing truth

Whatever people thought about the Christ of God in Israel it would not have included the thought that the Messiah would suffer. There was a real problem for the first Christians in communicating their faith that in Jesus God had acted for the salvation of the world. The problem was the cross. Indeed, Deuteronomy 21.23 says that anyone hanged on the tree is cursed by God. But there is Jesus saying that the Son of Man must suffer. And he is very stern with Peter. Why does he call Peter 'Satan'? Is it because in this kindly challenge to his God-given destiny Peter is restating the temptations in the wilderness?

Jesus has a vocation to suffering. The man who has done such mighty deeds for others, who can command even the wind and waves, has to suffer. Why? What is it that is so serious about our human condition that it can only be healed by the cross of the Son of God? It sounds cruel to say that the Son of Man *must* suffer. Yet only in this way can the full extent of love show itself. And that is why Jesus' disciples have a vocation to suffering too.

✴ *Suffering, Saving, Servant Lord, help us to follow you, and trust in your way to life.*

Transfiguration!

On top of Mount Tabor in Israel there is a monastery church that strikingly recalls the Transfiguration story. As you enter the door you can see the chancel stretching before you. But instead of there being one altar there are two, set on different levels. Below is a plain altar table and behind it a mural depicting Jesus walking the fields with the disciples. It is a very human picture of a man with his friends. We have met this person in Mark's Gospel.

But the second altar is set above the first. It is glorious in its colours of white and gold. In the dome above is a mosaic depicting Jesus in his transfiguration, talking with Moses and Elijah. He is lifted off the earth and shines in glory.

This Jesus too we have encountered in the Gospel, though in surprising ways. He is the Son of God. He is human and divine. He does wonders. He is the Suffering Servant of the Lord. But we must follow him, go with him, to the cross and the empty tomb to learn just who this man of mystery is.

✳ *Lord, help us to walk on with you,*
to the place of sacrifice and love,
that we may know who you are
and receive our own identity in discipleship.

For further reflection, group discussion and ACTION

- How would you describe the significance of Jesus to someone of another faith?
- Why do you think Jesus had to suffer?
- What does denying yourself and taking up the cross mean in your own experience?

LENT – True Fasting

Notes based on the New International Version by
John Hastings

John Hastings, a presbyter of the Church of North India and Church of Bangladesh, was a founder of community development organizations in Calcutta bustees, One World Week in the UK, and a people's movement for mass literacy in Bangladesh. He is well-known in many countries for his involvement in development, human rights, inter-faith co-operation, and literacy.

Lent begins on Ash Wednesday and lasts forty days. Some Christians follow a tradition of self-discipline, which in a token way, reflects our Lord's days of fasting in the wilderness. Friday may be a total fast, or without meat. Others decide to go without something they specially like, or to eat less. Finding spiritual and/or physical benefit from such discipline, some resolve to continue it when Lent is over. Some churches ban weddings and other celebrations in Lent. Other Christians, whose traditions disdain seasonal observances, keep every day of the year free of self-indulgent excess, with room to celebrate when occasion demands.

For many, public observance of fasting is quite wrong. But no Christian can escape the call to disciplined living, and even those who 'live as normal' during Lent can use this week's studies to ask themselves whether their 'normal living' matches up to what God requires.

7th Sunday before Easter, February 22   *Isaiah 58.1-8 *J*

God can't be bribed

Isaiah's denunciation of hypocrisy is devastating – and no doubt risky for him. He condemns the way his people pretend to be 'holy' (verse 2). He ridicules their idea that they could buy God by self-denial. They complained they had wasted their time fasting: it didn't work; they got nothing! That isn't true fasting, says the prophet. It hasn't improved your way of life. You go on serving your own interests, get bad-tempered, fight, and exploit your workers just the same. A fast is not intended to earn spiritual acceptance: God is not bribed! Can a few days' fasting make amends for a life given over to amassing wealth?

A true fast is (verses 6-8) caring for those in need, changing your way of life so that those in the chains of poverty are set free and receive justice. This new sort of fasting has a real effect. It leads to real righteousness and healing of society. You will not be getting the things you've been trying to get, but the new 'dawn' in your life will mean glory for God!

If you are making plans for Lent, make sure you don't make them for the wrong reasons. Decide before God first what you'll do to amend your life, then what you can do during the coming weeks to help you towards that goal.

✳ *Lord, teach me what true fasting is.*
Take my way of life and amend it for your glory.

Monday February 23   *Mark 2.18-22 *J*

Come on and celebrate!

Jesus was not interested in stereotyped formal religion, with ritual for the sake of ritual. In opposing it, he was distancing himself, not only from the religious establishment, but also from John the Baptist's way of doing things. At this time, he told them, my disciples have reason to celebrate. They are rejoicing in the discovery that the Kingdom is in their midst. They have a sense of occasion and are not bound by blanket rules and regulations. There will be other days when fasting will be appropriate. Such a time came when he was 'taken away' from them on Good Friday.

We may take verse 20 as a scriptural basis for fasting on Fridays (or every day). Or, on the grounds that the living Bridegroom is always with us, we may take Jesus' message to mean that, in the new era he has begun, the old style of fasting is obsolete, and we need a new-look, celebratory faith. Either way, the priority is to absorb and enjoy Jesus' message. Have we received it joyfully? Do we celebrate it enough?

✳ *Teach us, Lord, how to celebrate your presence today*
and every day.

Tuesday February 24   *Luke 4.1-13 *C*

Look out!

A group of young people designed some posters for a protest march against world hunger and the exploitation of the poor. One of them featured two anxious eyes looking out of a window which had just been flung open and bore the caption 'Look out!' It cleverly linked the need to care for the world outside us with what happens to our inner lives.

Jesus' three temptations did not just concern his 'spiritual life', but were about the work he had to do. They came to him, not only in his forty days of fasting, but throughout his life. And they come to all of us, whatever our duties, throughout our lives. Like him, we too have to learn (1) to love spiritual food more than meals and other delights of the body; (2) to seek God's glory rather than worldly fame or riches; (3) to rely on the One we know to be pure Love without looking for sensational proof.

Each of us needs to take time to commit ourselves to accepting this threefold discipline. For some, a weekend retreat for self-examination may serve this purpose, but for most of us longer is needed. It can be learned within the 'wilderness' of chores, the daily round and common task. It takes some of us years in an overseas 'wilderness' to relegate material comforts and delights to their right place, to spurn 'success', and to trust God wholly.

✳ *Lord, help me to look out,*
  both within me and into the world,
  to conquer my craving for material joys, success and
     honour,
  and to enjoy what for you is true food,
  true victory and true glory.

Ash Wednesday, February 25   *Matthew 6.1-6, 16-21 *C*

The happy faster

You can imagine a 'happy eater'. Can you imagine a 'happy faster'? If we have really overcome our passion for more food than is good for us, we will rejoice in God's manna, a parable or symbol to lead us to find our true food in God's Word (Deuteronomy 6.3). At first, fasting for self-discipline, including the 'fasting' that is constant control of excess, may seem burdensome. But eventually it should become a really happy experience.

One can often see Muslim communities taking great delight in the celebration of fasting during the month of Ramadan – the discipline itself, not only in the *Iftehar* ceremony of breaking the fast each evening. It would have been very different among the Jews of Jesus' day. It was a show of self-mortification, and it was very public. People sometimes even used trumpets to herald their acts of self-denial. Leaders may justify public displays of religion 'to get everyone moving'. But for Jesus, paraded religion is no religion: generosity, fasting and prayer should be secret. Only the Father should know.

✻ *Lord, help me to live your way secretly – and happily.*

Make me a blessing

In some early manuscripts, verse 29 reads, 'This kind can only come out by prayer and fasting'. Most scholars now think it is more likely that an early Christian sect wanted the last two words added to give credence to their ascetic practices and that is why they are omitted by others.

Yet the suggestion here is that fasting may also be used for the healing of others: fasting in solidarity with those who suffer and as a way of pleading for reconciliation.

Mahatma Gandhi used fasting in this way. It may be said that his motives were political, but his aims were justice and people's liberation. Christians too may engage in protest fasts and/or protracted sessions of prayer for prisoners and abused people. Fasting for a just cause is for the healing of society.

✻ *Lord, make me ever ready to give time to intercede*
   that others may be healed,
   that the innocent and the oppressed may be set free,
   and that peace and justice may reign in your world.

Not so much a duty, more a way of life

Rather than systematic fasting, Paul's self-discipline was hard work, hunger, sleepless nights, hardships, beatings, prison, ill-repute, poverty and the brink of death. He accepted these as necessary for others' sake. Tied up with them were patience, purity, understanding and genuine love – fruits of his life of communion with God. On the one hand, there was inner discipline, on the other, outward giving for others. Had he been asked what a true fast was he would surely have given this broad view, and underlined it with the prophet's definition (Isaiah 58.1-8).

In Japan (1920-40), Toyohiko Kagawa accepted this sacrificial way of life as part of his battle for justice. He lived in a tiny space in a crowded slum of Kobe. One of the diseases he contracted there left him all but blind. He wrote that he learned a great deal about love from 2 Corinthians. Another example comes from the 19th century: in Molokai (in the South Pacific) Father Damien cared for leprosy sufferers before any cure was known. One morning, when they heard him address them with the words, 'We lepers', they realized the depth of his love for them. These and countless other 'happy fasters' would say that you don't have to look around for occasions to fast if you live with consistent dedication.

✳ *Lord, every time we ask you to grant healing,*
peace and justice to our world,
remind us that your answer depends on us giving
ourselves
to bring about the changes for which we pray.

Saturday February 28   *Psalm 91.1-2, 9-16 *C*

Security without deposit

The words of this psalm were crucial to Jesus, and must have been a source of strength down the ages to all who have struggled to serve God amid threats and dangers. Yet it can be mis-read. Verses 11 and 12 were cited by the tempter in the third temptation (Luke 4.9-11), which might be called 'the temptation to take all scripture literally'. Jesus pointed to other words (Deuteronomy 6.16) to get at the real meaning. The security provided by God is not freedom from pain and suffering, nor an insurance against dying in an accident. It is an assurance that God will always be with us whatever the trouble (verse 15). In concluding this week's analysis of a true fast, it is fitting we remind ourselves to expect great things, not personal favours, from God, and simply to hold on to the truth that God is love and utterly reliable.

There is no deposit for this security and there are no conditions or small print. 'The large print giveth and the small print taketh away!' as a critic of the 'ad-men' has put it. God is not a gamble, but a safe-house for any refugee.

Though not about fasting, the Psalm underscores what the other passages this week have pointed to – not a succession of intermittent rituals, and certainly not paraded ones, but the true fast of a consistent, self-denying way of life.

✳ *Give me for joy, O Christ, the drying of another's tears;*
give me for light, the sunshine of healing their sorrows;
give me for shelter, the shadow of your cross,
and for my heart's content, the glory of your presence.
Amen

G A Studdert Kennedy (1883-1929)

For further reflection or group discussion

- Were the temptations of Jesus basically the same as those we face? As we acquire material things (and perhaps begin to regard luxuries as necessities) is it more difficult to overcome the temptation to hanker after material things?
- How far might this week's readings suggest that many Christians have yet to be fully converted?
- Consider one or two situations which have prompted people to organize 'protest fasts'. Do your think there is a scriptural basis for such action? Is there a current issue of injustice for which you might be persuaded to join a 'protest fast'?

FOR ACTION

Plan and take whatever action commends itself to you from this week's readings.

LENT – Christ our High Priest
The Epistle to the Hebrews

Notes based on the New Revised Standard Version by
Burchel K Taylor

Dr Burchel Taylor – who has been pastor of the Bethel Baptist Church, Kingston, Jamaica, for the past twenty-five years – is widely recognized as a leading Caribbean theologian.

Many do not find the letter to the Hebrews easy to understand. But if time is taken to become acquainted with it, it can be a most rewarding experience. The letter will prove to be very instructive, faith-sustaining, challenging and encouraging. There is a pastoral sensitivity to Christian commitment under stress, even in crisis. There is a vision of the possibility of Christian confidence and assurance in the midst of struggle. There is a sense of ministry and mission that calls the Church to solidarity in suffering, witness beyond its own narrow confines, and hope in the promises of God.

Everything is grounded on what has been accomplished by Christ, whose Person and Work have been represented in distinctive fashion. He is not only the unique Son of God, Apostle and Pioneer, but Great High Priest, sharing the very depth of our humanity and representing our cause in the eternal realm. It is Jesus, in terms of who he is and what he has done, who makes all the difference. He has made available an alternative vision of reality which throws true light on the meaning and purpose of the life and mission of his people.

1st Sunday in Lent, March 1   *Hebrews 1.1-4*

God's last word

God has spoken in Jesus in a way he has never spoken before, and in a way that cannot be equalled or surpassed. Jesus Christ is God's full and final Word to humankind. This is what these majestic opening words of the letter convey. He who is presented here remains in full focus throughout the letter as the Supreme Source, foundation and goal of the entire Christian commitment.

He shares a unique relationship with God as a Son to whom all things are designated. He is perfect Revealer of the divine nature and character, Agent of creation, Sustainer of the universe, Saviour from sins. He is the ultimate Fulfiller and Vindicator of God's purpose, witnessed in his exaltation to the place of supreme honour and authority at the right hand of God.

The appropriate response to the Work and Person of Jesus will be set forth in greater detail in the recurring exhortations, challenges and counsel. Already, however, we are here transported into an atmosphere of awe and grandeur, but – at the same time – we are given the implied assurance that the One who is introduced has been and will be there for us. Our life's real hopes are bound up with him from beginning to end.

✳ *Lord, help us to see you as you are*
and to respond to you as we ought.

Monday March 2 — Hebrews 2.5-18

The glory of humankind

Jesus has been introduced from the divine side in the opening words of the letter. This is now followed up by a presentation of him from the human side. The nobility, dignity and authority intended for humanity in God's creative purpose have not been realized in human experience. This does not, however, mean that either the promise has been withdrawn or the purpose ruined.

In Jesus we see the reality of the intended glory demonstrated, and its possibility remaining an offering of renewed hope. All this has been accomplished through a unique act of solidarity with us human beings displayed by Jesus. He shared the fullness of our human nature, plumbed the depths of our experience, and went all the way in suffering and sacrifice for our glory. In all this, he showed himself to be the Pioneer and High Priest, characteristic representations of Jesus in this letter. This High Priesthood will be the dominant portrayal.

In the world of daily life, the common experience is that glory is achieved and displayed at the expense of others; with Jesus it is done *for* others. Solidarity, service, suffering and sacrifice replace exploitation, oppression, coercion and manipulation. Herein lies our true hope of glory.

✳ *Lord, teach us true humility that reveals the honour*
and dignity of the life you have made possible and
available.

Exemplary faithfulness

Jesus, who fulfils the promise of glory, ought to be the centre of the full attention and concentration of the family of God. This is the family of his own creation, and he is Head of it. They ought to learn from him for the shaping of their own lives, in faithfulness to their calling as members of his household.

The way is that of sincere meditation on Jesus' own faithfulness as God's representative among his people, and as their given representative to God. He is worthy of this attention above any other, even the noblest in the past history of God's dealing with his people. This is so because of who he is and what he did on their behalf.

We witness to being members of God's household, inspired and motivated by the faithfulness of Jesus, by our own firm commitment and confident hope. Our greatest temptation lies in this area. The pressures of daily life and challenges to our faith from the hardship and opposition we often face – because of our commitment – can lead to unfaithfulness. We are warned not to let this happen. We have lessons from the past of the tragic nature of such unfaithfulness. A Christlike faithfulness is available to us to become the pattern of our lives. This is both a gift and a demand of our shared calling.

✳ *Help us, O God, by your Spirit, to be faithful to you after the manner of Jesus Christ our Lord. Amen*

A new exodus

There is a follow-up here of the warning issued against unfaithfulness in yesterday's reading. The emphasis now falls on the people of God as the liberated people of a New Exodus. They live towards the promised future of rest.

Memory of the Exodus experience of the ancient people of God serves as the basis of an urgent warning to the people of the New Exodus. They should not repeat the unbelief of the ancient people that deprived them of entry into the promised rest. The promise remains open to them by the liberation that Jesus has accomplished. The good news of this should be met with faith and ongoing commitment.

God's liberated people must bear in mind that the freedom of their liberated existence bears its own risks, entails its own responsibilities and faces its own challenges. These in different ways can constitute crises for faith by raising questions against God's promise of ultimate rest. The good news of God's promise, grounded on what God has already done, ought to be trusted without reserve, and the journey toward fulfilment of the promise ought to be pursued boldly and in confidence.

✳ *Lord, we confess that we too easily become weary,*
distracted, impatient pilgrims.
Forgive us and increase our faith in Christ. Amen

Thursday March 5   *Hebrews 4.14 to 5.10*

Perfect credentials

The High Priesthood of Jesus now takes centre stage. The credentials of the High Priest and their implication for the life of the people of God are emphasized.

He is *'the Great High Priest'*. Greatness undoubtedly conveys a difference from the traditional priestly order. Here he is presented as One with direct access to the throne of God, a factor that will be noted to be of immense blessing for the people of God. Yet, at the same time by divine appointment, he entered totally into our human experience. He shared all our human vulnerabilities, though not succumbing to sinfulness. In earthly life, he suffered beyond measure unto death, in obedience to God's saving purpose and for our salvation.

By virtue of his stated credentials, this great High Priest is eminently suitable and equally ready to sympathize with us. He can help us in our weakness, strengths, hurts and uncertainties. As High Priest, he offers us a basis for unswerving perseverance in commitment, and gives us a confident assurance in seeking the gracious and merciful presence of God. It is the challenge and comfort of having one like him on our side that undergirds life with purpose and hope.

✳ *Lord, we thank you for providing for us*
in such a meaningful and thorough manner
through Jesus Christ our Great High Priest. Amen

Friday March 6   *Hebrews 7.15-28*

Superior and sure

The High Priesthood of Jesus is not simply marked by impressive credentials. It is essentially superior to the priesthood of the old order in every way, and is guaranteed never to be found wanting or superseded. Important points of contrast are indicated to underscore this.

Inherent inadequacies and limitations of the traditional priesthood – related to the mortality, flawed spiritual and moral condition and transitoriness of their accomplishments – are noted. These are overcome in and by the priesthood of Jesus. His exalted Person, eternal Presence and effective accomplishments speak to the decisive significance of his High Priesthood.

The point is not necessarily to debase what existed. It is rather to emphasize the radical difference Jesus as High Priest makes to our human hope and destiny in the redemptive purpose of God. Upon this we are assured of a living Presence and ongoing concern of utter dependability which will transform and sustain life in true freedom and courage, even in the face of the most threatening of circumstances. The work of the High Priest remains intact.

✳ *Lord, we thank you for the assurance*
that the chances and changes of circumstance and time
do not lessen the effectiveness of your redemptive work.

Saturday March 7   *Hebrews 9.11-14*

The all-sufficient sacrifice

The thought continues to emphasize the superiority of the High Priesthood of Jesus. It is here extended to the sacrifice offered by Jesus the High Priest in his saving work and purpose. The significance of the sacrifice is brought out as it is contrasted with the all-important sacrifice executed by the High Priest of the old order on the Day of Atonement.

The all-sufficient nature of the sacrifice of Christ is highlighted in contrast with the limited and partial effect of the all-important sacrifice on the Day of Atonement. The all-sufficient nature of the sacrifice of Jesus is linked to its eternal association and 'once-and-for-all-ness'. We are shown the totality of its redemptive effect on human life, its identity and spiritual imprint.

What sacrifice could be more sufficient for our redemption and abiding assurance of it than Jesus himself, the High Priest, the eternal Son of God? It is a sacrifice of immeasurable cost, and an unparalleled expression of grace and mercy in one and the same act.

✳ *To God be the glory! Great things he hath done! Amen*

For further reflection or group discussion

- What are some of the benefits to be gained for daily living by meditating on the Person and Work of Jesus?
- What relevance do you think the concept of sacrifice has for our Christian understanding today?

2nd Sunday in Lent, March 8　　　　　　　　　　*Hebrews 9.23-28*

At the highest level

Much is said here that has been repeated elsewhere, even in yesterday's reading. Yet it seems that in the repetition there is special emphasis here on the ultimate setting of Christ's activity. This too is considered of much significance, in contrast with the setting of the activity of the priest of the old order. Not only the Sacrificer and the sacrifice are significantly better, but also the sphere of the operation.

Jesus' activity went beyond the historical into the eternal realm. This is the point of the repeated references to his entry into the heavenly sanctuary of which the earthly is but a copy. Work done for our redemption was carried out at the highest level. It was in the immediate presence of God in a way not open to the priest of the old order.

With the thought of the decisive redemptive act taking place in the eternal realm, with eternal significance, goes the assurance of continued representation at the same level by the same great High Priest. All that is to be done for our redemption has been well and truly done. When Christ appears again, it will not be to repeat what has already been achieved. It will be for accountability for what we have done in response to his redeeming work.

✳ *Lord, may your will be done on earth*
　as it is in heaven. Amen

Monday March 9　　　　　　　　　　*Hebrews 10.19-31*

Time for action

In the light of the work of the Great High Priest, there is assured basis and good reason for sincere practical response. This is the point of the concentration of exhortations and the stern warning to be found in our passage.

There is both opportunity and obligation for the life renewed through Christ's saving work. There is opportunity for fellowship with God and with fellow-believers. There is the obligation of faithfulness in the very opportunity given for fellowship, and in holding fast to the acceptance of God's promises grounded on Christ's accomplished work.

The practice of the cardinal Christian virtues of faith (verse 22), hope (verse 23), and love (verse 24) in worship, steadfast perseverance and mutual care and concern will be tangible evidence of the fellowship and faithfulness at work.

On the other hand, there is the stern reality that we incur severe problems for ourselves if, after all that has been done for our redemption and hope, we persist in rebellion and unfaithfulness. We are without excuse in the face of the judgement we incur. The way has been opened for a life of fellowship and faithfulness through Christ Jesus.

✳ *Lord, renew your Spirit within us,*
that we may be truly faithful, hopeful and loving. Amen

Tuesday March 10   *Hebrews 10.32 to 11.7*

The practice of faith

Faith is singled out from the cardinal Christian virtues in yesterday's reading. In a context of struggle, opposition and challenge, because of commitment to God in Christ, this is readily understandable. When faith is threatened, it puts everything else that is essential to faithful Christian practice at risk. There is, therefore, the assurance that all such trials, and any other, can be faced with utmost confidence. God's promise holds for ever. He faithfully and graciously rewards enduring perseverance. Faith it is that inspires, sustains and ensures such confidence.

It is faith that assures to our spiritual consciousness and understanding the reality of what God promises, even before such a reality is actually shared or entered upon. This faith is exemplified in the life and experience of persons cited from the past history of God's dealings with his people.

It is not possible to live a life pleasing to God without faith in God. Faith affirms the very reality of God, and entrusts itself to the promises of God believingly. Christian practice calls for faith which is both made possible and rewarded by God in Christ.

✳ *Lord, increase our faith in and through Christ Jesus.*
Amen

Against all odds

Faith takes risks as it responds to God's call and promise. It proceeds on the basis of what God requires, directs, assures and promises. It is prepared to do this against all seeming odds.

It often means abandoning standard necessities and desirable and popular ends. Abraham, in faith, abandoned the security of a settled life for the insecurity of a nomadic existence. He was sustained by faith's openness and commitment to God's promised future. He and others looked forward to a settlement to which faith gave meaning, even though it had not been realized.

Faith accepts the seemingly impossible and believes it to be possible on God's Word, which it holds to be true and trustworthy. Faith is not limited or restricted by our awareness of our own inadequacies. It opens and entrusts itself to the enabling power of God. Abraham and Sarah accepted the possibility of parenthood upon God's Word against all odds. God's enabling, when trusted, makes a great difference to the fulfilment of his purpose in, for and through our lives.

✷ *Lord, give us faith that inspires hope*
   and hope that strengthens faith.

Solidarity, success and suffering

Faith commits the people of God to a life of taking the side of the oppressed. They are to defy any temptation to seek their own comfort and neglect the oppressed, or to live at their expense. Self-renunciation and exposure to the wrath of the oppressed are challenges faith accepts.

Faith confronts and overcomes powers and forces which trust in their own strength and are contemptuous of faith's expression. It is a source of spiritual and moral courage that often perplexes those who think they would easily crush the Christian spirit and eliminate Christian confession.

Faith is at the same time prepared to suffer for righteousness' sake, and charged with the vision and confidence of ultimate vindication. Life's hope is not exhausted by current experiences, even death itself.

Faith inspires a vision of reality that sustains hope beyond death and the fulfilment of God's promised new order of righteousness and peace. God's people look to this, and are raised because of the resurrection and exaltation of Christ.

✳ *Lord, give us the self-giving,*
overcoming and enduring faith we need in the midst
and in the face of life's challenges. Amen

It can be done

Interestingly, after the exposition and illustration of faith, there is here encouragement to the people of God. In the imagery of a long-distance race, they are being urged to press on. The struggles and temptations of such an experience are envisaged: the hindrances might appear too great, the course too wearying and, in the end, too demanding.

The challenging nature of the way of life is not denied. Yet there is every confidence that it can be pursued with satisfaction to its end. This is the point of the encouragement. There are vast numbers of witnesses, who by their testimonies are examples that it can be done. Above all, there is Jesus, Initiator, and ultimate Fulfiller and fulfilment of the way. His own inspiration and example are enabling and empowering.

There is, therefore, encouragement to pursue the way with single-mindedness, steadfastness and strength of character: to run the race with a focused vision of Jesus, a determined sense of purpose and an acceptance of harsh experiences. These are of formative and disciplinary value as we grow towards maturity under God's care and nurture. With life set and shaped in this manner, the way of faith can be pursued towards its ultimate fulfilment.

✳ *Lord, grant us the grace of your ever-renewing Spirit*
for the way of faith.

Follow the lead

The calling of the people of God is a way of life that is devoted, dynamic and daring. The closing section of this letter reinforces this message. Readers are asked to emulate the pattern of the life and service of the leaders, from whose devoted service and commitment they themselves have benefited. There is no place for diversion and preoccupations that would detract from the challenge of a faithful pursuit of the Christian calling to mission.

There is an even greater challenge to a life of mission by appeal to the pattern of the ministry of Christ, the Pioneer and

Chief High Priest. It took him outside the wall where he was crucified. The abiding challenge to the people of God is to follow his lead. He must be followed along the admittedly dangerous path of going beyond the boundaries and barriers of class, race, gender, religion to reach the excluded, the marginalized, the dispossessed and the strangers. Such a path entails opposition, suffering and even death. Yet the vision with which the people of God are imbued holds before them a hope that death cannot diminish. It is a hope that catches the vision of the new order promised by God and guaranteed by the death and resurrection of Christ.

✳ *O Lord, give us faith, hope and love to follow you*
   to the end which is also a new
   and greater beginning with you. Amen

For further reflection or group discussion and ACTION

- How is our faithfulness to our calling as Christians tested by the dominant culture in which we live today?
- What are some of the ways in which you think solidarity with the oppressed is demonstrated in the mission of the church to which you belong?

LENT – Turning to the living God

Notes based on the Revised English Bible by
Bernard Thorogood

After serving in Polynesia for 18 years, mainly doing theological education, Bernard Thorogood served as secretary of the London Missionary Society/Council for World Mission, and then as secretary of the United Reformed Church in the UK. When he retired he settled in Australia as a member of the Uniting Church.

My eyes were opened. It suddenly came to me. It made sense at last. I could see it all ...

These are phrases for an experience we have all had at some moment in life. We saw reality in a new light. It may have been a death or an illness, or a sight of great beauty, but whatever the trigger, we faced truth and challenge. An encounter with God is this carried to the ultimate.

In these two weeks we shall be reading of moments when human life meets the Creator of life, to find wonder, glory, dismay, hope. This is part of our Lent readings, for at this time we think of how the extraordinary Christ touches our ordinary lives – and so brings to us that 'extra' which is life with and in God for ever.

3rd Sunday in Lent, March 15   *Joshua 5.9-15*

God beyond our vision

Joshua, as commander, was preparing for a tough campaign. All his thought was on the strategy for winning the territory of Canaan. All around, behind the hills, were tribes which would resist the incoming Israelites. So the question in verse 13 was very natural. Was this vision a sign of victory or defeat, friend or enemy? The reply was a shock for Joshua. 'Neither! I am not to be classified in that way for I am a messenger of God.'

We are all tempted to claim God for our own side in battles. In time of war both sides may pray to God for victory. But God is not to be kept within our categories of friends and enemies (that would make God a tribal deity), for the whole human family is equally loved by God. One side, or one party, may be closer to truth and justice than the other, but even so God is not their mascot, their flag to wave. We, like these ancient people, discover that God is greater than our vision can ever be.

✳ *Wonderful God, we say you are our God;*
But you are God of all people.
Today may we love and serve you
as the Lord of all.

Monday March 16   *Hosea 6.1-6*

God beyond 'religion'

Verses 1-3 give us words from the preacher. We can imagine similar words by preachers today, calling for repentance and faith after a time of trial and fear. Verses 4-6 bring us the thoughts of God – as Hosea understood them. God saw this unfaithful people who had to be confronted and corrected by the prophets, lifted beyond ritual religion to living faith.

Should preachers 'cut them' and 'slaughter them' with words? This does not sound like the merciful Lord. But then we remember the language of Jesus about the ritual religion of the Temple, when he denounced superficial worship and hypocrisy. We need prophets. We need their words of tough challenge, for we all slip too easily into the forms of religion and lose the spirit. But prophets themselves need love, not just anger, if they are to be effective voices of the Lord. Where do we find the prophets of today? We may have to look beyond the formal church to find them.

✳ *I love your word of grace;*
but I need your word of challenge.
Unsettle me, Lord, when ritual takes over
and faith sleeps.

Tuesday March 17   *Isaiah 55.1-9*

God of welcome

This great song of faith is a passage to read slowly, so that we can take each verse as a theme to think about. It is as though the living God is speaking directly to Israel, for the opening invitation is from the giver of life itself. We have to imagine the prophet waiting and praying, perhaps for years, until this voice of great power is given to him.

So we think of life, true life, as more than what we buy, more than education, investments, status and all the glory of the world. It is closeness to God, faithfulness to God's way, that is the key.

There is nothing narrow or mean or petty here. Indeed these verses (especially 6-9) offer the open door to the household of God, and so form a prelude to the words, 'Come to me, all who are burdened' – the welcome of Christ.

Can we say that our churches today offer that quality of welcome?

✳ *Let us rest in these words –*
God calls us to come and listen,
to seek, to return, to approach.
We come now,
believing that the God who is so far beyond us
is the God who calls us by name.

Wednesday March 18   *Psalm 63*

God of exiles and refugees

Yesterday we read of God addressing us. Here we find the singer calling on God. It is the cry of the refugee, the exile, the wanderer. Today in a world of refugees, millions of people without homes or security, the cry is very close, very true to life. To whom can they turn, if not to the Lord who holds the whole creation in his hands? How does God respond?

This is where I find the last three verses of the psalm difficult. I can understand that the cry of the exiles is for revenge on those who have driven them out. But that does not connect with my experience, or with my understanding of the one who said, 'Father, forgive them.' So I suggest that as we read these verses we are back in the era of tribal warfare, back to the elemental instincts, and still waiting for the grace of the Christ. But that too is true to life. In many places today people caught up in violence are still waiting for the advent of Jesus, the prince of peace, to heal bitterness of spirit.

✳ *For all those who today are wanderers,*
seeking peace and rest,
may there be hands reaching out to help
and justice done.

Thursday March 19   *Malachi 3.6-12*

God of justice

If you have time, please go back to chapter 2 verse 17 and read through to 3.12. The challenge begins with the question, 'Where is the God of justice?' The God who speaks to Israel is truly the one who defends the helpless and accuses the employer of cheating the workmen. God is the prosecuting counsel in court (verse 5). So what hope is there for Israel?

Then comes the real heartache of those who have cheated God, who have claimed his name but have never given God their love and devotion. That is a national disaster. But still there is hope, and the symbol of that hope will be when the people make their offerings to God with honesty and generosity.

To cry to God for help, but to reject God's way of justice and honesty, that is a recipe for failed religion, and a risk for us all. There are two sides to a covenant. The prophet asks, have we and our nation fulfilled our part?

✳ *Keep us true, Lord,*
to the way you have shown us;
let us live the Kingdom life and offer you ourselves.

Friday March 20   *Luke 15.1-10*
God of the lost ones
It is remarkable that, in response to a bad-tempered complaint (verse 2), we have three of the most wonderful stories in the world. In writing this part of the Gospel, Luke brought together parables which show, with absolute clarity, why Jesus was concerned for people who were lost.

Who are the lost ones? We can be lost in the jungle of business and busy-ness, so pressured by daily demands that life becomes a rat race. We can be lost amid the drug culture, not knowing where we are. Or lost as we reject the way of truth to follow some mad notions or ambitions of our own. Some people are lost in their worries, some in their pain. It is for all these that Jesus is seeking, and when one is found and restored, then it is as though all the angels sing with joy. The Church on earth has to share that passion too.

✳ *Untiring God, may we share your longing*
that all may be restored,
and your joy when the lost ones are found.

Saturday March 21   *Luke 15.11-32*
God of waiting
God seeks the lost. Yes, but here God also waits. In the story the father let the boy go, and waited until he was ready to come

home. It was waiting with hope. This is a reality for which we give thanks today. What patience there is in God. The human family has reached amazing technical powers but has drifted into such violence and inhumanity that in some places these years are the Dark Ages. And God waits. Some of us resist the way of God for years, believing that we can fashion our own destiny just as we like. And God waits.

This is a word about human freedom which the lad seeks in the far country where appetites are in control. Yet that is an illusion, for the lad becomes a slave. It is in the father's house that he finds freedom to love and to face the future in hope. And it is the tragedy of the elder brother that he could not see this, but is absorbed with his rights. Where are we?

If you can find it, look at a copy of Rembrandt's picture *The Return of the Prodigal*.

✳ *Reflect: tenderness, reconciliation, warmth, abiding joy, God's patient love for me.*

For further reflection or group discussion

In all these readings people meet the reality of God and are changed. Have we ever had such an experience?

● In what ways were we challenged?
● Do we expect this experience each time we pray and attend worship?
● Can we help others to enter into this meeting with the living God?

4th Sunday in Lent, March 22　　　　　　　*2 Corinthians 5.16-21*

A new creation

'New creation' is one of the most powerful phrases for the purpose of God in Jesus Christ. We catch the echo of the 'new birth' in John's Gospel, and the very act of birth in the Christmas story. 'New creation' means that what is done for us in the life of Christ is not just an affirmation of old laws and old preaching; it really brings something new into the world – a new way for people like us and the Creator of the cosmos to be at one.

This is the wonder that Paul describes here as reconciliation. It is not an easy 'let's all be friends again' reunion. It is showing, in pain and death, that the way of love is the way of God. Human nature resists that. Reconciliation happens when we have faith in

Jesus as the very character of God, drawing us into his light and spirit. To be ambassadors of this new start for the world is not a professional task for a few, but is the calling of us all. Each local church is an embassy of the new world.

✳ *Renew us, remake us, and lift us up*
today and every day.

Monday March 23   *Psalm 32*

A way of confession

In verses 1 to 7 we read the prayer of the penitent; in verses 8 to 10 the word of God as the teacher; then in verse 11 a chorus or conclusion.

For most of us verses 3 to 7 are the key, for they speak with total directness about the way of confession and how hard that is to follow. There is something in our nature which resists confession. We want to keep our status as being in the right even when we know that we are in the wrong. And then we wither in spirit, like the effect of a drought (verse 4). Here in Australia drought is a constant reality, with farmers forced to kill their stock after years of no rain. Everything is brown and dusty. What a picture of the human life resisting the reality of sin and separation.

So confession is a necessary prelude to pilgrimage. When we are open and true in our confession, then God welcomes us, guards and enfolds us (verse 7). The prodigal comes home.

✳ *When I want to conceal what I am*
from you, Lord, and from those around me,
help me to be honest, open and willing to change.

Tuesday March 24   *1 Peter 4.1-6*

No one is excluded

This letter of Peter was written to people who formed a tiny minority in a tough world where they suffered for their faith. So they were very distinct from the majority around them. That is why we read here of the great change that has come, a rescue from a wretched past. Small groups of Christians were living a new quality of life.

Verse 6 refers to the very ancient teaching that Jesus, on his death, 'descended into hell' so that all those who were lost might hear the voice of the good shepherd. It is not something that comes to us from the words of Jesus, and I cannot claim it as a historical fact like the crucifixion. Yet it holds a great truth. There is no one outside the gospel, or beyond the reach of God. The word of calling and forgiveness is for all, in every generation and condition and culture. When we ask, 'What about all those who died before Christ?' we hear this word, that God cares for them, just as for us.

✳ *What difference do people see in us?*
**God of grace, I pray that I may show
how meeting Jesus has changed me and kept me true.**

Wednesday March 25   *1 Peter 4.12-16*

A way of joy

Jesus did not promise an easy way for his followers. 'Blessed are you when people hate you and ostracize you, when they insult and slander your very name, because of the Son of Man' (Luke 6.22). Now, as the readers receive this letter, that is coming true. The first of the persecutions organized by Rome is upon them. So the apostle assures them that their suffering is truly part of following Jesus.

It has not been my calling to suffer in that way. I have been able to live in free societies where Christians can speak and sing and witness without penalty. If that is your situation too, then our calling is to be grateful, to work continuously to maintain freedom, and to help those who are suffering.

But if as you read this, you are facing penalties for your faith, then take the words of Peter for yourself. The way of Jesus may be a way of pain, just because there is opposition to his truth and light which shine into the dark places of humanity. But it is also a way of joy because we are united with the God who came in Jesus.

✳ **Let me follow you, Jesus, all the way.**

Thursday March 26   *Hebrews 13.1-6*

A way of life

It has been a privilege in my ministry to enjoy hospitality in many parts of the world. I think of small Polynesian villages on isolated islands where the fishermen spent the whole night fishing for the feast of welcome; of a black township in South Africa where the choir had prepared special songs; of a hill village in Myanmar and an excited gathering around the Gospels; of a dalit community in

South India offering their needlework and their fruit. Hospitality is a gift of the Spirit, a lovely aspect of the fellowship of Christ.

This passage reminds us that when we have met God in Jesus, there are results which follow. The experience is not just an emotional high. There are consequences for marriage (verse 4). Today it is not easy to retain the high standards of marriage that have always been the Christian aim. So we should be all the more grateful for steadfastness in marriage. Perhaps the Church could do more to celebrate faithfulness over the years, and the love that lasts.

✳ *The Lord is my helper;*
Be with me every hour of this day.

Friday March 27   *James 3.1-12*

A way of speaking

We come to a very powerful warning by the apostle, addressed in the first place to teachers. Every teacher carries a heavy responsibility because those who listen accept the words as having authority. So if the teacher (or the preacher) speaks what is false then the judgement will be very severe.

But this leads on to the passage about the danger of the tongue. It reads as though James had suffered from bad talk at some point and so sees the dangers. In verses 5 and 6 the power of the tongue is like the spark which starts a bush fire. Two years ago this city of Sydney was surrounded with fires, the smoke dimmed the sun, and black ash was sprinkled over our gardens and roofs. All that destruction from a spark! So the word we speak can have effects far beyond our sight and, once spoken, we can never call that word back. Malicious gossip is one of the worst failures that can hit a church. That is why we are to guard our tongues.

✳ *Let the words of my mouth*
and the meditations of my heart
be acceptable in your sight,
my Lord and my God.

Saturday March 28   *James 4.1-10*

Come close to God

In verse 4 the 'world' is seen as the enemy of God. Yet God 'so loved the world that he gave his Son'. Plainly there are different meanings for the one word. In John 3.16 the world is the entire family of humanity, beloved of God. Here in James the world is what human nature has become without God; it is the world of appetites, anger and violence.

Verse 5 is very hard to understand and translate. It probably means, 'the Spirit which God has planted in us jealously longs for our total devotion.' That is, there is no room for others to compete with God. The all-or-nothing to which God calls us.

Then two splendid sentences: 'Come close to God, and he will draw close to you' (verse 8). 'Humble yourselves before the Lord, and he will exalt you' (verse 10). Bound in the new covenant of grace, we trust that this is the deep reality of life.

✴ *We would be your friends, Lord Jesus,*
living in your way
living through your Spirit.

For further reflection or group discussion

● It has been easy for the church to point to the visible, obvious sins. But what do you understand from the New Testament to be the most dangerous – often insidious – sins that threaten our fellowship in Christ?

● To be reconciled with God – is it a vision, a hope, or a reality here and now? Are parts of our lives still unreconciled? How do we understand it?

A thought at the end of the section:

In the introduction I wrote of our ordinary life and the extraordinary grace of God in Jesus. Now I want to reverse that. The ordinary, natural, regular place for us all is to live as children of God. The extraordinary thing is our choice to live apart from God, as though we can rule the world.

FOR ACTION

As we approach Easter, seek different ways in which the cross has been seen through the ages – in pictures, statues, poetry, stories. What touches you most deeply? What offends you? Share this with a friend. Make this part of your Easter offering.

IBRA INTERNATIONAL APPEAL

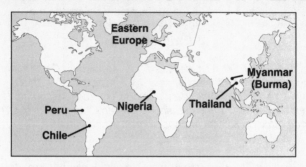

In five continents you will find Christians using IBRA material

Some Christians will be using books and Bible reading cards translated into their local language whilst others use English books. Some of the books are printed in this country but more and more of the books and cards are printed in their own countries. This is done by the IBRA International Fund working through churches and Christian groups and Christian Publishing houses overseas.

Each year we receive more requests for help from the IBRA International Fund, with greater emphasis on helping our overseas friends to produce their own version of IBRA material.

**THE ONLY MONEY WE HAVE TO SEND
IS THE MONEY YOU GIVE,
SO PLEASE HELP US AGAIN BY GIVING GENEROUSLY**

Place your gift in the envelope provided and give it to your IBRA representative, or send it direct to:

The IBRA International Appeal
1020 Bristol Road, Selly Oak
Birmingham Great Britain B29 6LB

Thank you for your help.

PASSIONTIDE – The Servant Lord

Notes based on the Authorized Version and the
Good News Bible by
J Emmette Weir

Emmette Weir is a minister of the Methodist Church in the Bahamas. He has also served as President of a theological institution and superintendent of a boys' correctional home. He is keenly interested in the contribution which Christians of the Third World make to biblical and theological scholarship.

The earliest Christian creed was simply 'Jesus is Lord'. In this short sentence the early Christians expressed the essence of their faith. Faced with the challenge of other religious cults, they boldly proclaimed their allegiance to Christ. Our purpose in these meditations is once again to examine our belief about Jesus and our relationship with him. Is he our Lord? And what challenge does his status as 'Servant' make to us?

Passion Sunday, March 29   *John 12.1-11 *C*

Hard choices

Should a church in a depressed area of a large city spend its money on renovation and expansion, or in the construction of badly needed housing for the poor? This dilemma is at the heart of today's reading. Mary, in a supreme act of devotion to Jesus, just a few days before his crucifixion, anoints him with an expensive ointment. Judas, treasurer of the apostolic group, sees this as needless extravagance in a poor world. Jesus, on the other hand, while recognizing Judas' concern, accepts the gift as an offering of devotion as he prepares to offer his life for the life of the world.

As Christians living in a world of gross inequalities, it is our responsibility to spend both time and money in acts of compassion – feeding the hungry, healing the sick and housing the homeless wherever we live. But it must always be clear that such acts are carried out in the name of Christ and under the constraint of his love.

✳ *Grant us wisdom in our use of the gifts*
you have bestowed upon us,
that we may not confine their use to our own comfort,
but use them for the benefit of others.

Monday March 30   *John 12.12-19*

Universal appeal

Sometimes those who oppose Christ express through their objections the most profound truths. Thus as Jesus entered Jerusalem, the religious leaders exclaimed, 'You see that you can prevail nothing; look the whole world has gone out to Him.' Frustrated by their defeat, they speak to us of the universal appeal of the gospel.

The multitudes, on the other hand, welcomed him as the long-expected Messiah, a nationalistic figure who would free them from Roman imperialism. But he came as the Suffering Servant, offering a new beginning, not only to his own nation but to all the world.

We live in a pluralistic age, and have to follow Christ and find our way amid the challenges and questions of belief which come to us from other religions and ideologies. This calls for respect for others' beliefs and experience of God, while we also share our faith with them. This means that we must know the Christ whom we follow; he must be our centre, our Saviour, our Lord. Unless we know him as such, and grow in our understanding of our faith, we shall have nothing to share!

✳ *Living Christ, grant us wisdom,*
courage and compassion
to proclaim your Lordship in the world.

Tuesday March 31   *John 12.20-33 *C*

Follow me

From India comes the story of an educated Hindu who had read the Bible and knew a lot about Jesus. When invited to become a Christian, he replied, 'A Christian? I'll be one when I see one!' The challenge he made is at the heart of today's reading.

Some Greeks asked the disciples if they might see Jesus. It is significant that the Gospel does not tell us whether they met him, or if Jesus made any attempt to see them. Instead we hear Jesus predicting his passion and challenging the Twelve to more costly discipleship.

Through the parable of the grain of wheat, he speaks of death as the means to new life, and urges them to die to their love of self and throw themselves wholeheartedly into following him (verses 25,26). He also indicates that in his death he will be 'lifted up', as a sacrifice to draw 'everyone' back to God (verse 32).

In his response Jesus implies that the disciples, by the quality of their ministry to others, are to be the means by which the Gentiles are to come to him. And so it must be with us.

✳ ***And they'll know we are Christians
by our love ...*** *World Council of Churches Song Book*

Wednesday April 1 *John 13.1-17 *C*

Servant Lord

In a large household, such as the one where Jesus and his disciples celebrated the Passover meal, washing the dusty feet of tired travellers was a menial task performed by the humblest of servants. No wonder the disciples held back. According to the other Gospels they were preoccupied with their discussions about which one was the greatest (Mark 10.35-37; Matthew 18.1-5). Jesus now reinforces his teaching about true greatness in this symbolic and unforgettable act.

He admonishes them, 'Ye call me Master and Lord: and ye say

well; for so I am.' He warns them to drop the pride which had prevented them from serving each other and to follow his example of service. Only so would they become the kind of disciples who would effectively draw others to follow him (John 15.8).

In a world which admires 'the show of force', we too must demonstrate this humility not only in the Christian community, but in the wider society where we are called to follow the way of Christ.

*Chinese paper-cut
From Nanjing Theological
Seminary*

If you have time, read Philippians 2.5-11.

✳ *Eternal Lord,*
who was prepared to serve those who called you Lord,
help us always to be mindful
that humility is the true sign of mature discipleship.

Thursday April 2   *John 13.18-30*

The challenge of Lordship!

A well-known Caribbean preacher, the late Rev Atheron Didier, once preached a sermon on Judas. After looking at the various theories of the apostle's treachery, he asserted that Judas was a revolutionary who wanted Jesus to be the conquering political Messiah. When it became clear that Jesus was committed to the Servant role instead, he betrayed him. Then, in a brilliant conclusion, the preacher challenged his congregation to accept the Lordship of Jesus!

It is interesting to note that this view is also followed by Western scholars who have identified Judas as 'the man who wanted a liberation struggle', and added that when Jesus refused to take this route, Judas betrayed him (*Who was Jesus?* Don Cupitt and Peter Armstrong, BBC, 1977).

Herein lies the key to understanding the tragedy of Judas. He did not want to follow Jesus' way. He wanted Jesus to conform to his own pre-conceived notions rather than accept Jesus' own understanding of his mission (Mark 8.31; 9.31; 10.33-45), or the challenge of Jesus' Lordship. Do we?

✳ *Thy way, not mine, O Lord,*
However dark it be.
Lead me by Thine own hand;
Choose out the path for me.

Horatius Bonar (1808-89)

Friday April 3   *John 18.1-11 *C*

Whose side?

The enemies of Jesus sent soldiers to arrest him. They were armed with lanterns, torches and swords, weapons of conventional warfare. Jesus rebuked Peter's impulsive act of defence (verses 10, 11). Why? Peter was resorting to the same hostile approach as the soldiers. Jesus had made it clear that he would not retaliate. He would win the world by love. Peter was acting according to worldly standards rather than the constraint of love (Matthew 5.43-45; cf. Mark 12.29-31; John 15.9-14). Jesus also made it clear that nothing would now deter him from the path of suffering (verse 11). His 'hour' had come.

In a world of declining moral standards, we are often tempted to adapt our Christian principles to the easy-going lifestyle of contemporary society. But compromise was not the way of Christ.

✴ *Lord, have mercy upon us.*
Help us to see our double standards
and false behaviour.
Forgive us, and help us to develop a Christlike
integrity.

Saturday April 4   *John 18.12-27 *C*
Is he your Lord?
Before rushing to condemn Peter for his threefold denial of Jesus, let us consider the circumstances under which he did so. Peter was under intense pressure from every direction. His master had been arrested and was hastily brought to trial by the High Priestly family – first century 'power brokers' summoning all the force that was available to them. While most of the apostles fled, Peter had the courage to venture into the Court of the High Priest. He was interrogated about his relationship with Jesus, though his Galilean accent did not make his disclaimer very convincing. Moreover, having attacked the High Priest's slave, he was a 'marked man'. Is it any wonder then that he instinctively distanced himself from the man under trial for charges of religious blasphemy and political dissension?

Would we have done any better than Peter? When we sit silently while others mock our Christian ideals, when we fail to speak out against corruption and injustice, or go about our work in such a way that our Christian commitment is unrecognizable – then are we not like Peter denying our Lord?

✴ *Lord, have mercy upon us,*
for we also, in the heat of the moment, deny you
and set your high standards aside for fear of
opposition.
Forgive us, and grant us courage and strength
that we may stand with you
and testify to your Lordship in every situation. Amen

For further reflection or group discussion

- How can we witness to the Lordship of Christ in a pluralistic world?
- How can we more effectively demonstrate the love of Christ every day?
- In what ways do we, inadvertently and deliberately, distance ourselves from Christ?

FOR ACTION

How can we overcome the most subtle temptations?

PASSIONTIDE –
The Son of Man is lifted up

Notes based on the Revised English Bible by
Penny Fowler

Penny Fowler, a former mission partner serving with the Methodist Church in Fiji in the South Pacific, is now Administrator of the Wesley & Methodist Studies Centre at Westminster College, Oxford, working with students of Methodist theology and history, and with ministers in training.

For the writer of the Fourth Gospel, Jesus (as Son of Man) is the link between earth and heaven (1.51). He came down from heaven and ascended again (3.13). The 'lifting up' of Jesus must happen in order for people to see who he is (8.28 and 12.34). A link is made (3.14) with Moses and the snake (Numbers 21.8-9), telling of the bronze serpent made by Moses and held up as a standard – a reminder to the Israelites of God's continuing care for his people.

The 'lifting up' has two meanings. Jesus will suffer a shameful and humiliating death lifted high on the cross for all to see, but he will also be raised to glory by God (12.23 and 13.31).

In John's Gospel, the timing of the death of Jesus is different from that of the Synoptic Gospels; Jesus dies at the time when the Passover lambs are killed. The Son of Man gives up his life as a sacrifice, but as the slaves in Egypt were led from despair to hope, so God will raise him again.

This week, as we read the story of the trial and crucifixion of Jesus, we will find that the passages reflect the feelings of the friends and family of Jesus. We can look at the story and try to understand what is 'going on', but at the end we can only stand with those at the foot of the Cross, look to the one who is lifted up, wait and wonder.

Palm Sunday, April 5   *John 18.28-40 *C*
'My kingdom does not belong to this world'
It was the time of one of the great Jewish festivals when the headquarters of the Roman governor was temporarily moved to

Jerusalem. Pilate is shown taking the trial of Jesus slowly, but trying to pass responsibility back to those who brought the charge in the first place. Jesus is at the centre of a struggle between the religious and political authorities, an innocent prisoner who is being used to strengthen both the authority of the chief priests, and that of Pilate who is anxious to keep the situation calm, and to preserve his position. For Jesus, the way forward leads to his death, a death that has become the symbol of God's infinite love for all people.

A teacher dies while trying to protect a pupil; a young and gifted priest is killed while helping one of those on the margins of society – we give thanks for the love of God that is seen through them and all who have laid down their lives for the sake of the Kingdom.

✳ *There is no greater love than this, that someone should lay down his life for his friends.*   *John 15.13*

Monday April 6   *John 19.1-16 *C*

'Here is your king'

We see Jesus at the mercy of his tormentors. Pilate is desperate to resolve this situation, perhaps by teaching Jesus a lesson, allowing a beating and then sending him away. The crown and purple robes are symbols of kingship and yet the wearer is subject to further humiliation. 'This is a man,' says Pilate. Can a man who has suffered all this really be a king? But Pilate eventually gives in to the demands of the crowds and Jesus is led away to be crucified. Not only is Jesus the *Logos* – the Eternal Word – but that Word became human and lived among us.

It is Passover, the time when Jews remember the years of suffering of their ancestors living as slaves in Egypt. God's care for his people, leading them from shame to restoration is the strong theme of Passover celebrations. We see Jesus, mocked and beaten, but we know that God will lift him up, leading him from humiliation to glory.

We are often tempted to despair and forget that God's purposes will be fulfilled. We pray that God will give us the strength to trust him when all seems hopeless.

✳ *Who is he, this king of glory?*
The Lord of Hosts, he is the king of glory.

Psalm 24.10

'The tunic was seamless'

'It was all in a day's work. There were three of them that day. One was a young man. They had beaten him but he was able and determined to carry his own cross. We carried out the executions, and waited for them to die. There were four of us and we were allowed to take the clothes of the prisoners, and share them between us. The young one had a tunic. It was woven in one piece – too good to tear up and share – so we tossed for it. Must have been my lucky day – I won it. It was good cloth, perhaps a friend gave it to him. He had friends – they waited near the cross. I needed the money so I sold the tunic, got a good price for it, too. I wonder where it is now?'

The Son of Man is lifted up on the cross and even his clothes are passed on to others, into the world of the Roman soldiers.

Reflect on the symbolism of the seamless tunic. Does it mean that Jesus is our High Priest (Exodus 28.32), or is it a symbol of the unity of those who are joined together by the death of Jesus?

✳ ***There is one mediator between God and man, Christ Jesus, himself man, who sacrificed himself to win freedom for all mankind.***   *1 Timothy 2.5-6*

'The Son of Man is lifted up' – on the cross

There are several people or groups of people to whom Jesus shows concern, even as he suffers:

- his mother who is given a home and support;
- the loved disciple who takes his place in the family;
- the executioners who are able to ease the pain of the dying man.

In death, as in life, the love of Jesus is shown to all. He makes provision for two people close to him but extends his concern to those who are his 'enemies'. He is allowing them to gain merit (Proverbs 25.21-22), and accepts the wine they offer. Read also and reflect on Romans 12.20.

For John, Jesus remains in control. He lays his life down of his own free will (10.18), triumphant that he has completed the work that God gave him to do.

✳ *May we seek to have the love of Jesus so that we can*
reach out with hope to the sad and desperate,
even when we, ourselves, are at our lowest,
and have no hope.

Thursday April 9   *Job 14.1-14 *C*

'If a man dies, can he live again?'

The disciples' hopes are dashed. Jesus was one they thought
they could rely on and now he has gone. How could they be so
wrong? Why does God treat them like this? Do they recall the
story of Job? He faced the loss of all that was precious to him,
and his friends could offer no comfort. Is there any way forward
for those who have lost everything?

Today's words, from earlier days, assure us that there is hope.
Help will come even if it seems a long way off. God is with the
poor and vulnerable; as a parent suffers with a child in pain, so
God sheds tears with us in our despair.

Spend some time thinking about the tree. Picture a tree in your
mind – its shape and colour, its leaves that will fall but that allow
new life to grow – the fruit that develops. Reflect on your life
growing in similar ways. Does this help you in your understanding
of God's care and provision?

✳ *'I would not lose hope' (verse 14)*
We confess those times when we have lost hope for
the future.

Good Friday, April 10   *Psalm 31 *C*

'In you, Lord, I have found refuge'

Traditionally, the sacrament of Holy Communion is not observed
on Good Friday, emphasizing that this is a day of serious
reflection, a day of deep sadness and feelings of abandonment.
As Jesus utters the cry, 'Why have you forsaken me?' (not
recorded by John) so Christians may decide to deny themselves
the comfort of the offering of bread and wine.

Read Psalm 31 or, if you would prefer a shortened version,
read verses 1-5, 15-16. Then read the verses through again as a
basis for your prayers, giving thanks for those special times when
God has been your 'rock' and 'stronghold'.

'Into your hands I commit my spirit' (verse 5). Reflect on these
words of Jesus from the cross. What new insights into the death
of Jesus have you gained today?

✳ *My God, my God, why have you forsaken us?*
We see the suffering of your people -
those driven from their homes by the actions of others,
children facing abuse from those who should be
    providing safety,
the hopelessness of young people without homes or
    work,
the fear and confusion of those suffering from mental
    illness or incurable disease,
our own fears for the future ...

Spend time in prayer for those who today are not able to say
'My fortunes are in your hand'. How is God leading you to act?

Saturday April 11   *John 8.21-30*

'When you have lifted up the Son of Man you will know that I am what I am'

We have read this week of how Jesus was lifted up – before
Pilate, in front of the crowd, and on the cross. There were those
who 'put their faith in him' (verse 30) and those who followed him
right up to the moment of his death – Mary and the other women,
and the beloved disciple. Joseph was a secret disciple who made
the arrangements for the burial of the body.

There was a choice – to deny his authority and to lift Jesus on
to the cross, or to recognize who he was, and where his authority
lay. Human beings made the wrong choice but the power of God
raised Jesus up.

There are no 'wrong choices' for God's power will overcome.
Thanks be to God!

✳ *We know that in all things God works for good with*
    those who love him.   *Romans 8.28 (GNB)*

For further reflection or group discussion

● Jesus moves from an active role to a passive one. What does
  this teach us about the Kingdom of God?
● Job writes of a tree that is cut down. What images are helpful
  to you when thinking of God's power and strength?

EASTER – HE IS RISEN INDEED!
1. Seeing and believing

Notes based on the New Revised Standard Version by
Bao Jia yuan

Bao Jia yuan graduated from Nanjing Union Theological Seminary in 1966. Unable to work as a minister during the Cultural Revolution, he was sent to the countryside for many years. It was not until 1987 that Bao could begin full-time church work. In 1988 he was finally ordained. The Revd Bao is currently Deputy General Secretary and Director of the Nanjing office of the China Christian Council, where he is responsible for overseas relationships.

During the Cultural Revolution (1966-1976), churches were closed down, along with universities and other institutions, and ministers were assigned secular jobs. Christians in China passed through 'the valley of the shadow of death'. Reflecting on words from the New Testament, Bishop Ting (Chairman of the China Christian Council) reminds us: 'The Cultural Revolution was a great period for Christians to understand that when we are weak and dying, life is in the offing, and to learn that strength is found in weakness, and life in dying. Christ's own resurrection tells us that the meek are to inherit the earth.'

Since 1979 in China, the number of churches has increased and we are experiencing a revival. In recent years, there has been a conspicuous growth in congregations and church membership. According to our rough estimate (in 1996), there are over 10,000 churches open for public worship, among which more than 4,000 have been newly built, and there are also some 20,000 groups of Protestant Christians meeting in homes. The total number of Protestant Christians in China is estimated at between eight and ten million.

Easter Day, April 12   *Mark 16.1-13*
The stone has been rolled away
A careful reading of the resurrection story in the Gospel of Mark shows that the first Easter morning was not filled with joy, peace and excitement as we tend to say today. Mark draws a different picture.

The women were exhausted, not only in body, but also in soul, after experiencing the severe blow of losing Jesus whom they deeply loved. That was why they said to one another, 'Who will roll away the stone for us from the entrance to the tomb?' To their surprise when they got there, the stone had already been rolled away. The entrance was open and they could enter. It was unbelievable! Jesus had been raised! Ironically, the women were so scared by what they saw and what they heard from the young man in white, they could not accept the fact! Their hearts were overcome by doubt, fear and terror. They fled and said nothing to anyone, for they were afraid.

Like those women, we are often depressed by the heavy stone of fear and uncertainty, sadness from misfortune and shadow of insecurity. How can we roll away the stone from our hearts? Free ourselves from the burdens? Have you met the risen Jesus? There is nothing too hard for God!

The open tomb is the open door of possibility for us. The open tomb is the open door of the future for our world. Why do you not believe?

✳ *Risen Lord, cleanse our hearts of all deceit;*
   teach us to be true and help us to have integrity
   in all we say and do.

Monday April 13   *Acts 10.34-43 *C*

Christ is Lord of all

In his first sermon to Gentiles, Peter stressed the impartiality of God towards every nation. Anyone who fears God, and does what is right, is acceptable to him. This message was obviously very much appreciated by non-Jews, and gradually a breakthrough was made in the barriers that had built up between Jews and Gentiles.

In a nation like China, where people have been strongly influenced by the ideas of the great Confucius for centuries, and where the majority of Chinese are non-Christian today, how do we share the good news with others? As Christians, there is no reason to isolate ourselves from non-Christians, or to feel superior to them. It is important to explore common ground and to enter into dialogue with one another, that we may share God's blessings to us all. Christian tolerance and a broad vision are indispensable for the sake of the gospel. Jesus is Lord of all. What do we really mean when we say that? Through Jesus' words, the life of the Church and our communities will be renewed, and the life of our nations and the world will prosper.

✳ *Our Lord, you are the Lord of forgiveness, healing and*
     hope.
   We thank you that your own experience of death
   and heartbreaking trauma enables you to understand
   our sin, sickness and sorrows.

Tuesday April 14   *1 Corinthians 15.1-11 *C*

If you hold firmly to ...

Christians must hold firmly to the essence of the good news, as
did Paul who was 'not disobedient to the heavenly vision'
received on the Damascus road. What was that vision? It was
that Christ died and was buried for our sin, in accordance with the
Scriptures; that Christ was raised on the third day to make new
life possible for us all; that he appeared to his disciples to leave
for us some visible proof of his resurrection to help us believe.
Paul tells his readers that he too saw the risen Christ in that
decisive experience.

   If we hold firmly to God, he will hold us fast when we fall,
because he is all-powerful, the source of all wisdom and all love.
He promises abundant life. The power of resurrection will never
fail, but will be seen in the insights which come to us through the
generations and in all places. When you are weak and dying, do
not forget that the grace of God is sufficient for you, and that life is
always being transformed.

   Along with the growth of the Church, dramatic changes in
Chinese Christian life have taken place. Mutual love has been
restored and harmonious family relationships have been established through reconciliation. Christian values have been demonstrated through the many witnesses to our faith in our society.

✳ *Lord, grant us your peace that we might impart your*
     grace and truth to those in doubt.
   Grant us your love that we might guide the world to the
     Father's heart.

Wednesday April 15   *1 Corinthians 15.12-19 *C*

If there is no resurrection ...

Paul argued with those at Corinth who did not believe in the
resurrection of Christ, and the resurrection of the dead. If there is
no resurrection, he says, there is no Christian faith, and the faith of
many converts has been in vain; those who believe in Christ are to
be pitied. You are not only living in your sins and going to perish

without hope, but will be blamed for a new sin: misrepresenting God. But Christ was raised in his own time in history. We are surrounded by a 'great cloud of witnesses' who saw Jesus, touched him and believed in him, and their lives were transformed.

The resurrection story has a direct impact on our lives. It is easy to lose faith, and this leads to a deterioration in moral standards in a materialized and secular society.

Today China ranks with developing countries; it has gained great achievements in economic growth and social reform. In a changing society it is not enough for us to seek individual salvation and personal piety. We are called to present our faith in a spirit of hope, service and witness and in ways that challenge contemporary morality. Is Jesus in our daily life?

✳ *Jesus, help us to open our eyes to recognize you; encourage us to dedicate every day to live for you and for values that will last.*

Thursday April 16   *1 Corinthians 15.20-28 *C*

The first fruits

After the period of so-called Cultural Revolution (which actually was neither cultural nor revolutionary), the first publication of Chinese Bibles was delivered into the hands of Christians whose Bibles were confiscated and burnt in the years of suffering. They knelt down to receive them with tears gushing from their eyes. They understood the significance of 'first fruits', and rejoiced in the resurrection they were now experiencing. They were hungry and thirsty for the Word of God which, through the power of memory, had sustained them in their pilgrimage through the 'valley of the shadow of death'.

God is walking before us and paving the way for us. There is a Chinese proverb 'When the mountains and streams come to an end, and we think there is no path, the shady willows and bright blossoms bring us to yet another village.' The resurrection is like that in our experience. Like the shady willows and bright blossoms, Christ brings the hope of eternal life. His marvellous care of the Chinese Church in the mist of bewilderment once again tells of his faithfulness.

✳ *Lord, you are the one who overcomes all enemies and brings us the first fruits so that those who are identified with you through faith will be raised at the time of your coming.*

Living a Christian life

As the two sides of a coin are different, you must consider yourselves both dead to sin and alive to God in Christ Jesus. After believing in Jesus, you are no longer enslaved to sin; you are freed from it. The resurrection of Christ brings new life. Human limitations no longer have control over you. Living and enjoying this new life in Christ is so important to you and to others as well. A Christian life must be like that. Let your light shine before others, that they may see your goodness and offer praise to God (Matthew 5.16). A Christian life will challenge others to see the value of having faith; it will be full of joy, patience, kindness and righteousness; it will have strength to overcome the temptations which come from materialism and secularism. A Christian life makes its contribution to the spirituality of the whole people in any social context.

The person who follows Christ in China must learn how to appreciate those who are different – people who have no faith. Bishop Ting says, 'The very attempt to deny God at least raises before the people the question of God, and that is of evangelistic significance.' Is that also true in your context?

✳ *God, giver of life, teach us to deny ourselves,*
 to carry the cross,
 to follow you and to serve one another.

The rock was turned into a pool of water

Israel never forgot the desert journey from Egypt to Canaan, and neither will Chinese Christians forget their deliverance. The first part of this psalm praises the power of the Lord's salvation, and the latter part describes God's presence in all creation. Verse 8 recalls Exodus 17.6. In the desert-water was hard to find. The people quarrelled with Moses and protested to God. It seemed to Moses like the end of the way. He too cried out to God, and was shown a rock and commanded to strike it. And water came pouring out. Isn't God's providence amazing?

Like the rock in the desert, Christ was struck and crucified, and for this he is also glorified. Risen and ascended, living water flows from him to sustain and refresh us for ever, and to flow on from us to refresh others (John 7.38). And there is enough for the whole world to come and drink.

✳ *Lord, let us receive your living water*
which will become in us a spring of water transforming us
and the world for ever.

For further reflection or group discussion

● Imagine that you are experiencing adverse circumstances. How will the story of Christ's resurrection help you to experience the presence of God?
● What fresh insights have come to you through the Chinese experience?

God of many names
  Shangdi
    Tianzhu
      God of all peoples
        God of China

No great wall
  can keep you out,
no great dam
  stop your love flowing.

From mountain to sea
in paddy field and city
you walk with your people,
  you see
    smile
      suffer
        weep.

In you
strangers become friends
and so
we weep for China's pain
  sing of China's faith
    pray for China's people
      hope for China's future

Lord of all peoples
  Tianzhu
    Shangdi

Prayer from the China study pack, A Future and a Hope
(Council of Churches for Britain and Ireland, 1996)

FOR ACTION

While seeking to be changed yourself through the power of the risen Lord, appreciate the differences in others, including those of other faiths and those of no faith at all.

EASTER 2. Exploring truth

Notes based on the New International Version by
Luis V Veagra

Luis Veagra, a Costa Rican minister of the Methodist Church in the Caribbean and the Americas and former Chairman of the Panama/Costa Rica District, is World Church Secretary for the Americas and the Caribbean in the Methodist Church in Britain.

Christians continue to wrestle with the truth about the resurrection of Jesus and its meaning: 'Did it really happen; does it assure us of a life after death?' Doubt is deepened when believers are scorned and accused of believing in a 'hallucination of Jesus' disciples'. This week's readings and notes are about people like us who struggle with disappointment, confusion, fears, doubts and pain, and through encounters with the risen Lord, discover the truth about his resurrection and its power to meet their everyday needs.

2nd Sunday of Easter, April 19   *Luke 24.13-35 *C*

Exploring truth in the midst of complexity

The two disciples who walked with Jesus on the road to Emmaus had a problem with the truth about his resurrection. They had expected Jesus to subdue the Romans and liberate his people. Now that Jesus had been crucified and buried, that hope had vanished. That confusion was deepened by the women's claim that Jesus had risen. The truth dawned on them when, in the intimacy of a home, Jesus blessed, broke and shared bread with them. With this act the story of the women was confirmed and their confusion was dispelled.

In life we wrestle with circumstances we cannot explain. In an article entitled 'Searching for truth in Sri Lanka', Kenneth Mulder, an American mission intern, tells how he struggled to find the truth about the war in that country: 'There I was forced to deal with the question of truth in a tense, explosive context. Once again my faith was shaken. In an environment of violence and conflict, I found historical truth under heavy assault.' Not having discovered the truth about who is to be blamed for the war, he left, a disappointed and confused person.

✳ *O living God, when circumstances around us baffle*
and confuse us, join us in our search for truth
and help us to find it in your Son, the risen Christ.

Monday April 20   *Luke 24.36-49 *C*

Exploring truth in the midst of fear

To strengthen their grasp of the reality of his resurrection, Jesus showed himself to the disciples (verse 36). Showing them his hands and feet where the nail prints were visible, and eating a piece of fish, revealed that he was not a ghost, but a living person. Though the resurrection transcended the limits of time and space, it was real, and manifested itself in everyday life. And so it does today.

Maggie and David Stringer, mission partners in Bolivia, were faced with a dilemma. Marcela needed blood desperately for an operation. There was none in the hospital at Montero and no money to buy it from elsewhere. But her relatives and friends had blood to give. And so, encouraged by Maggie, they all went to the hospital. Maggie and David wrote of their experience: 'We were a community of friends, sharing our faith by giving the only useful thing we had, blood. Everyone knew that Marcela was fighting for her life; we were all there to fight for her ... we were united as one body, sharing the hope that it was not too late to renew the life of Marcela.'

✳ *Lord, draw near to those who are suffering*
and show them your wounded hands and side,
that they may know that you are suffering with them.

Tuesday April 21   *Isaiah 25.6-9 *C*

Exploring truth in the midst of death

In the eighth century BC the people of Judah suffered drought and famine, and at the same time invasion and threats from foreign powers. Today's reading offers a message of hope – a vision of the banquet God will provide for all humankind, and contains one of the clearest statements in the Old Testament that God will overcome death:

'... he will swallow up death for ever.
The Sovereign Lord will wipe away the tears
    from all faces' (verse 8a).

See also Isaiah 26.19; Psalms 49.14-15; 73.24.

To a people who had endured mourning and sorrow, this word responded to their greatest yearnings. Many fear death because they have no hope beyond this life. Ruben, a school teacher and friend of mine, was dying of cancer in the hospital in Colon where I was minister. He hadn't been to church for some time. But his wife called me to his bedside one day before he died. As we spoke, I shared with him the words of Jesus, 'I am the resurrection and the life. He who believes in me will live, even though he dies; and whoever lives and believes in me will never die' (John 11.25-26). After praying with him, he held my hand and said, 'I believe'.

✳ *Pray for those you know who are suffering a terminal illness, that they may be assured of life beyond death; and for those who mourn the death of a loved one, that they may discover Christ in their bereavement.*

Wednesday April 22   *John 20.24-31 *C*

Exploring truth in the midst of doubt

The post-resurrection stories are full of doubt. In the Gospel of Mark, the disciples were afraid and trembled with amazement (Mark 16.8-14); in Luke, they dismissed the women's story as nonsense (Luke 24.11); in Matthew, when they met Jesus in Galilee 'some doubted' (Matthew 28.17). But it was Thomas who expressed that doubt most explicitly (verse 25). From doubt, Thomas was led to discover the living Lord.

My son grew up in a Christian environment. He took part in daily prayer at home; he attended a Methodist school, Sunday School, youth group, Sunday worship, and at times Bible studies. Yet, at the age of 27, he continues to struggle with certain aspects of faith with which he has not yet come to terms. When we talk on the telephone, he insists on raising questions with his mother and myself. We always respond, saying, 'Fermin, your doubts are valid; don't give up; keep searching and you will discover the truth in Jesus Christ.'

✳ *Lord, help us to be honest with our doubts,*
and keep us searching until we find our answer
in your living presence.

Thursday April 23   *Psalm 118 *C*

Exploring truth in the midst of worship

This psalm is the last of six psalms known as the *Hallel,* hymns of praise which were used during the celebration of Passover. For centuries the Church has used it on Easter Day, since it speaks of God's enduring mercy. Verse 17 gives the assurance of God's gift of life: 'I will not die, but live.' The words bring to memory God's great act of deliverance in Egypt, and guidance through the wilderness to settlement in Palestine. We cannot read into this cry the New Testament belief in life after death, but – from the perspective of Christ's resurrection and promise of eternal life – it reinforces hope: that we can find new life in all adverse circum- stances. Death is experienced in many ways. Any loss which destroys our sense of well-being, and throws us into a state of meaninglessness, is death – the breakdown of a marriage, the loss of a job, a failure in business, or the death of a relative or friend. To affirm that 'I will not die, but live' is to say that in Jesus Christ we can face any loss.

✳ *Loving God,*
   who is with us in every experience of life,
   open our eyes
   to see signs of resurrection
   in situations where hope is hard to find.
   Deepen our commitment
   to share others' pain,
   so that in dying to self
   we may find life.

Friday April 24   *Acts 8.26-40 *C*

Exploring truth in the word of God

The Ethiopian eunuch was reading a passage from Isaiah which spoke of the Servant of the Lord who suffered on behalf of his people (Isaiah 52.13 to 53.12). Responding to the man's inquiry about its meaning, Philip proclaimed to him the good news that Jesus was God's Suffering Servant who had been denied justice in his death, yet vindicated in his resurrection. The story is told as a divine encounter in which God is the primary actor.

God's word continues to confront and convince people of the saving power of the risen Lord. Saray, a nine-year-old found a portion of the Gospel of John in the road. She picked it up and began reading. 'I have found a wonderful book,' she said. 'Can I go to the church where it is explained?' Both parents agreed and she began to attend the Methodist Church in Pedregal, Panama. From that day her life was changed. Today, at the age of 60, she says, 'I still find the Bible fascinating. It is new every day and rich in content. Above all, it led me to Jesus Christ.'

✳ O send thy Spirit, Lord,
  Now unto me,
That he may touch my eyes,
  And make me see;
Show me the truth concealed
  Within thy word,
And in thy book revealed
  I see the Lord.   *Alexander Groves (1842-1909)*

Saturday April 25   *2 Corinthians 12.1-10*

Exploring truth in the midst of weakness

Paul testifies to the triumph of grace over weakness, and to the truth that divine power is more evident in human frailty. He speaks of a thorn in the flesh (verse 7b), some chronic, painful physical suffering, and weaknesses, insults, hardships, and persecution (verse 10). Though these are painful, he prefers to boast of them, rather than of deep mystical experiences, since it is in suffering that he finds the power of God's grace. Paul's faith is based on Jesus Christ who, in extreme powerlessness, was raised from the dead by the power of God (13.4).

Mrs. Benn, a member of Trinity Church in Colon, Panama, suffered greatly from migraine headaches, glaucoma, arthritis and an enlarged heart. I was to take her to an Easter Sunday morning service, but because it was one of her bad days, I did not insist. 'Reverend', she said, 'I am not going to allow Satan to keep me back on this Easter Day. The grace of my risen Lord is enough for me. I am going to church today.'

✳ O God, through the cross of your Son
you have chosen to show redemptive power.
Through our weakness grant us genuine strength.

For further reflection or group discussion

● Reflect on the Old Testament passages read this week and think how far we can see in them a development of belief in life after death.
● Stories have been shared this week. Recall similar experiences you have had of the living Christ, particularly in crises.

FOR ACTION

Spend some time with someone who is terminally ill.

EASTER 3.
Responding to challenge

Notes based on the New Revised Standard Version by
Jil Brown

Jil Brown, a local preacher of the Methodist Church, is a post-graduate student at the University of Birmingham, exploring the relationship between Black women and Jesus Christ.

'All authority in heaven and on earth has been given to me.' The disciples were now challenged to continue the mission to which they had been called, only this time Jesus would not be physically with them. From here began a journey fraught with challenges, and of uncertainty, adversity, accusation and witness. And history has shown countless others sharing the same painful journey of obedience, believing in the ultimate victory of their cause.

3rd Sunday of Easter, April 26   *Matthew 28.16-20*
The promise of Jesus' presence
Sojourner Truth was once asked by a preacher if the Bible was where she gained her material for preaching. She replied, 'No, honey, can't preach from de Bible – can't read a letter. When I preaches, I has just one text to preach from, an' I always preaches from this one. My text is 'When I found Jesus' (from *Sojourner Truth: Narrative and Book of Life 1850 and 1875,* Olive Gilbert).

Sojourner Truth had been a slave. She had witnessed the enslavement of her people, the selling of her own parents by slave owners. And yet she still testified to the love of Christ. Where did her conviction come from? After all, she had not, like the disciples, been physically present with Jesus during his earthly ministry? Yet she, and others like her, believed firmly that Jesus Christ was not only with them but endured what they endured. It was this conviction that enabled her to fulfil the task to which she had been called – to preach the word of God.

Jesus said, 'And remember, I am with you always to the end of the age.'

✷ *Ever-present Creator, thank you for those past and present, whose lives testify to your promise. Amen*

Beyond all expectations

'I never expected that!' Certainly these words could be echoed by the man who had never been able to walk. His expectations were determined by his circumstances, and Peter's expectations were determined by his faith in Christ's promise and the authority that he had given the disciples.

During the years of slavery, there were many slave revolts. Slaves believed that as surely as God had saved Daniel from the lions, God would perform the same redeeming act for them. Their expectations exceeded the reality of their circumstances, but their encounter with the risen Christ challenged them to expect and demand more.

> All the broken hearts
> shall rejoice;
> all those
> who are heavy laden,
> whose eyes are tired
> and do not see,
> shall be lifted up
> to meet with
> the motherly healer.
> The battered souls and bodies
> shall be healed;
> the hungry
> shall be fed;
> the imprisoned
> shall be free;
> all her earthly children
> shall regain joy
> in the reign
> of the just and loving one
> coming for you
> coming for me
> in this time
> in this world.

Sun Ai Lee Park, Hong Kong
(In God's Image, Asian Woman's Resource Centre 1986)

✳ **Creator God, teach us to expect the unexpected.**

To obey or not

The persecution of Christians ensued. The events surrounding Stephen's death (Acts 7.54 to 8.1) were firmly on Saul's mind as he set out on his journey to Damascus, so determined was he now to extradite Christians he knew to be there. What could have been further from his mind than the possibility of an encounter with the risen Christ!

Saul was challenged to accept the voice in his vision as the authentic voice of Christ whose followers he was persecuting. But the greater challenge came when, unable to see and totally dependent on others, he was instructed to get up, continue his journey to Damascus, and wait: to wait until he was told what to do.

Jarena Lee, an African American woman who was called to preach, was told directly that as a woman the pulpit was certainly not the place for her. The Revd Richard Allen's response to Jarena Lee's vocation was to point out that '... our Discipline knew nothing at all about it' – that it *did not call* for women preachers. Jarena remained faithful to her call despite the obstacles, and some eight years later began her preaching ministry.

✳ ***Creator God, may we discern when it is time to act
and time to wait. Amen***

Just like that!

Two men, who had once been openly hostile toward all Black people, told, on a television chat show, how their attitude had been changed by meeting and getting to know one Black person, so that they were ready to embrace the very people they once despised. Likewise Saul, vehemently opposed to Christian believers, encountered the very source of his hostility on the road to Damascus.

We are often sceptical of people whose value systems 'change' so radically for the positive. We question their sincerity and expect this transformation to be short-lived, and sometimes we are proved right. Ananias' response was understandable! In Saul's case, however, his confrontation with the risen Christ was permanently life-changing.

We may not be persecuting others, or engaging in activities to demonstrate resentment towards people of different belief systems and cultures. Yet are we, by our lack of effort to show solidarity with those who are marginalized and to speak out on their behalf, failing to respond to the challenge of Christ to love as God loves?

✳ *Transforming Creator, challenge us again.*

Thursday April 30   *Acts 26.19-29*

Whose side are you leaning on?

Paul has been arrested and is on trial before King Agrippa, accused, as Stephen was, of speaking against the Law and the Temple. In his defence, Paul testifies to his life as a Jew; to his previous hostility to the very name of Jesus; and to his encounter on the Damascus Road with the risen Christ. He is no more afraid to testify in front of the king than he is to those in the Temple, such is his conviction.

History has many examples of people, such as Nelson Mandela and Steve Biko – both vehement opposers of South African apartheid – who in their time were called to account for their words and actions, to validate who they were and what they stood for. The challenge for them was to hold fast to what they believed, even knowing that their defence might prove detrimental to them.

✳ *Enabling Creator, strengthen us*
that we may have the courage of our convictions.

Friday May 1   *Psalm 30*C*

A cry for freedom today

I light this candle, O Lord,
to burn the darkness of my soul.
Burn my hatred, burn my fears,
burn my shame and burn my pains,
and melt me to newness.
help me to become a new being.
Then I will ask from you, O God,
the burning of his soul ...
him who caused this hatred and these fears,
him who caused this shame and pain.

Burn his darkened soul ...
Burn his arrogance and pride ...
By the light of your love, melt his heart

101

so that he will return to you.
Let him return to you, O God!

Psalm by a Filipino woman

✳ **Pray for those who have lost faith in human goodness, and in God.**

Saturday May 2   *Revelation 5.11-14 *C*

This vision of John assures us of the victory that is ours through Christ's earthly sacrifice. Verses 5 and 6 demonstrate that the victory has already been won, and so the scroll (representing the last stage in God's redemptive plan for the world, including God's purposes of blessing and judgement) can be opened.

The time will come when all recognize and acknowledge the source of all our hope. Those of us who profess to know this source *now* can share our hope with others.

Millions of African people were earthly sacrifices. They were brutalized, raped and murdered during slavery, and their subjugations were 'justified' in the name of Jesus. Rather than be earthly slaves, some chose freedom by taking their own lives and the lives of their children. Their only source of hope was God.

✳ **Reflect on the words of verse 12.**

For further reflection or group discussion

● Martin Luther King said, 'If you don't stand for something, you'll fall for anything.' What are the issues you feel strongly about and why?

● How are you putting your feelings into action?

FOR ACTION

Borrow from your local library a book *(see Friday's example)* giving the stories of ex-slaves and reflect on their relationships with their owners and with God.

QUALITY OF LIFE
1. From here to eternity

Notes based on the Revised English Bible by
Ralph Lee

Ralph Lee, who was formerly on the staff of the Hong Kong Christian Council and chaplain at the United Christian Hospital, served with the World Church in Britain Partnership in South Wales from 1990 to 95. He is now the Superintendent minister of the Kowloon circuit of the Methodist Church in Hong Kong.

Although these notes are being written in 1996, by the time you read them Hong Kong will have been politically part of China for almost a year – since July 1997. For some years, people have been asking what quality of life we will experience after the change-over. This question and others will continue in the minds of people, both here in Hong Kong and overseas, particularly on issues of human rights, freedom of movement and religious tolerance. What message will the Christian faith be able to share with the people of Hong Kong? Will we be able to identify with Christians in China and respond with them?

4th Sunday of Easter, May 3   *John 10.22-30 *C*

Eternal life

In Hong Kong, on the peak of Lantau Island, there stands a huge statue of the Buddha. It was built recently by the Precious Lotus Monastery. Lantao Peak is one of the highest mountains and the statue the tallest in Hong Kong. Having climbed the many steps to the feet of the Buddha, we can see far across into China and yet feel wondrously close to heaven. Touching the statue, we are aware both of the history of our peoples and of a sense of eternity. There can indeed be oneness, harmony and the reality of eternal life here on earth. In the Fourth Gospel, 'eternal life' is not about something that will only happen to us in the future, but a new quality of life which we may experience here and now, and which can never be destroyed.

Yet Lantao Peak can also symbolize disharmony. At the official opening, the last Governor of Hong Kong and the Chinese Official were invited. After the ceremony, the Governor held out his hand for a handshake, but the Chinese Official returned it with a symbolic Buddhist gesture – with both hands clasped and making a polite bow. There was no touching, no friendship, no compromise on either side, no reconciliation – no oneness.

Often, for deeply religious reasons, we build or make symbols that are meant to uplift our human nature and make peace between ourselves and God. Yet, because of our differences and vested interests, we fail to be changed.

✴ *Jesus, Messiah, who walks on our streets*
and relates to people in the market-place,
give us that eternal quality of life which reflects
your own oneness with the Father.

Monday May 4   *Acts 9.36-43 *C*

Life and work live on

Tabitha was dead, washed and laid to rest, waiting to be buried. But Peter raised her to life again. Can a 'frozen body' be revived nowadays? A medical expert was asked by a television network to comment. She gave a definite answer: 'No way!' Yet the miracle is that the quality of a person's life is by no means dead. Tabitha's 'acts of kindness and charity' lived on. And we can see this happening all around us.

I took part in a memorial service for a secondary school principal recently. The feeling of loss was so great that all the speakers cried and the whole assembly of students (apart from those who had not known her well) sobbed with tears. For ten years, the principal had struggled with the increasing pain and physical weakness of cancer but her commitment to her work had not wavered. Her life had touched many colleagues and students. A few weeks later, I visited the school again to attend their graduation service. It was a joy to be among them. It is a school of excellence in every way. The new principal carries forward the achievements of his predecessor.

✴ *Living Christ, through your life among us,*
may God's love and acts of kindness and charity
continue to live among us daily, everywhere.

Tuesday May 5   *Romans 8.1-11*

Let life be directed by the Spirit

On the night before the arrival of the Foreign Secretary of the People's Republic of China to Hong Kong – for the inauguration of the 'Selection Committee' of the Special Administrative Region – a small number of pro-democrats had a sit-in and a hunger-strike outside the meeting premises. They protested against the 'closed shop' selection procedure and the unacceptability of forming, after 1 July 1997, a future 'Provisional Legislature', which by international law is illegal.

This small minority of citizens knew perfectly well that their action would have little effect. They risked being blacklisted by China and perhaps even prosecuted. Time and time again they refused to give up the struggle to secure a higher level of democracy. Yet the majority of people are giving in to the inevitable force of power for the sake of personal safety. They continue to move along a lower level of life – bound by human weakness.

Being a Christian, life is transformed by the Spirit so that it is no longer ordinary. We are given a spiritual outlook and our lives are directed by the Spirit. The Spirit brings hope for the future, and that remains in our hearts. The Spirit also witnesses to that life and peace which is envisioned by Christ for all the earth.

Hong Kong, as it is now, owes a lot to a courageous few who are not intimidated by man-made laws or threats to life.

✴ *Open our hearts to feel your Spirit,*
Open our hands to touch your people,
Open our lips to denounce injustice and incompetence,
Open our ears to hear the voices of victims of exploitation,
Open our eyes to see your hands at work in the world,
And give us courage to follow the pace of Christ.

Anesia Nascimento, Brazil
from More Living Prayers for Today (IBRA 1997)

Wednesday May 6   *2 Corinthians 4.1-15*

Out of darkness light shall shine

Light is always there. In spite of all the blockages, darkness cannot shut it off. We admire those who dare to bring fresh light to the world and awaken our conscience, even though at times it is shamefully painful.

At the close of 1996, Wang Dan, the student leader of the 1989 'Tiananmen Square' democracy movement, was imprisoned again. This time he was sentenced to eleven years. Quietly and peacefully he accepted the unavoidable consequence of speaking up for the truth of his belief. His harsh sentence stirred the conscience of the world, while at the same time sending a warning to many in Hong Kong. 'Today Wang Dan, tomorrow you and me,' said one devout Christian community leader.

Such courage against all odds is remarkable. People like the young man in Beijing and many in Hong Kong inspire others to bring hope and light to situations of darkness and oppression. They may be 'hard pressed, but never cornered ... struck down, but never killed' (verses 8-9).

Never lose heart, for God is with us.

✳ *Living God, strengthen us that we may never feel isolated.*
Remind us again that truth cannot be silenced.
Wherever people are in darkness,
make them brave and open their eyes
to see the light that is never dimmed.
And make us your candles!

Thursday May 7   *Philippians 1.18-26*

What makes people fearless?

For someone to declare that 'death is gain' – what a tremendous impact that message has, whether in prison or free. From prison in Rome, Paul was able to encourage those outside – believers at large and perhaps even the general public. We can sense there is no fear in him, for within him is the life of Christ. That fearlessness springs from courage and compels one to proclaim the gospel in harsh situations. Such fearlessness comes from God's indwelling love and from a genuine love for others.

In the months prior to the handing over of Hong Kong to China, a small minority of people fearlessly campaigned for freedom of speech, the protection of human rights, and a more democratic society after 1997. A few entered more risky situations to express their convictions. Their disregard of their own safety and security, then and for the future, was a thorn in the eye of the incoming power.

Yet such a display of belief is an example to all of us. It is also a sign of hope for others. Can we be challenged by people like that and remain selfishly quiet and passive?

✳ *O Lord our God,*
who for our sake made the ultimate sacrifice
on Calvary's cross, forgive our sins.
Cleanse us from the stain of guilt.
Renew us in heart and mind,

and grant us the courage and power to fight against all evil.
Enrich our lives with the presence of your Holy Spirit.
Teach us the life of righteousness,
that we may walk faithfully in your footsteps.
Give us confidence to exercise self-control
in paths of temptation,
that we may be truly free to serve you,
to the honour and glory of your holy name. Amen

Lesley Anderson, Panama/Belize
from More Living Prayers for Today (IBRA)

Friday May 8   *Colossians 3.1-11*

Life in Christ

While I was living in Britain, I asked: 'Why do old people always look down when they walk?' I was told that the roads were uneven, particularly when it rained and in the dark. It sounds reasonable, and it might be an epitome of our lives. Also in Britain, I lived in a house surrounded by trees and often saw birds on the tallest branches singing. In Hong Kong, I see dogs sitting on the higher ground of a hill and watching. Perhaps we human beings and animals alike look downwards when we are not sure of the next step. Yet as Christians we are reminded to fix our thoughts on a higher realm.

Citizens have left Hong Kong by tens of thousands since 1984, after the signing of the 'Joint Declaration' between Britain and China, but many returned before the hand over and quite a number rushed back recently to be registered as residents just before 1 July 1997. People are afraid to be left out or trapped in. Hanging on to what one can get gives a sense of security – perhaps. But, whatever happens, neither a place overseas nor Hong Kong can offer permanent security.

The best choice is not in earthly places. It is in Christ, and in God's Kingdom of peace and strength.

✴ *God, enlighten us to seek you*
and to look up to you as we journey,
for in you we become strong to face all uncertainties in life.

Saturday May 9   *Colossians 3.12-17*

An everlasting garment

God's creation is continuous. His purpose is to 'bind everything together and complete the whole' (verse 14), to be moved and motivated by love, for God has first forgiven us.

Yet we often move far away from such thoughts and deeds when our primary concerns are personal interests and powers. When we are self-centred, there is no 'wholeness' but only 'individualism'. We forget the whole and turn away from unity. The overall is sacrificed to selfish ambition and comfort.

As you read this, Hong Kong has again been part of China for nearly a year. The long-term goal for China is to bring Taiwan back into the one country, so that there will be one people. There is no argument against this on either side of the China Sea, if only people are governed with 'compassion, kindness, humility, gentleness, patience' (verse 12); if we could be governed with love rather than by force.

To attain the wholeness of all God's people together, all of us, ordinary citizens and those in powerful positions, have to realize that we are only God's co-workers in completing his purpose on earth. We need to be concerned with the people around us, or under our authority, to make peace with God, and then be enwrapped in his garment of love.

✳ *Lord, give us a new cloth for our hearts*
that will reveal your purpose for humankind,
so that all may live in peace and love.

For further reflection or group discussion

● Reflect again on these notes and readings in the light of current news from Hong Kong and China.
● How have these readings challenged you in your social and political context?

QUALITY OF LIFE
2. For all the world

Notes based on the New Revised Standard Version by
Hyacinth Sweeney

Hyacinth Sweeney, who is Caribbean British, is a young local preacher and youth worker from Slough (UK). At present she is reading Theology at the University of Birmingham. Her special interest is Urban Ministries – working on the cutting edge of society, locally, nationally and internationally, within the whole 'diaspora'. Her aim is to liberate people from oppression and to enhance empowerment and justice throughout the world.

The real quality of our lives is often limited by what society allows us to do. To improve that quality we may need to step out and behave differently. This includes accepting the unacceptable; it involves opening our homes to everybody, especially *those we don't see*. We are challenged to make a new beginning. For the good news is that Jesus is our Saviour and Protector. If we move to another place, away from home, he will be our guide if we put our trust in him. Jesus wants us all to enhance the quality of our lives by finding 'holy places', within his sacred and special world. Eternal life – which begins here and now – is for all the world and we should treat it like a precious stone and want to share it.

5th Sunday of Easter, May 10   *Acts 11.1-18 *C*
Accepting the unacceptable
We go through life taking in the parts of it that we like and fitting them into our models of what life should be. But models all too easily become fixed and resist change.

Peter received a vision which showed him things that were outside of his model, but not beyond the Kingdom Jesus proclaimed (or Jesus' own model). At first, Peter could not understand the vision. It contradicted the strict food laws and traditional rules against contact with non-Jews. But when the vision was repeated a third time, he realized what God was saying to him. When the three men appeared at his door, he knew that he should go with them without further question.

109

We are all made in the image of God and this is something that we need to believe, deep within ourselves. It needs to be projected outwardly to the whole world. We are all the children of God, as were the children from many different backgrounds I met while working at Camp Bennett in Maryland, America. Some of them knew Jesus and some did not. These children are like others we tend to turn away from – we put them outside our 'models' and do not place them within our lives, as children of God. But they, and many people like them, need our open arms to welcome them with love.

✱ *Lord, we come to you in different forms,*
  from different places we make up your world.
  Together, we add to the quality of the world's life,
  together we make a patchwork model, just for you. Amen

Monday May 11   *John 13.31-35 *C*

Leaving us with a new commandment

I received a phone call from my sister, who told me that she was leaving us next week and going to live abroad. I was shocked. No one so close had ever said that to me before. The disciples too were shocked and could not understand when Jesus talked about leaving them, and his reason was even more surprising – that God's glory might be seen through him (verses 32-33).

When we look at our children we never picture the day they will leave our homes. This image is too hard to bear. In the same way Jesus explains who he is and what he is doing for the world's people. He gives the disciples a new commandment – to love one another as he had loved them. The quality of such love will be plain for all to see in our Saviour's house.

We need this quality of love today throughout the world, a love which surpasses all barriers and social boundaries. I offer you a challenge – look at the quality of your love: are you as open to others as Jesus was?

✱ *We are your precious children, Lord,*
  and we know that you will never fail us,
  for we believe in you. Amen

Tuesday May 12   *John 4.43-54*

True belief

Many Jews who met Jesus believed in him, for they were waiting for a Messiah whom their religious tradition had taught them to expect. The writer of the Fourth Gospel tells us that, despite their cultural differences, a Roman official responded to Jesus' words. Jesus reached out to someone of a different culture and brought a new way of life to his whole family and those who worked for him. The Roman officer's belief came from deep within him. In many parts of the world today, people respond in surprising ways to the challenge of faith.

Inter-Faith dialogue is one of our greatest challenges – seeking to listen to one another and working together to build bridges and pull down the barriers that exist between so many peoples.

What are you doing in your life to gain wisdom from others?

✳ *We too need to believe,*
deep belief from within.
We too need to be true,
true from within.
Creator, allow us true belief
so that we can proclaim
your saving grace for ever. Amen

Wednesday May 13   *Luke 10.1-12*

For you and for me?

Recent statistics show that the number of British Church-goers is declining. Pews are not being filled, though churches with a participatory style of worship are more popular, and the Church worldwide is growing. Jesus said, 'The harvest is plentiful ...' and that is still true. Many hear and long to hear the 'good news'. Jesus said, 'If anyone is there who shares in peace, your peace will rest on that person; but if not, it will return to you.' However hard we try, our message will not be accepted by everyone. We must expect rejection.

Jesus was rejected by his townsfolk in Nazareth. Like him, we need to be aware of rejection and move on. We need to respect everyone's freedom to choose whether they should hear and believe or not.

Many Christians and people of faith believe that if you walk in Christ's way and share in Christ's family, you will never be alone, but will find the life for which you have been searching in his Kingdom.

✳ *All who believe shall say:*
My God shall answer my call,
we are the family, Lord,
and you are here beside us, always. Amen

Our Saviour and Protector

In this vision, written at a time of great persecution, John sees ahead to the wonders of heaven, and all the power and glory attributed to God. The persecuted and rejected have come through their suffering. They have faithfully served the Lord. This vision was written down by John to bring encouragement to those who were facing martyrdom.

In the city of God, there will be no more suffering, and God will wipe away all the tears. This remains true. Again, this vision is for all the world – the multitudes beyond number from all the nations (5.9). And in the centre of its life is Christ – the Lamb of God – with renewal for all those who come. It will be a place of peace and protection for all.

✳ *Saviour and Protector,*
watch over us your people of the world,
as you watched over the peoples of the nations.
For we worship you all day and all night, for ever.

Friday May 15   *Revelation 21.1-6 *C*

A new beginning

Whilst on a period of research in Washington DC, I stayed for four days at a shelter for the homeless. There I felt denied as a person. I lost all sense of self-worth and dignity. The staff of 'Carers' treated me as if I was a 'non-person'. And it seemed to me as though the Carers looked down on the homeless because their luck had run out. It was a case of 'us' and 'them'. Yet the people who lived in that community needed someone whose heart was with theirs, who cared enough to live among them as Jesus did. They had reached their lowest point, and had lost everything material, and now they were robbed of a new beginning.

In today's reading, we are given a vision of a new heaven and a new earth where there will be no more pain, discrimination, persecution, or patronizing attitudes.

Jesus was humble and walked, talked, ate and slept with the people. He gives us a second chance to make a new beginning: to humble ourselves and give 'the invisible people', those who live on our streets, a new beginning too.

✳ *Lord, we all need new beginnings in our lives,*
let us observe your example and give to others
what we gain from you. Amen

Holy places

In our last two readings, John – exiled on the isle of Patmos – had a vision of perfect, universal worship being offered to the living God. In earlier times, the Psalmist also saw the whole universe, the earth, the natural world, kings, leaders and ordinary people offering uninhibited praise to God.

On a visit to Israel, I crossed the still, calm sea of Galilee, and heard the voice of Jesus; at the Mount of the Beatitudes, I saw the awesome power of God's creation; in the Garden Tomb I felt the presence of Jesus. These things happened to me in the Holy Land, but a holy place can be anywhere that God chooses. We need to take off our blinkers, take out our earplugs and look into our world and see the temples of love, hear the voices of praise and feel alive. God loves each of us and we need to tell the whole world about this precious thing. If you open up your heart and let God's power in, you will be able to do wonderful things, for God will be your guide forever.

✳ *Watch the mountain tops and the trees,*
see the tower blocks and the streets.
Watch the open lands and our front doors,
and see people just where they are,
on holy ground. Amen

For further reflection or group discussion

● Ask yourself: How good am I at choosing difficult tasks?
● Jesus took up the cross and died for you. Are you willing to sacrifice all that you have around you to go and live in another place, with people you don't know and who don't see Jesus as you do?
● Do you then choose to take the narrow path of Jesus or the wide path of the world?

FOR ACTION

Open your eyes to the invisible people. Let them into your heart, mind, body and soul, physically. Reach out and touch them with your own hands.

QUALITY OF LIFE
3. Becoming one in Christ

Notes based on the New Revised Standard Version by
Cindy O'Shea

*Cindy O'Shea is a North American living in Ireland since 1983
and worshipping and working in the Church of Ireland. She works
in children's ministry, training lay people who work with children in
the church, lecturing to ordinands and speaking to parish groups.
She has written several publications including a Sunday School
curriculum and Christian nurture material for adults. Cindy is a
member of General Synod and serves the Liturgical Advisory
Committee and another committee exploring the issue of children
and Communion.*

The most awe-inspiring aspect of Christian faith, personally, is
knowing that God's love is unconditional. I think of the exhortation
in the service of the Eucharist in the Church of Ireland's
Alternative Prayer Book, which begins, 'Almighty God, to whom
all hearts are open, all desires known, and from whom no secrets
are hidden', and I marvel. How can God know every thought,
every deed, every 'speck', and still love me for who I am? For me
it implies that all are accepted. All are welcome. All are valuable
members of the community of faith – that is, our faith communities or congregations.

6th Sunday of Easter, May 17   Acts 2.42-47
A just community
Imagine what our parish lives would be like if we took this
example of Christian community seriously? If we really believed it
possible for the members of parishes to live today, as they did in
the community in Acts 2, would we be persecuted? Ridiculed?
Embarrassed? Could it be done at all? Is it too idealistic? Imagine
a vibrant, miracle-filled community: a community where the
dignity of every member is respected, where members are
committed to peace with justice for all. Couldn't that be a real
possibility, even for the most marginalized individuals or groups in
our communities, if we aspired to those six verses in Acts 2? The

season of Easter is a good time in the cycle of the Church year to consider this. To look at what we have done, what we can and intend to do, and most important, what help we need to make good those intentions. Consider the unconditional love referred to in this week's introduction. With that God-given gift, nothing is impossible. The people of the Acts community were special people indeed, but they were not supernatural beings. They were mothers, fathers, sisters, brothers, daughters and sons, labourers and teachers, thinkers and preachers. They accepted and lived life in the knowledge of God's love and grace.

✳ *God, enable us to let you love us as we are.*

Monday May 18   Acts 16.9-15 *C

A vision of seeking Christ in everyone

How easy it is to assume someone is not interested in sharing your faith. How tempting to stay quiet when some faithful words may be appropriate. How much simpler to stay right where you are and not venture into the unknown. For Paul it was a vision which led him to a particular Roman colony where he found Lydia, a worshipper of God. I wonder if, after this dream, Paul was tempted to stay right where he was, or better yet, go back to a place where he knew he would be surrounded by fellow worshippers. God called Paul to a new place, however, just as God calls us: a calling to seek out our brothers and sisters in Christ; to value each as made in the image of God and as a worshipper of God; not to make assumptions which exclude certain people, nor to fear their disinterest, but to seek their faith. Lydia's whole household was baptized, not just herself and the women found in the place of prayer by the river. It is a story of inclusion; of seeking Christ in each person.

✳ *Cross over the road, my friend,*
  ask the Lord his strength to lend,
  his compassion has no end,
  cross over the road.   *Pamela Verrall*
          Irish Church Praise; APCK/Oxford University Press

Tuesday May 19   Philemon 1-25

All persons in Christ

In this letter, Paul is not just asking Philemon to take back Onesimus, a runaway slave, and treat him as a beloved brother, but to look deeper. Paul is asking that Philemon value Onesimus as worthy. Don't judge him by his accounts, nor as if he has wronged you, but welcome him as you would welcome me. Surely that echoes Jesus' own teachings and even evokes particular Gospel passages for you as it does me. The Church of Ireland, as most Christian Churches, includes people of very different and wide-ranging experiences. Those experiences, our experiences, our 'life stories', shape and form the variety of unique individuals which make up the Church: unique individuals with a common faith. ALL are worthy of welcome and acceptance, of being valued. Look back to Paul's words again – don't judge him by his experiences or life story, but welcome him.

✳ *Dear Jesus, open my eyes to the worthiness*
of all my sisters and brothers in you;
let me be as you would be;
let me welcome them as, I pray my friend,
I welcome you. Amen

Wednesday May 20   *Galatians 3.26-29*

Different but one – all children of God

We are a community of faith. For some it is a new, experiential, intuitive faith. Some affiliate to the traditions and rites of the faith community, focused on the 'belonging' aspect. Some have searching, questioning faith, or are doubtful and perhaps even despondent. Some are blessed with confirmed, owned, affirmed faith. John Westerhoff III, a prominent theorist in faith development, writer, and teacher, describes these four styles or types of faith by offering us the vision of a tree, cut so that you can see the rings of growth. Westerhoff says that all these styles or types of faith are valid, one no more so or less than the other. For a tree with one ring is still a whole tree, and no less a tree than one with four rings. The one with four rings is simply an expanded tree. So it is with the children of God, a faithful people. We are all different, by gender, by experience, by age, by race ... yet we are all valid and valued in the eyes of God.

✳ *Loving God, Father, Son and Holy Spirit,*
you have made us different
that we may learn
to appreciate one another's gifts and skills,
and work with you
for the benefit of all humankind.
Make us one body, as you are One.

Witness without ceasing

All are called to witness: all, by our lives, to show our faithfulness to God. Because we are children of God, sisters and brothers in Christ, we have the courage, strength and purpose to live as witnesses. Not just to gaze heavenward in praise, but also to praise Jesus, whose ascension we commemorate today, in our words and actions. We are sustained in this great task by God's Holy Spirit. We are not to know the length in time of our mission, nor its boundaries. Rather we are to witness without ceasing. We are to go out in the name of Jesus and, because we believe, others' belief will be conceived ... born ... strengthened. I look to Matthew when this mammoth task of witnessing by the way in which we live our lives seems too much. Impossible! Not for me! This is someone else's job! Jesus says to us, 'And remember, I am with you always, to the end of the age' (Matthew 28. 20).

✷ *Send us out in the power of your Spirit*
   to live and work to your praise and glory. Amen
        Alternative Prayer Book 1994 according to the use of
        The Church of Ireland (Collins Liturgical Publications)

A vision of fulfilment

The Book of Revelation, for me, is more like watching a series of great paintings, or an artistic film, for the words cannot remain just words on a page or in my head. I can see the open gates and accept the absence of night – no need for sun or moon to shine. I can hear and feel the peoples of all nations in this 'city of God'. For me, it is a challenge to believe in the 'alwaysness', the 'everlastingness' of God. It would be ridiculous to think that any of us could remain on this earth as we are, for ever, but are we willing to believe that one day we will see God face to face? Or is that the part we find too hard to accept? If our journey in life is a journey of 'becoming one in Christ', of accepting our worthiness and that of our sisters and brothers, and witnessing to that by our lives – then, also, can we not look forward to a time of fulfilment?

✷ *Dear Lord, in you, through you, and by you,*
   may we believe in the fulfilment of your plan for us,
   trusting in your love and forgiveness,
   through Jesus Christ our Saviour. Amen

Let all the peoples praise you

The 67th Psalm, a hymn of praise, is a right and fitting end to this week's theme. We began with the Acts community, journeyed with Paul to the place of prayer where he baptized Lydia and her household, listened to Paul's plea to Philemon to welcome Onesimus, and read the Galatians' affirmation of our oneness in Christ. Finally we visited 'the city of God' through the imagery of Revelation 21, and we finish our week with pure praise!

Verses 3 and 5 act as the chorus or refrain to our hymn of praise, and the remaining verses echo the themes of the reflections on our daily readings this week – all are worthy: 'for you judge the peoples with equity'. We are sustained in our task of witness; 'God, our God, has blessed us.'

✳ *Let the peoples praise you, O God;*
   let all the peoples praise you.   *Psalm 67.3*

For further reflection or group discussion

● If we believe that there is 'room for all', that we can live in Christian community as the early church in Acts 2, what implications does this have for you, your family, your parish community?

● If you **cannot** accept that all are worthy of acceptance and welcome, who would you exclude and on what basis?

● If you **can** accept that all are worthy of acceptance and welcome, what help and support would you need to accomplish this within your community?

FOR ACTION

Seek out one person – at work, in your parish or community – from whom you feel furthest away, or with whom you have the least in common. Show him or her by your words and actions that s/he is welcome, accepted and worthy, maybe through a gesture, invitation, or conversation.

PENTECOST –
Filled by the Holy Spirit

Notes based on the New Revised Standard Version by
Melvyn Matthews

Melvyn Matthews is the Vicar of Chew Magna with Dundry, two commuter villages south of Bristol. Here he ministers to working and retired professional people in a strikingly beautiful rural setting. He was a University Chaplain and Lecturer for many years and has worked as the Director of an Ecumenical Centre for reconciliation and peace. He has written a number of books on the spiritual life.

The Holy Spirit is the ancient power and life of God poured into the world from the beginning. In the Hebrew Scriptures the Spirit is constantly poured out on the whole of creation. Its gift is not limited to the children of Israel, nor to any particular time or season. It does not come and go, nor is it given in response to any particular offering or activity. It is the gift of God. The Spirit moves over the waters of chaos bringing life, order and relatedness to things (Genesis 1.2). The Spirit brings life to all things. Plants, animals and humans alike look to God for life (Psalm 104.27-30).

So when Jesus speaks of the gift of the Spirit, he is saying that what the disciples had been told about the Spirit of God in the Scriptures was being and would be delivered in and through his person. Faith in Jesus as the Son of God would reveal to them what God had been doing from the beginning of time.

The author of St John's Gospel points out that to grasp this the disciples had to pass through the narrow point of faith in Jesus. This faith in Jesus Christ crucified and risen will bring us, says the evangelist, to know something of the universal activity of God watering the whole earth with his Spirit.

Jesus' words of promise are spoken almost secretly, deep in the heart of the story of his death at a very narrow point; but they say, 'Do not be afraid, you have been brought to this point so that you may receive what has been given to all things from the beginning, but which has been kept from you by the hardness of your heart and dullness of sight. Your hearts, like the body of Jesus, will be broken, but this is really not destruction or death but a breaking open to show that what your heart contained was the

119

infinite love of God. Your life is greater and more wonderful than ever you could have imagined. It is full of the Holy Spirit.'

The place of life
Around Lascaux in France, there are caves containing the most beautiful prehistoric paintings. To get into them you have to pass through the narrow entrance. Once you are inside, gradually, your eyes become adjusted and you see more than you had bargained for. Every now and again in life we come to a narrow place, a point from which we do not appear to be able to escape. We have to go forward but our hearts quail and we draw back, wondering how we ever reached such a difficult point. This is 'the place' that the disciples and Jesus have come to. He calls them forward to accept the cross, 'the place' that is prepared for them. When he spoke to the Samaritan woman at the well (4.7-42), Jesus said that 'the place' where people would worship God was neither Samaria nor Jerusalem, inferring that he himself was 'the place'. At that place they would also realize that 'God is spirit'.

This 'place', where we realize that 'God is spirit', is where the disciples are to remain. This is their resting-place. The word 'place', which occurs too often in this passage, is related in the thinking of the evangelist to Jesus' exhortation to his disciples to 'abide' in him. We have constantly to abide in the place to which we have been called. We are always, if we are his disciples, passing through that place, the cross, where we have to abide in the love of God without fear.

✷ *God, you often place the cross on our shoulders*
and ask us to abide in your love;
help us to bear its weight and to pass through
the narrow door into your eternal love. Amen

The spring of life
When Jesus promises the Spirit to his disciples it is his own life he promises. The Spirit is the Spirit of truth just as Jesus is himself the truth (verse 6). So it is the life of Jesus which is promised. But the life of Jesus is also the life of God the Father. So the Spirit and Jesus and the Father are all bound up together. But that is

not all, because those who love Jesus and those who keep his commandments are caught up in the love of the Father, and the Spirit will be revealed to them.

Jesus is saying that through love of him and obedience to him the disciples will be caught up into the life of God and filled with the Spirit. Indeed the words here (especially a word like 'reveal') are used in the Hebrew Scriptures to talk about a revelation of God. So in his parting words Jesus is in fact talking about the same things which happened to Jacob, or to Moses, or to the prophets of the Jewish past. What begins as friendship between the disciples and Jesus ends as participation in the revelation of God to humankind.

Often in Hebrew Scriptures the life of the Spirit is portrayed as a river flowing across dry ground, or like a spring of life (see Joel 3.18 or Isaiah 35.6). Jesus seems to have discovered something of that eternal spring within himself and believed that it came from God, and that those who loved him and followed him were caught up in that same spring. There is within all things a deep well of life springing up from God the Father to refresh and renew. It is this life which Jesus brings and releases. When we do not share in that life then, in Jesus' words, we are orphans – worldlings – because we cannot see or know our parentage, the source of our lives. Being a disciple of Jesus means believing that in Jesus' person the entire activity of God, past, present and future, is available. Being a disciple means that you cease having no home, cease being an orphan, and come home to God.

✳ *God, help us each day*
to allow the spring of life you have placed within us
to well up so that we may live, as Jesus did,
in the power of your Spirit and in union with you. Amen

Tuesday May 26   *John 14.22-26 *C*

Drawn by love

When we come to the Father, it is love which has drawn us. Elsewhere Jesus says, 'And I, when I am lifted up from the earth, will draw all people to myself' (John 12.32). He draws us to himself by divine attraction, by a loving desire. This love between God and the disciple is mutual. God is as drawn to us as we are to him. This again is one of the secrets of the universe which has been hidden from our eyes, namely that God draws us to himself by his great desire for us. He wants us and that wanting is reciprocated in us. The mission of the Son is to reveal this.

121

So often Christians suppose that God is some sort of invader, who has to break down our resistance and take us captive. Although the language of Christian devotion has often used such imagery, the reality is that the encounter between the soul and God is much gentler – it is a meeting of hearts prepared for one another from the beginning. We were meant for this; there is a special place for each person in the heart of God, and the human soul is meant to find its home there. The great exponent of the union of love between the soul and God in Christian history is St Bernard of Clairvaux. In his great treatise *On Loving God* he says, 'God is the cause of loving God. He himself provides the occasion. He himself creates the longing. He himself fulfils the desire ... His love both prepares and rewards ours. Kindly he leads the way. He repays us justly.' And so we realize that we were made by love for love and that when God draws us to himself, this way has been prepared for us from the beginning.

✴ *Lord, you are good to the soul which seeks you. What are you then to the soul which finds? But this is the most wonderful thing, that no one can seek you who has not already found you. You therefore seek to be found so that you may be sought for, sought so that you may be found. Amen*

St Bernard of Clairvaux (1090-1153)

Wednesday May 27   *John 14.27-31*

'My peace I give you ...'

Any visitor to modern-day Israel is struck by the usual word of greeting and farewell: *'Shalom'* – peace. But in Hebrew *shalom* means far more than peacefulness: it signifies peace, justice, wholeness, completeness. In the Bible it is used to indicate, for example, that peace which God wrought upon the chaos of things at the beginning. In the peace of the garden of creation God comes to share his peace with his children. They are shown as helping him to build and sustain it. This peace was one of settled and just relationships where no one part of creation existed separate from, or in superiority to any other part. All the parts work together for the harmony of the whole. It is this same peace, peace with justice and respect for the integrity of the creation, which Jesus promises to his disciples at the end of his ministry.

No one who claims to speak for the Spirit but whose actions are unjust, isolating or fostering lack of harmony in the world, can be speaking the truth. Too many speak of being in the Spirit but by their actions promote injustice or disturb the harmony of creation. This quest for justice and harmony is opposed by the prince of this world.

✳ *God, we crave your peace. Our own peace never seems to last. Draw us by the bonds of love deeper into your love so that knowing you we may live without fear and with deep and humble respect for all that lives. Amen*

Thursday May 28   *John 16.5-11*

The hidden scenario

Sometimes something happens which makes you think, 'Oh, so that is what has been going on' and everything falls into place. This is what the Spirit of God does; it brings home to us what God has actually been doing. The function of the Spirit is that of revealer. Here Jesus makes the point that the arrival of the Spirit will reveal what has been the case – that the world has been sinful. The context makes it clear that 'sinful' means without aim, homeless, chaotic and that God has been righteous, dealing rightly with the world (while we thought it was all chaotic and so what we did didn't matter), and that the Prince of this world has already been judged. It is not that the jury is still out and we do not know what is right and what is not; no, things have been settled from the beginning.

This is the inner, hidden scenario which the Spirit reveals. God has been at work in the world. What the words and work of Jesus do, if we trust and obey his call, is reveal the actual truth. At times in the Gospel of John, salvation is like the shining of a torch, a sudden realization, a dawning of light in the mind. This is reflected in the saying in Acts, 'when they heard this they were cut to the heart' (Acts 2.37).

✳ *God, we need to learn to trust that you have always been at work redeeming the world with your righteous love. Shame us, by the presence of your Holy Spirit, into trusting that love more and more each day. Amen.*

Friday May 29   *John 16.12-15 *C*

Doing the Truth

The great obstacle to faith for the modern mind is its understanding of truth. We think it is a mental possession of our own. When Jesus speaks of the truth in John's Gospel; it is always something which is God's and it is always something which is done, enacted rather than thought. Jesus embodies in his life, death and resurrection the truth of God. The text tells us that the Spirit will tell us the truth. This truth cannot be something which we can simply hold in our mind as an interesting piece of information. It is something which will happen to us. Just as, in the Hebrew Scriptures, God led his people into the wilderness; just as, in the New Testament, the Spirit led Jesus into the wilderness to be tempted; so the Spirit leads us into the truth. We too will be led to a place of testing and conversion. There has to be an abandonment of our 'knowing' so that we can 'know' God in the cross and self-emptying of Jesus. Who we are has to be abandoned so that the truth can set us free.

✳ *God, help us to allow your truth to be done in us and in our lives. Amen*

Saturday May 30   *Acts 2.1-13 *C*

Reversal of Babel

In Genesis 11 we are told of the Tower of Babel and of how the inhabitants of the earth, who had at first spoken one language, were scattered because of their pride. The Lord confused their language so that they were unable to understand one another's speech. Here in the Acts of the Apostles, we see that the gift of the Spirit reverses the effects of Babel and that every one of those present, whether they were Jews or Elamites, residents in Mesopotamia, or wherever, could hear what the disciples were saying, each in their own language. In other words the outpouring of the Spirit brings about a reversal of the effects of pride and unites things into a single whole such as they had been at the beginning.

This story is not about the gift of tongues. Paul in 1 Corinthians reproaches those who speak in tongues because they risk making the good news incomprehensible. Both Paul and the author of Acts are clear that the gift of the Spirit enables the whole world to hear the good news each in their own way and so an original but lost unity is restored.

✳ *God, your Spirit brings us back into a single whole where we are each heard and can each hear what the other is saying. Prevent us from making so much noise of our own that we do not hear your voice speaking over our chaos. Amen*

For further reflection or group discussion

● Think about the words of St Bernard of Clairvaux: 'God is the cause of loving God.' In particular think how this short sentence gives each of us an infinite dignity and worth, for it indicates that God has already implanted within us the capacity to love him in return for his love. His grace has preceded our own desire to love him.

● Be sorry for your own pre-occupation, but be glad that God is there within you, and has been from the beginning.

Pentecost, May 31   *Acts 2.14-21 *C*

The point of breakthrough

On the Feast of Pentecost the disciples are brought to that point where they glimpse the possibility, within their own concrete existence, of the life of God which the Scriptures had promised for the last days. They had remained with Jesus and that abiding had brought them into touch with what God does, namely, pour out his Spirit.

The Scriptures use the images of past time (the moving of the Spirit of God on the waters of chaos at the creation) and future time (the predictions of the poetry of Joel) as metaphors for the transcendent activity of God who is beyond all time. So there is an initial gap, a distance between our concrete activity and the activity of God. What is celebrated on Pentecost Sunday is that these gaps have been broken down: the disciples, by their reflective faith in Jesus, have come to know that the gap is no more, and that God's activity is readily available for all to receive.

✴ *God, sometimes we know that the end of time is but a moment away. Give us lives which are filled with your Spirit so that the world may know that the barriers between you and us are of our own making. Amen*

Monday June 1   *Acts 2.37-41*

Repent and believe the gospel

The gift of the Spirit is linked, inexorably, to repentance. Turning from self to God is the channel through which the Holy Spirit can and does flow. Repentance is difficult because it requires giving up a stance of self-protection, but when we allow ourselves to do that then grace and pardon flow through us into the world. We cannot underestimate the effects on others of what happens when we repent. Our repentance is life-giving, not just for ourselves, but for the whole world. This is also why the texts about the gift of the Spirit are never limited: there is always a universal element. The Spirit is no one group's exclusive possession.

✳ *O God, we know that when other people repent, we benefit. Help us to be sure that when we are called to repentance we will be participating in something of universal consequence. Amen*

Tuesday June 2   *Acts 13.1-5; 16.6-8*

Freed for true living

I have just been talking with a remarkable priest who recently gave up the security of his position as Vicar of a large south London church and embarked upon a ministry of spiritual direction unencumbered by the structures of the church. His move came after a crisis in his life which somehow enabled him to live from God alone. This is what happens in the Acts of the Apostles. Of course, much of what is described in Acts is very stylized and artificial, written from hindsight after the event. Whether it was exactly like that at the time is difficult to say. Probably, like us, Paul and his companions had to trust that God was at work somewhere in all that was happening to them. But in the end that is the remarkable thing – they could and did trust that this was the case. Encounter with Jesus (and once again, as in John's Gospel, the text makes it clear that the Spirit is the Spirit of Jesus) enables people to live with remarkable freedom and energy. It seems to free them from constraint, enables them to let go and live from God. They can go to Cyprus suddenly; they can set sail without bother, move off into the unknown.

✳ *God, lift us out of the grip of ourselves so that we may live from you alone. Amen*

Wednesday June 3   *Romans 8.14-17 *C*

'I'm learning to trust'

We have to allow ourselves to live out of God, for God is already living within us. We do not easily allow that, preferring to live according to other forces, what St Paul calls 'the elemental spirits of the universe'. These spirits are things like fear or mistrust, resentment or jealousy, or simply greed and selfishness. We have to abandon our reliance upon them and live according to the Spirit.

I have in front of me the newsletter of my friend the priest who gave up his Vicarage to follow a ministry of spiritual direction. He talks about how he has set out in a rather precarious way, 'But this has proved very faith-building for me. It really does feel as if God is carrying us along, and that while life is often precarious, it always seems to be all right. I'm learning to trust.' He goes on to say that one of his prime aims in his work is to help people to be in relationship with 'the God they already know', by which he means the life of the Spirit they have been given but which has been waiting to be the source of their life. He says, 'It continues to amaze me that people have such a rich treasure buried within themselves, lying, for the most part, ignored and untapped. A large part of what I am doing is concerned with helping people to unearth this God-given gift, and to start to trust it and to live out of it.'

✳ *God, our lives sometimes feel precarious,*
like a boat in a storm.
Help us to trust that you are in the boat with us
waiting to be called upon. Amen

Thursday June 4   *Romans 8.24-27*

The river within

I talked earlier about the caves in southern France which my wife and I visited on our summer holiday. Often within these caves there was a river, an interior stream, flowing at great depth, cold and clear. Once again this is an image of the human person. Deep within each one of us there is a river of prayer which lies 'too deep for words'. The art of prayer is not to live on the surface of our minds and wills, forcing ourselves to pray as if it was a sort of duty like mowing the lawn, but to live at one with the depths of oneself, allowing that river within to be our prayer. That river is the life of the Spirit placed within us by God and which carries the prayers of our hearts into the being of God. This silent river has to be recognized and owned, come more to the surface and flow out into the light full of strength and praise, full of energy. Too often we regard prayer as a chore, the source of which is in our wills, and so we find it difficult and uncreative, a sort of trying to persuade God to do things. If we could recognize prayer as a deep stream already running within us, we would know that it is the Spirit of God who prays within us, interceding with sighs too deep for words.

✳ *God, you are already praying within us.*
Help us to join our prayers with yours. Amen

Friday June 5   *Galatians 5.16-26*

The fruits of the Spirit

The Anglican Church in Zambia – with which my Diocese of Bath and Wells is linked – has a custom of welcoming visitors with three handclaps and the words 'Love, Joy, Peace' as the claps are made. People come back from Zambia remarking on how these Zambian Christians have learned to live by the Spirit and so are full of the fruits of the Spirit. Small gifts delight them, everybody is welcome, the Lord looks after them and they live entirely by faith. One of the characteristics of the United Church of Zambia is enormous generosity and good humour. The Kwacha Parish to which we are linked decided in faith to build a new church without knowing where the money would come from. For a long time they had walls but no roof and simply lived in faith that the roof would come. Now it looks as if it will do so soon.

All of these characteristics are the fruit of the Spirit within them. The Spirit cannot be seen; it can only be seen in its fruits in their lives as they continue to live over against death, disease, poverty and lack of resources.

✳ *God, you are the source of life.*
Fill our lives with simplicity and praise
and let us be content. Amen

Saturday June 6   *1 Corinthians 12.1-11*

'I'm only ...'

During a period of high unemployment, while I was Director of an Ecumenical Conference and Retreat Centre, we ran a number of courses for those who were long-term unemployed. One of the exercises they were asked to do was called 'I'm only ...' Each member said, for example, 'I'm only a checkout girl', or 'I'm only a housewife', as if these were insignificant jobs. The others then had to tell the 'checkout girl' what skills she needed and used in her job. It was amazing how the players discovered their skills were far greater than they knew. A checkout girl needs to be numerate, to have hand and eye skills of a developed nature, to be able to relate well and be patient with people with no manners or money and so on. In the end all the members of the group came away convinced that they had something to give to life.

It is like this with the Holy Spirit who gives us gifts. Yet often we do not think we have any because we may feel that we are not articulate, not able to write well ... We think gifts are only associated with education and riches. But everybody has some of the gifts of the Spirit and these are all needed for the life of the Church. The skills of the humble parish visitor are just as much a gift of the Spirit as the gift of tongues. The humble listener, who makes other people feel good is as full of the Spirit as the one who speaks a lot and impresses everyone with a capacity to expound the Bible. In the end the important thing is that we are one Body where each part is equally valuable and all are bound together by love.

✷ *God, bind us together in love. Amen*

For further reflection or group discussion

Think about those times when you have been brought to 'the place' of the cross and have had to abide there with Jesus. Think of times when you felt crucified by forces beyond your control. Then try to recollect what you discovered about yourself or about God at those points. How did your life change as a result? What was it that you began to do or say as a result of this time of testing? Why did the Holy Spirit lead you into the wilderness?

FOR ACTION

Think what one thing you have always felt the Spirit wanted you to do and plan how you might do it within a particular period of time. Then get on with it.

PERSONALITIES OF THE BIBLE
1. Jeremiah

Notes based on the Hebrew Bible by
Jonathan Magonet

*The texts here are translated directly from the Hebrew Bible by
the writer, who is the Professor of Bible and Principal of the Leo
Baeck College, a Rabbinic seminary in North London. He is
author of three books on the Bible – A Rabbi's Bible; Bible Lives;
A Rabbi Reads the Psalms – and a frequent broadcaster on the
BBC World Service.*

A prophet in biblical Israel was probably trained to undertake the
'profession'. Many served in the royal court and simply gave
divine sanction to the policies of the government. But others
emerged with a very special quality and independence. Their
words and stories have been preserved in the Hebrew Bible.
They were critics of the leadership (political and spiritual) of their
society, even at the risk of their lives. They judged the world
against the traditional values of the covenant and out of their own
experience of hearing the word of God. Jeremiah stands out as
one such 'God-intoxicated' person.

Sunday June 7   *Jeremiah 1.1-19*
No illusions
Jeremiah, at the very beginning of his activity as a prophet, has
no illusions about what lies ahead of him. He marshals his
excuses much like others before him: Moses (I cannot speak!);
Amos (I'm not qualified!) and Isaiah (I'm not pure enough!).
Jeremiah claims to be only a *na'ar* which means 'young man' but
often someone who serves a religious leader, perhaps something
like an 'apprentice'.

From his training as a prophet, he may have understood the
risks involved in the prophetic vocation. God's words of comfort
are not very comforting: 'Don't be scared of them or I'll really
make you scared!' (verse 17). God will make him a 'fortified city'
against all his opponents – which may assure his ultimate safety
but condemns him to a life of isolation and constant threat. No

wonder he evokes the memory of his call, being chosen from within the womb, at the time of his greatest despair – would that he had never left his mother's womb (20.18).

Perhaps Jeremiah's uniqueness lies precisely in his self-doubt. The word of God is not always available to him, as it seems to be to his 'successful' contemporaries.

✴ **Even though I walk through the valley of deep darkness,
I fear no evil, for You are with me.** Psalm 23.4

Monday June 8 *Jeremiah 2.1-3, 14-19*

First love

It is possible that the words of verse 2 were intended to preface all of Jeremiah's prophetic utterances. However harsh and bitter his words may be about the coming fate of Jerusalem and of his people, all such threats were to be contained within God's memory of that first love: 'I remember the *hesed* of your youth'. This complex word, *hesed,* parallel here to *ahavah,* 'love', is the binding force within a covenant; a kind of faithfulness that turns a mere legal contract into an expression of mutual loyalty.

It is as if God forever waxes sentimental at the memory of those early days of trust when Israel was prepared to risk everything, leaving behind the security of slavery for the unknown dangers of the wilderness out of trust in God. It is a beautiful metaphor but a dangerous one, for the faithful, beloved wife can be turned around to the unfaithful, adulterous one. Both reflect attitudes to women within a patriarchal biblical society that we are still trying to disentangle. But God's *hesed*, which lasts for a thousand generations (Exodus 34.7), outlives the social forms in which we try to understand, and thus limit, it.

✴ **Do not remember the sins of my youth and my
wrongdoing, but remember me in love (hesed).**
Psalm 25.7

Tuesday June 9 *Jeremiah 9.1-8*

No hiding place

Who speaks here? Jeremiah so identifies with God that it is not clear who it is that wishes to escape. Strong as these words of condemnation are, the reader of the Hebrew text can hear behind them the echo of an older traditional tale. 'Let everyone beware of his neighbour; for every brother is a supplanter' (verse 4, Hebrew

131

verse 3). The word for 'supplant' is the root *aqav*, which gives the name *ya'aqov* 'Jacob', the same word-play being used by Esau (Genesis 27.36) on learning that Jacob has stolen his blessing. Verse 6 (Hebrew verse 5) reads: 'you dwell in the midst of *mirmah'*, 'deceit', which is the word used of Jacob's deception of his father Isaac on that same occasion (Genesis 27.35).

Jeremiah evokes painful lessons from Israel's past as if pointing to an inherent flaw in the people. Yet he cannot entirely leave them. In a 'lodging-place' he could at least affect and influence the few who came into his world.

But this is a dream and ultimately an illusion. It is in the midst of Jerusalem, in the daily struggle with political and religious corruption, that Jeremiah is doomed to act out his prophetic ministry.

✳ **Blessed are You, our Living God, Sovereign of the Universe,**
who has not made me a stranger to You.

Jewish Morning Service

Wednesday June 10   *Jeremiah 18.1-6; 19.1-13*

God the Creator

In 18.1-6, Jeremiah has visited the potter and seen how he can mould a clay vessel, but if dissatisfied simply break it and remould it using the same raw materials. So can God do with nations, breaking them and re-forming them if they do not conform to the divine will.

The image of God as 'artist' or 'craftsman' is disturbing, for great art exists in a realm outside of conventional morality. It has an arbitrariness and even cruelty utterly different from the God of justice and fair play we would like to imagine. Yet all too often it is hard to square human suffering with the loving God of our conventional faith. Could we cope with the implications of an 'artist' God?

Jeremiah plays with the image and the word for an earthenware bottle – *baqbuq* (19.7): 'I will *make void, empty out,* the counsel of Judah' uses the root *baqaq*, I will 'unbottle' their wisdom. The punishment is measure for measure. This place, where they slaughter their children, will be filled with more corpses than they could have dreamed of!

The warning is savage, but, all too often, so is the damage one generation inflicts on the next.

＊ *May the will come from You to annul wars and the*
shedding of blood from the universe, and to extend
peace, great and wondrous, in the world.

Nachman of Bratslav

Thursday June 11   *Jeremiah 19.14 to 20.6*

Conflict within

Jeremiah is addressing a society faced with a powerful enemy
and an uncertain future which is also at war with itself. Pashur
has the power and authority, as a priest in charge of the Temple,
to put Jeremiah in stocks. But Jeremiah also has the public ear
and the authority of a prophet to speak. Religion for the Hebrew
Bible is not simply something for the private sphere, but is deeply
interwoven with the political. So how does anyone who observes
these struggles judge the respective merits of two such powerful
protagonists?

There is bitterness and anger in Jeremiah's words as he utters
what is effectively a curse against Pashur. But in this he is
echoing the action of Amos when similarly confronted with the
voice of authority, Amaziah the priest of the royal shrine at Beth
El (Amos 7.10-17). Both prophets translate the fate they see
befalling the entire people into the personal life of their opponent.
It is the priest and his family who will personally experience the
horror of the destruction to come. He will go into exile to die there
on foreign soil. Perhaps this may penetrate the layers of
bureaucratic authority and power to reach the man himself.

＊ *Blessed are You, our Living God, Sovereign of the*
universe,
who opens the eyes of the blind.

Jewish daily morning service

Friday June 12   *Jeremiah 16.1-9*

Bridegroom and bride

Jeremiah's personal life is to model in part the fate of his society.
He is to have neither wife nor children, the two central norms for
an Israelite man. Never to see children is sad; but to see them die
is worse – and to know they will die without burial or mourning is
bitter.

As Jeremiah will not personally experience the joy of marriage
festivities, so will such rejoicing cease. The phrase *qol sasson*

133

v'qol simchah qol hatan v'qol kallah, 'the voice of mirth and the voice of joy, the voice of the bridegroom and the voice of the bride' became part of the Jewish marriage ceremony. It stands for the continuity of life, of the generations and of hope. But Jeremiah can also see a time when this too will be restored (33.11).

These verses come too close to another Jewish experience of destruction this century and to an experience repeated time and time again in the charnel houses around the world. Throughout his prophecies, Jeremiah holds out hope that a change of heart, of action, can change this seemingly inevitable destruction. But at this low point in his life no other fate seems likely.

✳ *May it be Your will, our Living God, that the sound of happiness and rejoicing be heard in the streets of Jerusalem, the voice of the bridegroom and the voice of the bride, the song of friendship and the voice of peace.*
Based on the Jewish marriage service

Saturday June 13   *Jeremiah 15.10-11, 15-21*

Inside out

So closely does Jeremiah identify with his people that even his personal anger with God, his feeling of betrayal at times when most in need of support, can express the sentiments of the nation as a whole.

The passage contains a bitter irony. He appeals to God for support against his enemies, even though God seemingly deserts him at the time of his greatest need. But God's answer is to cast everything back upon Jeremiah himself, as God warned at the time of the call (1.17).

'If you, Jeremiah, turn back to me then I will turn you back, you will stand before Me (as a prophet who 'stands before' God). If you can bring out the precious from the worthless then, and only then, can you be as My mouth.'

Jeremiah has to transform his own bitter feelings about his role, his fate, his relationship to God, if he is to serve God effectively. It is not God who must change but Jeremiah. He must himself subsume his ego to the divine will. To bring out the precious from the worthless is not merely an incidental part of his task as prophet. It is his task.

✳ *Turn us back to You, God, and we shall return; renew our lives as of old.*   *Lamentations 5.21*

For further reflection or group discussion

- Did prophecy end with the closing of the canon of the Hebrew Scriptures?
- How do you distinguish a 'true' from a 'false' prophet?
- Is the quality of the person primary in judging the 'true' prophet, or the nature of the prophecy?

Sunday June 14   *Jeremiah 29.1-7*

A letter to the exiles

No wonder Jeremiah was accused of being traitor. His letter to the exiles contains two 'sins' that no national pride could possibly tolerate. Firstly, to accept defeat as the will of God and set about surviving in an alien land of exile. He takes his stand against the jingoism of his contemporary prophets who play the national rallying cry at every moment – 'in two years the yoke of Babylon will be broken' (Hananiah in 28.4). Yet Jeremiah's message, that Israel's God is undefeated, has actually used Babylon for God's own purposes, will utterly transform the experience of exile.

And then the second outrageous idea – to pray for the peace of the city to which they have been exiled! Has the prophet no shame? Can he so readily ignore the Israelite blood that was shed, the bereaved families, the destroyed land and lives? It is scandalous! And yet, more than just the enlightened self-interest of a people living in subjugation, Jeremiah affirms the possibility of life for a people without a territory or state to give them identity or power. He envisions an autonomous people, sufficiently secure in its relationship with God to wish to share its blessings with all.

✴ ***God, may we always seek the peace of the city in which You have placed us and pray on its behalf to You.***

Based on Jeremiah 29.7

Monday June 15   *Jeremiah 32.1-27*

Standing before God

It is Jeremiah's paradoxical task, already known when he was called, to be a prophet who brings the word of destruction but also of rebuilding. From his prison cell, condemned for prophesying doom to Jerusalem, he enters into this transaction to purchase a field in his native Anatot.

Even Jeremiah is bewildered by this act of hope in the middle of imminent destruction and prays for God's answer. His prayer,

135

using the language of the tradition, rehearses the great events of the exodus and the granting of land. But since God dispenses justice to people according to their deeds (verse 19) where is there room for a restoration of this people who have indeed abused their situation?

Is this a genuine question for Jeremiah, or a rhetorical one designed to evoke the positive answer God gives – is anything impossible for Me (verse 8)? That is precisely the strange intermediary role of the prophets – to stand in such intimate relationship with God that they can pre-empt God's response, as it were, leading God on to a positive answer. But the price they pay for that intimacy is their isolation from their people.

✳ *Blessed are You, our Living God, Sovereign of the universe, who has not made me a slave.*

Jewish morning service

Tuesday June 16   *Jeremiah 38.1-13*

Prisoner of conscience

There is something deeply troubling about these chapters that seek to fill in the historical background to the life of Jeremiah, and the particular contexts of his various prophecies. They are disturbing because they confront us with all the immediacy and reality of a newspaper *exposé*. Hearing Jeremiah's voice alone, especially in his time of despair, one wonders about his sanity: the voices he hears in his ears calling for his death (20.10). But here we learn the truth of his situation. There are those in power who do wish to destroy him, out of the very best 'reasons of state'. 'He is too dangerous to be at large.'

That the king accedes, whether out of political or personal weakness (verse 5), is the final seal on Jeremiah's fate.

But one individual had the courage to intervene and save him. To the nation's shame, it is someone not of Israel, Ebed-melech, the Ethiopian, whose initiative persuades the king to release Jeremiah from certain death.

How many 'prisoners of conscience' rotting in jails throughout the world, like Jeremiah tortured and facing death, have no Ebed-melech to save them. He might be recognized as the patron saint of Amnesty International.

✳ *Blessed are You, our Living God, Sovereign of the universe, who frees those who are bound.*

Jewish morning service

Choices

It comes almost as a surprise to find Jeremiah's caution here. But he has been too close to death to want to risk his life at this moment. He may curse the day of his birth at the time of his deepest despair (20.14) and wish he had never been born, but this is no time for rhetoric.

Of course Jeremiah's advice remains totally unacceptable in terms of '*realpolitick*'. No one surrenders to Babylon while some illusion of victory remains. Most pathetic is the personal fear of the king of being mocked by the party that has gone over to the Babylonians.

At stake for the king, as well as his personal fate, is the tradition of the Davidic dynasty, the independence of the Judaean state, and a way of life, cultural and religious. Hard to risk that on the promise of a single renegade prophet that all would somehow be restored in the end.

The king chose to make no decision – and so chose to seal his fate and that of his nation. But he honoured his promise to Jeremiah with a white lie. And Jeremiah too, this once, let common sense override his passion for truth.

✳ ***Blessed are You, our Living God, Sovereign of the universe, who gives strength to the weary.***
                                        Jewish morning service

Decisions

One wants to know so much more about the characters involved here and the historical background. Presumably these different factions among the remnant of the nation were known to the author and readers. Johanon the son of Kareah had warned Gedaliah, the governor appointed by the Babylonians, of the plot against his life. But Gedaliah had ignored the threat and was assassinated. Clearly this act could only lead to Babylonian reprisals, hence the wish to escape to Egypt. But that would mean finally abandoning their land. There is honesty and urgency in the question addressed to Jeremiah, for their very survival is at stake.

I wonder about the ten days it took Jeremiah to respond. God never gave instant replies – a source of constant concern to him. Yet Jeremiah was on good terms with the ruling powers in

Babylon. Ten days might have been time enough to have got a message of reassurance from them if Jeremiah had asked for it.

That his hearers were suspicious of him is also clear – else why accuse his scribe Baruch of inciting him? The generals made their decision, and took Jeremiah down to Egypt with them.

✷ **Blessed are You, our Living God, Sovereign of the universe,**
who raises those bent low.

Friday June 19   Jeremiah 44.15-23

Idols

The attitude of the Judaean exiles is perversely logical. They have lost everything. They remind us forcibly that the worship of Israel's God was not uncontested and came with no guarantee of success. God had proven ultimately to be a failure, a disaster, the cause of their current distress. Logic is on their side – and fear, dismay and anger. No threats or promises from Jeremiah can change their minds.

It is a sad end to a spiritual revolution that had sustained them for over a thousand years. Now it was all to end in defeat and tragedy in an Egyptian backwater where the last great prophet tried in vain to hold them to the word of God. According to Rabbinic tradition, Jeremiah died in Egyptian exile, assassinated.

But other voices took up the message. Like Jeremiah they promised a return and a new beginning. For was it not already forecast in the words of Moses. 'You shall seek the Eternal, your God, from there and you will find, if you seek Me with all your heart and all your soul' (Deuteronomy 4.29). And as Jeremiah added: '"I will let you find Me," says the Eternal' (29.14).

✷ **God, we put our hope in You. Soon let us witness the glory of Your power when the worship of material things shall pass away from the earth, and prejudice and superstition shall at last be cut off.**
From the traditional 'alenu prayer

Saturday June 20   Jeremiah 31.31-34

Written on the heart

Too much theological ink has been spilled over this passage, and ultimately too much blood. It would have puzzled Jeremiah to have seen what became of it. But for centuries after the closing of the canon, the Hebrew Bible became the template by which all truth was measured – and in which every controversial idea had to find its 'source' and justification.

Is it possible to capture the 'original' meaning of Jeremiah's words about a 'new covenant'? A Jewish view would simply read it as a poetic expression of the renewal of the old covenant, with Israel and Judah newly restored to their land and reunited. That covenant made when they left Egypt they broke and God punished them for it. But that does not change the essence or continuity of that relationship. If anything it is now stronger. No longer carved on stone tablets alone, for God will write it on their hearts.

A Christian reading would emphasize the 'new' and redefine Israel as a wider community of belief. The prophetic word remains ever open to be re-experienced and re-defined.

In his time, Jeremiah may have seemed a failure. But his words remain to haunt and challenge us today.

✳ *May the words of my mouth and the meditation of my heart, be acceptable to You, my Rock and my Redeemer.*
Psalm 19.14

Acknowledgment

The prayers in this section are taken from *Forms of Prayer Vol. I* edit. Lionel Blue and Jonathan Magonet (Reform Synagogues of Great Britain).

For further reflection or group discussion

● Do we have prophets today? Are they any more 'successful' than Jeremiah?
● What can we learn from Jeremiah for today?
● What do we understand by exile today?

FOR ACTION

Jeremiah was what today might be called a dissident. Certainly he fought against the 'received wisdom' and power assumptions of the regime of his time. He paid the price in personal danger, near-death, mockery and isolation. The work of Amnesty International is to explore the fate of such people and offer support wherever possible. A project might be to learn more about its work and consider the possibility of joining in its activities (see page 229).

PERSONALITIES OF THE BIBLE
2. Elijah: accuser and preserver

Notes based on the Holy Scriptures according to the
Masoretic Text JPSA, by

Albert Friedlander

*Rabbi Albert H Friedlander is the Minister of the Westminster
Synagogue and the Dean of the Leo Baeck College in London
training Reform and Liberal rabbis. His books on Jewish theology
and philosophy have appeared in Europe, the USA and Great
Britain. He is Honorary President of the World Conference of
Religions for Peace, and is currently a visiting Fellow at the
Wissenschafts Kolleg in Berlin.*

The prophets of the Bible come in all shapes and forms. There
are the major and minor prophets with their own books: priests,
peasants or princes like Jeremiah, Amos, or Zephaniah;
professional court prophets like Nathan – and then there is the
wild man himself: Elijah, the troubler of king and court. In our texts
for this week, we walk alongside him in his vision of social justice
and his struggle against idolatry. In Elijah, we discover the
religious vision moving through human strength and weakness,
part of Israel's growing awareness of the will of God.

Sunday June 21   1 Kings 17.1-24
The tribune of the people
Elijah flees into the desert after leaving his message of Divine
punishment at Ahab's court. He becomes the people's prophet,
surrounded by marvellous stories of ravens who feed him, of the
brook Cherith in the desert, and of miracles he can do for a poor
widow and her son who are resigned to die of starvation. Elijah
saves them. The cruse of oil and the jar of meal which will not
cease giving food are an old tale among the poor; behind it lies the
firm conviction that God will not let the righteous starve. But death
calls on every home, and the widow confronts the prophet with her
child's body. Was it not mockery to be given hope and then
despair? Elijah takes the child to his chamber and restores life.
Was it the first recorded case of mouth-to-mouth resuscitation –

no miracle as they knew it, but inspiration from God which is a continuing miracle within human life? It doesn't matter. The child lived; the woman believed; and Elijah found strength for his tasks. Sometimes, in order to believe in a prophet, the people need to see what seem to be miracles. And often, in the dark moments of self-doubt, the prophet needs confirmation that God is at his side.

✸ *God, let me see the miracles of daily life.*
Let them come to me from every encounter with the
*   world:*
the starry sky, the clear brook of water,
the movement of the trees which feed my hunger
and my need for beauty.
And let me know that in the dark nights there will be help,
so that I can awake in the morning and help others.

Monday June 22   *1 Kings 18.1, 16-40*

Challenging the waverer

Ahab's address to Elijah is the familiar attack upon the voice of social conscience: 'Is it thou, thou troubler of Israel?' Elijah's reply sums up the evil done by the king who has forsaken God's law. The prophet challenges 450 false priests to a combat of faith on Mount Carmel. The stage is set for one of the most dramatic encounters in the Bible; and the people love it. Elijah addresses them and the priests with powerful images. 'How long will ye halt between two opinions? If the LORD be God, follow Him; but if Baal, follow him.' In a troubled society, the people can be uncertain in their faith. In the test, rigged in favour of the enemy, the false priests fail. Elijah mocks them with brilliant irony. Why doesn't their god answer? 'Perhaps he is on a journey ... perhaps he is sleeping ...' and the impotence of idols is displayed to the people. Then Elijah moves to the centre of the stage: a water-logged altar, and no fire – until it falls upon the altar from heaven and consumes the sacrifice. The false priests are slain – a cruel moment. But the final image is that of faith triumphant.

✸ *O God, I often waver in my faith;*
I stumble between truth and lie.
Let me be more secure in faith
and see Thy truth in all its power.
We worship material things; we listen to false prophets.
Give me the inner strength to seek the truth
and pursue it.
Then I can truly serve Thee. Amen

141

Striving with God and oneself

We expect too much from our prophets. Once they have proved themselves, they must always produce what is needed. The prophet as 'rain maker' is an old image, and Elijah has to battle with God, to make demands, so that the gift of rain can finally serve the suffering people. King Ahab is impressed – more, mocked by the power of the prophet. And Jezebel recognizes the danger of a prophet with true power in a land which she and the king rule through violence. She tries to kill him and he flees into the wilderness, ever the place for renewal.

There are times when one must withdraw to confront the religious vision totally outside the materialistic world. Perhaps one wants to escape completely. This time, Elijah confronts God with the plea to grant him death. Instead, he finds himself sustained by God. An ancient pattern is repeated: 'And he arose, and did eat and drink, and went in the strength of that meal forty days and forty nights unto Horeb, the mount of God.' On that mountain, in a time of deep soul searching, renewal can come.

✳ ***God, give me the strength to retreat, on occasion,***
from the strife of my society.
Let me reach out to Thee, and re-examine myself.
Perhaps I will return to my world with deeper faith.
But even if I doubt, let me have moments
when I feel myself standing on Thy mountain. Amen

The still small voice

Finally, the great vision comes to Elijah, confirming the truth of his life to him. Elijah stands on the mountain, and sees himself as the one survivor, the one fighter for God standing in his loneliness. Will he now see God? The Bible tells us: 'And behold, the LORD passed by, and a great and strong wind rent the mountains, and broke in pieces the rocks before the LORD; but the LORD was not in the wind; and after the wind an earthquake; but the LORD was not in the earthquake; and after the earthquake a fire; but the LORD was not in the fire, and after the fire a still small voice.' At that moment, Elijah hears God, and confesses all his weaknesses to Him. But also at that moment, the heaviest task is laid upon that servant of God. In his weakness, he is – stronger than ever – bidden to appoint new kings, and to select a successor in his work of prophecy. The second task seems smaller, but it is the bigger one: he must cast the mantle of prophecy upon Elisha, remove him from his family, to carry on a task which the kings he appoints cannot achieve: the religious vision must remain within the people.

✳ *O God, let me listen to my conscience,*
to that still small voice which sounds louder
than all the turmoil of the world.
Let me be reminded of what I can do, and what I cannot do.
Grant me the wisdom to leave space to others,
to my friends and members of my family,
so that my vision and hopes can be realized through them.
Let me know that I am a link
in the chain between past and future. Amen

Thursday June 25   *1 Kings 21.1-26*

Naboth's vineyard

There are times when we believe that corruption within government is new in the world; but power has always corrupted. Ahab, in this story, is not yet totally evil. He tries to purchase the property he desires, and he desists when the owner refuses the offer. The queen has no scruples, but does not simply use violence. Forgery and false witnesses permit Jezebel to use the judicial system to murder Naboth and to acquire the property 'legally'.

The prophet realizes that the royal house and government are beyond redemption. And so he confronts the king. The very act of which Naboth had been accused, 'cursing the king', now becomes the act of justice through which the prophet confirms the doom of Jezebel and Amos. They are condemned not only for the murder of Naboth, but for their worship of false gods and the evils they have brought into the land. Jezebel's death is foretold in graphic detail: the dogs will eat her body. Ahab can say to Elijah: 'Hast thou found me, O mine enemy?' But Ahab is *the enemy*. And it is God's judgement which speaks through the mouth of the prophet, a figure radiant with inner fire.

✳ *God, save me from the abuse of power.*
When I have authority, let me not misuse it,
but let me be aware of the rights of others.
And when I see the poor and weak oppressed and
*   burdened,*
let me not be silent. Let me speak out against evil,
so that justice may prevail in the world. Amen

More confrontation

The Bible is a harsh and honest book, recording the often brutal clash between king and prophet. Ahaziah is ill and sends for Elijah, who refuses to come: the king will die for having prayed to Baal-zebub instead of turning to God. The king is amazed at his message: did it really come from the prophet? The messengers describe him: 'A hairy man ... with a girdle of leather about his loins'. It *is* the Tishbite! Promptly, the king sends out a large arresting party. Promptly, the prophet proves his powers as a fire of God comes down to destroy the captain and his soldiers. This happens twice, until the third officer humbles himself and Elijah, secure in his faith, goes with him to the king. God's judgement is unchanged; he tells Ahaziah: '"Thou shalt not come down from the bed ... thou shalt surely die." So he died according to the word of the LORD which Elijah had spoken.'

The religious vision differs from the self-understanding of secular rulers. And the kings of Israel were judged by their adherence to the faith. Ahaziah's work, the Bible says, was 'written in the book of the chronicles of the kings of Israel'. No such book has been found. But Elijah's works and teachings have lived on for three thousand years.

✳ *Let me be humble, O God,*
 when confronting the vision of faith;
 and let me be proud and unyielding
 when commanded by the arrogance of evil.
 My judgement will often be faulty, but let me be strong
 against tyranny. And, at times,
 give me strength to challenge my teachers as well,
 so that we may learn from one another. Amen

Accepting the task for the next generation

Elijah was different from all other prophets. They lived and died in this world. It was granted to Elijah to go to heaven in a fiery chariot, and in all generations of Jewish life the dream exists that Elijah visits them, that he rewards virtue and that he will announce the coming of the Messiah. In this final chapter of his life, on his way to a final revelation, he is accompanied by his disciple Elisha. Elisha will wear the prophet's mantle; he will continue his work, but he will be less than his master. Elijah asks him what he wants, and Elisha replies: 'Let a double portion of thy spirit be upon me.' His master responds: 'If thou see me when I am taken from thee, it shall be so unto thee,' and this *does* happen. In a whirlwind, upon a fiery chariot, Elijah is taken up to heaven.

Elisha is more of a court prophet, less of the wild man of the desert. His vision is not as great as that of his teacher, but perhaps the 'double portion of spirit' was needed in the materialistic world he had to instruct. But the vision of the fiery chariot continued to instruct him, as it instructs all of us. *We need the mystery and the fire of religion alongside its ethical commandments.* The fiery chariot belongs to every generation of those who seek God.

✳ *O God, preserve the sense of mystery within my soul.*
Let me find Thee in the darkness of my life
as well as in the daytime.
Let me carry out the instructions of the past,
knowing how much strength I will need
to keep the light of faith burning.
If I cannot be the prophet, let me be the disciple.
In this way I will learn to serve others
and grow closer towards Thee. Amen

For further reflection or group discussion

● What was the role of the prophet within ancient society? Is there such a role now?
● Was Elijah a 'good' person? How could he kill all the priests of Baal, and the soldiers sent to take him prisoner? Elijah killed in the name of God. How far can we justify this, if at all?
● The story of Naboth's vineyard shows corruption in high places. What about now?
● Elijah's ascent into heaven in a fiery chariot gives us new insights into the prophet and his relationship to the world and God. Discuss.
● Did you like Elijah as a person? Why? How does he appeal to you as a figure in religious history?

PERSONALITIES OF THE BIBLE
3. Peter

Notes based on the New International Version by
Eileen Jacob

*Eileen Jacob, a member of the Church of South India, is retired
and living in Hyderabad. Previously she taught in a city grammar
school and was superintendent of a village hostel for girls.*

Peter would probably rank first in any popularity poll of early
disciples. Most of us can identify with his impulsive attempts to
show devotion to Jesus, and his failures to live up to the
standards of love and loyalty he set himself. Peter was a good
mixer. Because he knew what others were thinking and feeling,
he was able to speak for them. As we try to walk with Peter, may
his story help us as we too blunder along the way of discipleship.

Sunday June 28   *Luke 5.1-11*
What's my job?
Peter's job was fishing. But he was willing to offer his services
and make his boat available for Jesus' work. And he was more
than amply repaid by the catch of a lifetime!

In this interaction, Peter knew he was 'hooked'! He was ready
to leave everything and follow Jesus. This involved launching out
into the deep. To succeed as a 'fisher' of people, no shallow
commitment would do; it had to be an 'all or nothing' response.

Following Jesus involves a willingness to change. This may
not mean moving to new employment, but requires us, through
lives in which the presence of Christ is clear for all to see, to draw
others into his Kingdom. Our qualifications and resources will
always be inadequate, and we will often need the help of partners
in other boats. But the reward is a whole world of new relationships (Mark 10.29-30).

✸ *In spite of my unworthiness,*
  you can call me to work with you, Lord.
  Grant that I may help and not hinder
  as you seek to draw all people to yourself.

Monday June 29 *Matthew 16.13-23*

Could this be the Christ?

The Samaritan woman (John 4.29) came very near to making a confession of faith, but it was Peter who actually confessed, 'You are the Christ, the Son of the living God.' His words were inspired by God, and not based on public opinion as so many of our views are. Peter became 'the rock', the first of many 'living stones' with which Jesus began building the new people of God – the Church.

But Peter's clear vision of Christ was at once clouded by preconceived and erroneous ideas about the Messiah. How could the promised Saviour possibly undergo suffering and shame? How could he help others if he himself must die? So for Peter, as for so many others, the cross became the 'stone that causes men to stumble and a rock that makes them fall' (Romans 9.33).

So often, our moments of vision, when we are uplifted with fine thoughts, are followed by humiliating experiences of our own earthiness, our blind and stupid opposition to God. To know and accept our own weakness is the first necessary step to accepting God's way of the cross for our salvation.

✱ ***Jesus, by your wounded feet, direct our path aright.***
Jesus, by your nailed hands, move us to deeds of love.
Jesus, by your pierced side, cleanse our desires.
Jesus, by your broken heart, knit ours to yours.

Richard Crawshaw (1613-49)

Tuesday June 30 *Mark 14.26-31*

The flesh is weak

Peter had plenty of physical courage. Fishing on the Lake of Galilee was no job for cowards! So he trusted his courage, with the help of a sword, to carry him through the coming crisis. But it was not physical prowess that was to be tested. Peter was to be challenged again to take up his own cross and follow Jesus. Was he willing to identify himself as the disciple of one who stood dumb and defenceless before his accusers? Without any attempt at self-defence, was he willing to follow Jesus as he went to die? Everything masculine in Peter was revolted by the idea. Wasn't this the weakness that ends in defeat?

It is only those who have ever tried to walk the way of the cross who can think like this. It takes superhuman strength to follow this way. Jesus knew that Peter lacked this strength. Peter did not. But why did Jesus forewarn Peter? His prediction of

Peter's denial is very specific and does not suggest that he expected Peter to heed his warning. Perhaps it was the memory of those words of Jesus that helped Peter, after his denial, to find tears of repentance and the hope of a new beginning.

✳ *Grant, O Lord, that your love may so fill our lives that we may count nothing too small to do for you, nothing too much to give, and nothing too hard to bear, for Jesus Christ's sake.*   Ignatius Loyola (1491-1556)

Wednesday July 1   *John 21.1-19*

To die is gain

Life teaches us many lessons. When we are young, we are encouraged to stand on our own feet and reach out to attain worthy goals. As we mature, there are even harder lessons: how to let go, retire gracefully, accept help, and allow others to take decisions for us. The lessons are not contradictory, but appropriate for the stage of life we have reached.

Peter, humbled by the experience of his denial, and lovingly reinstated by Jesus, is now ready to face the unknown future. He has to learn to stretch out his hands to accept whatever life brings, to let others clothe him – even in garments of mockery; to let himself be led – even to a cross. To learn these lessons, Peter must deny himself and let his ego be destroyed.

The world will seldom applaud those who learn and apply these difficult lessons. It is more likely to crucify them, as it did Jesus. But there are those who glorify God by learning how to die.

✳ *Lord Jesus, you have shown us how to live and how to die. Help us daily to learn the lessons you set us, so that we can say with Paul, 'For to me, to live is Christ, and to die is gain'.*
                                                   Philippians 1.21

Thursday July 2   *Acts 4.1-19*

New life in Christ

The authorities were greatly disturbed. They saw very ordinary men exhibiting extraordinary courage, performing healing miracles and capturing the crowds with their teaching. In face of this phenomenon, the 'powers that be' were helpless. They could only utter ineffective threats to try to silence Peter and John.

The transformation in Peter was no less wonderful than the healing of the lifelong cripple now 'walking and leaping and praising God', a living proof that the crucified Jesus was alive. Gone also was the Peter who had been ashamed to confess that he was a disciple of Jesus. He was freed from all his disabling doubts and fears to witness boldly for his risen Lord. 'Praise be to the God and Father of our Lord Jesus Christ! In his great mercy he has given us new birth into a living hope through the resurrection of Jesus Christ from the dead' (1 Peter 1.3).

✳ *If you*
in devastating love,
can create an Easter dawn
from Friday's deathly night,
then can there be a stronger sign
that we are loved eternally?

So we add our voices
to the praise of all creation
and,
reborn every day,
we will proclaim your victory
in lives of hope
and words of joy
and deeds of courageous service,
all because of Jesus
our loving, Risen Lord.

Further Everyday Prayers (IBRA)

Friday July 3   Acts 10.34-48

Live and learn

Entry into new life in Christ is often spoken of as being 'born again'. Birth involves a separation from the past and a radically new beginning. But it must be followed by a process of growth.

Acts 10 tells how Peter's openness to new encounters, and his willingness to reflect on their meaning, enabled him to outgrow traditional prejudices against Gentiles and be ready, as God was, to welcome them into the new fellowship of believers in Christ.

The idea that they were God's chosen people was not a Jewish illusion. They had indeed been chosen by God for a purpose: 'All people on earth will be blessed through you,' was God's promise to Abraham. There is no question of privilege for its own sake. The Jews were called to share their faith with other nations. The same is true of the new Israel, the Church. In the encounter with Cornelius, Peter was true to his Jewish ancestry and responsive to the pioneering, cross-cultural spirit of Christ.

✴ *'We have the Spirit of God. And in the midst of all the imperfections in the world, in us, he is at work ... God is working His purpose out. He is not idle. Perhaps we are impatient. We want to see His Kingdom come at once. But God is infinitely patient.'*

Bishop Sumitra to the CSI Sisters, 1960

Saturday July 4   *Galatians 2.6-14*

I could be wrong

Both Peter and Paul had been amazed to discover that all the laws regarding ritual purity and the Jewish food restrictions were irrelevant to God. For both of them it was their personal experience of seeing Gentiles responding to the gospel and coming to new life in Christ that convinced them of this. The revelation would have been even more astonishing to Paul, the orthodox Pharisee, than it was to Peter (Galileans were not noted for orthodoxy). Paul continued his missionary work among Gentiles. Peter became an establishment figure, a pillar of the Church in Jerusalem.

Maybe Paul's theological training under Gamaliel and the intellectual discipline it involved, enabled him to see farther than Peter. How crucial it was to the propagation of the gospel, and to Church unity, that the dos and don'ts which obsessed some Jewish believers should not frustrate free admission of Gentile converts, or table fellowship with them in the Church. Peter received a passionate and public reproof when he compromised on this issue. But this is the kind of debate and creative tension through which the Church grows. Hopefully Peter was humble enough to accept criticism and learn from it.

Although there is no written record of Peter's death, tradition has it that he died a martyr in the Neronic persecutions.

✴ *Lord, help me to welcome criticism,*
even when it hurts and humbles me.

For further reflection or group discussion

● List Peter's strengths and weaknesses. Think of how God used both.
● Identify one strength and one weakness in yourself – or in each person if you are meeting in a group – and see how God uses these traits.

PERSONALITIES OF THE BIBLE
4. Some other personalities

Notes based on the New International Version by
Ebere Nze

Eberechukwu Nze, a Nigerian theologian and former Principal of the Methodist Theological Institute in Umuahia, has travelled widely and represented the Methodist Church Nigeria in many international conferences and seminars. He is now Bishop of the Nneochi Diocese, Abia State, Nigeria.

This week we turn to some lesser known personalities, whose stories are recorded in less detail.

A personality is to a great extent influenced by the group – family, community, nation or culture – in which s/he grows up. But as followers of Christ, we are challenged to estimate a person's significance according to the way in which the love of God is reflected in his or her life. It requires the eye of faith to discern Godlike qualities and to emulate these in our lives.

Sunday, July 5   *Judges 4.4-10; 12-15*

Deborah – 'woman of spirit'

It is interesting to see how in male-dominated societies God sometimes raises women to undertake leadership roles. It reminds us, whatever our culture, that God's image is reflected in all humankind; this is part of the mystery of God.

Deborah was both judge and prophetess in the hill country of Ephraim, rather like Samuel who later became judge and prophet over most of Israel. She had been used by God to settle the many disputes which the people brought to her. She is described as 'the wife of Lapindoth' which may be translated 'fiery woman', or 'woman of spirit'. She was obviously a strong personality. Barak refused to go into battle unless she came with him. The Canaanite army, with its iron chariots, was stronger than his own army.

Deborah's trust in God and her humility in accompanying Barak into battle earned her honour. Barak ran from the scene to pursue and kill Sisera, and perhaps win the greatest honour, but it was another woman – as Deborah had prophesied – by whose cunning Sisera fell (verses 17-22).

Some governments still promote repressive attitudes towards women, but God loves and uses both men and women to bring peace to the nations and honour to individuals and groups.

✳ *Gracious God, whose choice of leaders*
is not restricted by race or gender,
touch the hearts of those who practise discrimination,
that they may learn to honour all people.

Monday July 6   *1 Samuel 8.1-22*

Samuel – a prepared leader

The circumstances surrounding the birth of Samuel, and his dedication to the Lord, were well known. All Israel recognized Samuel as a prophet appointed by the Lord (1 Samuel 3.20). In 7.3, he called for national repentance and rededication. He was deeply exercised spiritually, well prepared for the teaching of true religion. As judge and prophet, he made himself accessible to the people. He became deeply involved in public affairs and was entrusted with the anointing of the nation's first king.

Yet Samuel was both surprised and disappointed that Israel should turn from a theocentric form of leadership to look for a monarchical government. Through Samuel's leadership, and led by God, the Ark of God's presence had been restored and the Philistines partly subdued. Why did they want a king to be like other nations? God asked Samuel to warn Israel of the consequences of such a demand – conscription, taxation, serfdom – and yet they persisted.

God had prepared Samuel as a dedicated leader who constantly pointed Israel to the rule of God. There are many such prophets all over the world. We will be wise to listen to them that we may receive the blessings and victory that come from God.

✳ *Dear Lord, help us to discern*
the difference between your rule and human government.
Make us obedient children of your Kingdom,
that we may attract the disobedient to your will
rather than lose our identity as citizens of the Kingdom.

Tuesday July 7   *Jeremiah 26.20-23*

Uriah – a true prophet

Truth is provoking and challenging. When spoken either by an ordinary or a well-known person, it threatens the security of the corrupt. Not much is known about the prophet Uriah, but we read that he supported Jeremiah's challenge to both king and government. Jeremiah had warned of the consequences of their continued flaunting of public morality and the laws of God: 'I will make this house like Shiloh and this city an object of cursing among all the nations of the earth' (verse 6).

Uriah had no army and no personal power to threaten Jehoiakim, so why did the king seek to put him to death? It was the truth that made the king, the priests and professional prophets of Judah uneasy.

In many nations today, people who stand by the truth are silenced, while others resist the truth and spend large sums of money to defend their indefensible falsehood. Rich nations and wealthy, powerful individuals do not want to hear the truth spoken by developing nations, and the ordinary people within them. Even among the developing nations, the cries of the poor are not listened to. But God persists in many ways, through known and unknown people, to declare truth and justice.

Uriah knew the danger that faced him, but God gave him courage to be outspoken. God can use us in the same way.

✳ *No one and no place is obscure before you, O God.*
Tune our hearts to recognize that whoever listens
to the truth of your word will be challenged to do your
will.

Wednesday July 8   *Luke 10.38-42*C*

Mary and Martha – their conflicting priorities

Here are two sisters who loved Jesus and were loved and appreciated by him. Acting from differing perspectives of kindness and love, they offered different hospitalities to Jesus. Jesus was on his way to Jerusalem, knowing that he would die there, when he called at the home of Mary and Martha. His thoughts were not on food and hospitality, but on the spiritual devotion which could give him strength to face the ordeal. Mary sensed his feelings, but Martha acted on her own presumed priority. Experience has shown that when we spend time meditating on God's word, God provides strength and wisdom to enable us to face physical pain and weakness.

Have you, like Martha, been kind to someone who did not appreciate your kindness? Did you discover that person's real need at the time?

When our priority is physical need, it becomes a burden when we fail to achieve it. When it is spiritual, we gain the divine directive on how to pursue and achieve it.

✻ *O God of love, purify our intentions and temperaments.*
Enable us to obey the directives of the Holy Spirit
that our kindnesses may really meet the actual needs
of our neighbour. In Jesus' name we pray. Amen

Thursday July 9   *Mark 15.21; Romans 16.13*

Simon of Cyrene – the first African follower

The story of Simon is an interesting one. Wherever he is mentioned in the Gospels (Mark 15.21; Matthew 27.32; Luke 23.26), only one verse in each case is written. All we know about him is that he carried the cross of Jesus. No book has been written about him, but a single act of service for the Lord has placed Simon's name in each of the Gospels where it stands for all time.

Mark tells us that he was the father of Alexander and Rufus, which suggests that his sons were well-known to his readers. Could it be that this is the Rufus referred to in Paul's letter to the Romans (16.13)? If so, then we could assume that Simon's encounter with the Lord at Golgotha may have led to his conversion and to his family accepting the Christian faith.

Simon came from Cyrene. As far as we know, he was the first African to follow Christ and suffer with him, lighting the first candle of faith in this great continent. In many African countries today, over half of the population are practising Christians.

✻ *Help us to help each other, Lord,*
    Each other's cross to bear,
Let each his friendly aid afford,
    And feel his brother's care.   *Charles Wesley (1707-88)*

Friday July 10   *Acts 4.36-37; 11.19-26*

Barnabas – the encourager

African names, especially in Eastern Nigeria, are very significant. Names tell stories and mark events. In most cases, the meanings of names reflect the life and characteristics of the person, and so do many biblical and Jewish names.

Barnabas means 'a son of encouragement'. In our first reading, he encouraged others to share by his example (Acts

4.36-37). On another occasion, he was sent by the Jerusalem Church to Antioch to encourage those who had fled there to find safety from persecution (11.22-23). He then went in search of Paul and brought him to Antioch. They spent a whole year teaching the community of Christians there, and it was from Antioch that Paul and Barnabas set out together in the wider mission of the Church.

Barnabas' whole life reflected the meaning of his name. He may have been overshadowed by the exceptional pioneering spirit and ability of Paul, but leaders like Paul depend on the support and encouragement of people like Barnabas. And we can all help in this way. The quality of our lives can console (or the lack of it can discourage) our neighbours and friends, and give support to those who lead us.

Does your name have a meaning? Everyone needs a name today for Jesus.

✴ *Eternal Lord,*
there is something special about your name.
Help us to bear names
that reflect the demands of the gospel.
And may the example of others of whom we have read,
or whom we encounter,
challenge us to more effective living.

Saturday July 11   *Acts 16.16-34, 40*

A girl whose name is not recorded

Here is another glimpse of the power of Christ over the wind and waves, and over the powers of demonic forces. Demons trembled in the presence of Christ. And in earlier stories of Acts, the apostles had confronted Jewish magic (Acts 8.9-24; 13.8-12). Here is a first encounter with pagan magic. This slave girl, who received omens and was able to tell people's fortunes, was mercilessly used by her masters to their gain. Like those, in the Gospels, who were 'demon possessed' and who recognized Jesus as the Son of God, this girl divined that here were obedient servants of God (verse 17), and that they would proclaim 'the way of salvation' – as indeed they did to the jailer (verse 31). This is an often repeated paradox in the New Testament that the spirits of madness recognized the truth of God's power where religious or powerful people failed to do so.

Part of the mystery of God is that he works with both good and evil forces. The casting out of the spirit of Python from the slave

155

girl actually advanced the cause of the gospel. Paul, who lost no opportunity to share his faith, was able to preach to prisoners and to the jailer and his household who believed with joy.

It is also true that wherever Christians attack vested interests, trouble follows. The greatest obstacle to the cause of Christ is materialism.

When we suffer for well-doing, let us bear in mind that it could lead to the transforming of lives that need the touch of God. And let us also remember how God loves the poor and oppressed – like the girl in this story – and can use us to transform their lives as we oppose those who exploit them and as we seek to build a more just society.

✳ *Holy and mighty God,*
banish greed and pride from our hearts,
so that desire for ill-gotten wealth
may never creep into our minds and destroy us. Amen

For further reflection or group discussion

Make a list of your own strengths. Then select one of the personalities you have studied this week, and see whether your strengths match with any of hers or his. If so, thank God, and if not, kneel and pray that God may help you to grow in grace.

FOR ACTION

Choose another country of the world and learn something about its people's culture. Select two or three aspects of that culture and compare them with your own. If Jesus lived in that culture – or your own – what would he say and do?

CALLED TO LEAD

Notes based on the New English Bible by
Donald Hilton

*Donald Hilton is a minister of the United Reformed Church (URC),
and has served in three local churches. Additionally he has been
the national Christian Education Secretary, Moderator of the
Yorkshire Province of the URC, and Moderator of the General
Assembly (1993/4). He has written and compiled a number of
books published by NCEC.*

Leadership is critically important. It can empower those who are led
but also has the ability and opportunity to cripple others. Leaders
can give vision to communities or plunge them into despair.

What kind of leaders do we want? For Christians the Bible is a
major resource in answering this question. These notes explore
some of the guidance and warnings that the biblical record offers
and leads us to see Jesus Christ as the faithful model of effective
and godly leadership with integrity and purpose.

Although these notes are written with leadership in the Church
in mind, those using them should reflect on the message for
political, commercial, industrial, and other leaders.

Sunday July 12   *Exodus 3.1-10*
Personal leadership; political action

Never assume when or how God will call you to be a leader.
Some have heard God's call through silent prayer. Alan Boesak
found his call to leadership in the turmoil of South African
apartheid politics. It was 'a holy anger about things that are wrong
in the world' and the realization that little children 'die of hunger
whilst the tables of the rich are sagging with food'.

The call to Moses was both personal and political. It came:
- **as he was doing his daily job** Leaders don't hang around
  dreaming that God may one day speak to them. They get on
  with daily life.
- **through the injustice in the world** Israel was oppressed by
  Egypt. Someone must act! William Booth led his Salvation
  Army with the conviction, 'While women weep as they do now,
  I'll fight; while little children go hungry as they do now, I'll fight.'

- **by God's initiative** The symbol of a burning bush declares that Moses' call involved God's action as well as Moses' choice. The first Christian leaders also understood that. Jesus told them, 'You did not choose me: I chose you.'

A minister recalls his very first church responsibility: he agreed to clear up after the youth club. Then followed lay preaching, ordination, and a lifetime's service. Would the greater jobs have come without his 'Yes' to God in the first smaller challenge?

✳ *Lord, open my eyes to the world around me,*
and the life within me, and then, hearing your voice,
strengthen me to obey.

Monday July 13　　　　　　　　　　　　　　　　*Exodus 3.11-15*

Human leadership; rooted in God

In the 1960s there was widespread persecution of Christians in the Congo; any African who protected a white person was likely to be killed. A black pastor was brought before the military court and accused of giving such help. 'Why did you shelter a white woman?' he was asked. 'Because she is my sister in Christ, the child of my own heavenly Father', he replied. He was sentenced to be shot but the effect of his dignity and belief was such that he was set free. Behind his testimony lay the conviction that the way we live springs from the kind of God we worship. If God is fatherly, we must live as a family of sisters and brothers.

Moses knew he would have to convince others to follow. How? They wouldn't listen. The answer came: Tell them who I am – your action springs from the kind of God you worship and serve. Jehovah is an I AM God – a God of the present tense who comforts and challenges his people in the present living moment. Although we can trace his presence and power through previous generations, and although we know he goes before us into the future, his call to us is always NOW. On that conviction Moses can accept the call to leadership.

✳ *Where you have placed me, there Lord let me serve.*

Tuesday July 14　　　　　　　　　　　　　　　　*Exodus 4.10-17*

Shared responsibility

Leadership does not belong only to important people who get their names into history books. God calls each of us to be a leader but the places in which we lead and the gifts we each bring to the job are varied.

Moses declined to lead because he was a slow and hesitant speaker. Was he being modest? Was he trying to evade responsibility? Did he stutter? 'No excuses!' God said. 'You can do the thinking and your brother the speaking.' It was probably the first job-share!

The principle runs deep in our belief about the Church. All the resources we need are present but they only emerge when people work as a team.

The Indian church-leader Daleep Mukarji challenged his church to stop being a 'receiving church' dependent on the West and start being a 'sharing' church. 'When will we realize', he asked, 'that we can share our experience and resources? Mission and partnership must be a two-way process of love, trust, and a willingness to learn and grow together.'

Think about your own church. Is it a team? Do you make room for newcomers to bring their gifts? Have you accepted young people as leaders? Recall when a child gave you a new idea.

✷ *Ever-rich God, you offer your gifts to us*
from the hands of so many people.
May we despise none but welcome all.

Wednesday July 15   Numbers 11.10-17

Sharing the burden

The cost of leadership can be unbearable. Nervous breakdowns and 'burn-out' are realities in our own society. Leadership can also be dangerous. Hitler was a leader in Germany. As a result, a nation was crippled and other nations suffered. Even so precious a gift as leadership needs checks and balances to remain creative.

Verse 16 marks an important step in understanding leadership. As the task grows so other people share it. Moses is both helped and kept in touch with the rest of the community; the seventy elders become a go-between.

✷ *Lord God, this we have learned in the community of faith,*
for this we give you thanks:
Until we hear with each other's ears
your word is indistinct, unclear.
Until we see with each other's eyes
we live in shadowed half-light.
Until we walk as pilgrim friends
we stumble and are quick to fall.
Until we love and let love conquer all mistrust and fear

we are pale shadows of the Christ we serve.
Give us ears and eyes and strengthened steps
and make our common search for truth
a gift of love we offer to each other.

Thursday July 16   *Judges 17.1-13*

Morals decline; a believer speaks

This sad picture of moral decline describes a community lacking effective leadership. A son steals from his mother. Shamed by her curse (would he have acted otherwise?) he gives it back. She dedicates it all to the Lord but in fact keeps most for herself. Then, they all worship an idol.

The reason for this decline is offered in verse 6. 'In those days there was no king in Israel; every man did what was right in his own eyes.' Compare that with the following story.

During the Nazi occupation in France, ministers and priests were instructed to read a statement in their churches urging people to conform to Nazi rule. A Breton priest read the offensive statement and then preached a sermon denouncing fascism. He said to his congregation, 'If anyone wishes to report me to the Germans, tell them they will find me in my presbytery.'

There are times when Christians have to offer clear leadership, regardless of the consequences. Martin Luther, seeking to reform a corrupt Church, preached boldly and lived dangerously with the words: 'Here I stand, I can do no other'. Desmond Tutu has been an example in our own times. Tomorrow it might be any of us – at school, in the office, at college, or at home – or even in the Church.

✸ *Lord, even if the earth crumbles, skies darken,*
and our hearts are fearful,
still your truth prevails in faithful lives.

Friday July 17   *1 Samuel 8.1-9*

Leadership styles

These words were written long after the event they describe. They are best understood as a parable about different styles of leadership. Samuel represents the example of a leader so faithful to God that such leadership becomes God's leadership.

The elders know his sons won't follow Samuel's footsteps so hereditary leadership could be dangerous. Instead they think they might like a monarchy. But the author of this parable has seen kings at work. They can be good but they can easily become oppressive. And why do they want kings, the parable asks? Because they have rejected God himself as the only ruler ever needed. Is this a romantic and unrealistic view of God's kingship, or are there ways of organizing national life so that God's influence is made known?

- In a democracy the people influence the choice of national leaders. Elect godly men and women!
- A free press can comment critically on a nation's leaders.
- The Church has a political as well as pastoral job to do.
- Ordinary people in daily conversation can raise a nation's sight to higher ideals and larger visions.

✻ *Rejoice, O land, in God thy might;*
  His will obey, Him serve aright.   Robert Bridges

Saturday July 18   *1 Samuel 8.10-22*

Crippling leadership

The author of these words has had a bad experience of kings. He has discovered that some leaders can be oppressive. They can cripple other people. Does this only apply to national leaders or can it happen in ordinary daily life?

Raymond is a minister in a local church. He has noticed that when he is in a discussion group everybody defers to him. Few people volunteer their ideas and everything depends on him. Yet if he steps out of the group for a time they all have something to say. He knows his leadership is inhibiting others and wishes it was not so. What should he do?

'The trouble with you', a female colleague said to Richard, 'is that you assume that women are worthless and so you don't listen to what they say'. The idea took Richard by surprise.

Think about the following: Can white people cripple leadership offered by black people (or vice versa)? Can older people block the leadership gifts of younger people?

If there are 'born leaders' must there be 'born followers'?

✻ *Reflect: Leaders are best when people barely know they*
  exist.   Lao Tzu, China

For further reflection or group discussion
- Recall leaders you have known. What have been their essential qualities?

161

- Think about the life of your local church. How is leadership shared around the congregation? Are there clear ways in which new leaders can emerge? Recall occasions when leadership by newcomers, young people, or the elderly was welcomed and used.
- In many nations there seems to be a decline in moral standards and honest behaviour. What leadership can the Church give?

Sunday July 19   *1 Kings 3.4-15*

When silence speaks

A woman with severe depression tells of a friend who used to visit her. She was not her only visitor; she was the one she most looked forward to seeing. Others would offer good advice and suggest how she might overcome her depressive illness. They told her of God's goodness and assured her that one day she would come through the dark tunnel. The special friend was different. She said little or nothing but listened as the sick woman talked aloud about her problems and anxieties. Sometimes there would be total silence between them for more than a quarter of an hour, but always as her friend left the woman felt encouraged and knew a little corner had been lifted on her depression.

Appointed as king, Solomon asks God for just one gift – 'a heart with skill to listen so that he may govern thy people justly' (verse 9). Friendship needs few words and there is a quality in some leadership that remains silent.

✳ *Reflect on these further words by Lao Tzu:*
Of good leaders who talk little,
When their work is done
And their aim fulfilled
The people will say, 'We did it ourselves'.

Monday July 20   *Isaiah 52.13 to 53.6*

The leader who suffers

Our reading offers a picture of the kind of leadership that is ready to be a servant, even to the point of suffering. Consider three possible interpretations:

1. Written in the 6th century BC, it describes a Hebrew leader who became the victim of gross injustice. As Israel was exiled in Babylon at that time it might even be the story of the suffering

nation since later verses of the chapter speak of renewal and vindication.

2. It foreshadows the passion of Jesus Christ who was despised and rejected for 'the Lord laid upon him the guilt of us all'. This is the interpretation in Handel's oratorio 'The Messiah' and has deepened our Christian understanding of Good Friday and Christ's death.

3. It offers us a model for all effective leadership, suggesting that true leaders do not lord it over the followers but live their lives alongside them and accept anxiety, suffering, and even death for the sake of those they lead. It speaks today to politicians, church-leaders, parents and others.

All these interpretations are helpful. This 'Servant Song' can be sung in any language and by any generation.

✳ *We may not know, we cannot tell,*
What pains he had to bear,
But we believe it was for us ...   *Cecil F. Alexander (1818-95)*

Tuesday July 21   *Matthew 4.18-25*

Called and sent

These verses are so familiar that we may be tempted to think we fully understand them, but the call of Jesus has to be re-interpreted in every generation. To what are we called? Consider the following:

To suffering

'To those who obey him he will reveal himself in the toils, the conflicts, the sufferings which they shall pass through in his fellowship.'   *Albert Schweitzer*

To intimacy

'Take me to you, imprison me, for I
Except you enthrall me, never shall be free,
Nor ever chaste, except you ravish me.'   *John Donne*

To anger

'The ability to rage when justice lies prostrate on the streets and when the lie rages across the face of the earth.'   *Alan Boesak*

To personal commitment

'God has committed some work to me which he has not committed to another. I have my mission.'   *John Henry Newman*

To obedience

'I heard the Lord saying, 'Whom shall I send? Who will go for me? And I answered: "Here I am; send me".'   *Isaiah 6.8-9*

This page could be filled with similar quotations since the call of Jesus comes to each one in a distinctive voice and with a special challenge. The lakeside, the office, the motorway, the kitchen, the laboratory, the pew and the pulpit are amongst the many places where he still confronts men and women, girls and boys. Many hear but some are not listening.

✳ *Here I am, Lord; send me.*

Wednesday July 22   *Matthew 5.13-16*

Salt and light

During the Japanese conquest of Burma (now called *Myanmar*), British troops were retreating. A small group of Burmese Christians gave the fleeing soldiers shelter and food. Other Burmese informed on them and they were hauled before the military. 'You have been helping the enemy so you must die', they were told. Pleading for their lives in vain they asked for time to prepare themselves by prayer. As they knelt they were cut to pieces. One girl was just seventeen. After the war a confirmation service was held and the Bishop noticed that one of the people to be confirmed had been a prominent anti-Christian leader. He asked how he had become a Christian. 'It was those girls in the village,' he said. 'I knew they had something I did not have.'

> **'You are light for all the world. A town that stands on a hill cannot be hidden'** *(Matthew 5.14).*

The church grew in Africa not primarily through ordained missionaries, but through lay people, most of them indigenous, black and white. A junior government officer was transferred to a new area, a nurse started at a hospital, or a trader moved through the country. Some gathered groups for worship, others asked for a little plot of land to build a church, all lived lives of integrity and love. As they lived so the leaven of the gospel was spread.

> **'You are salt to the world'** *(Matthew 5.13a).*

✳ *Lord, let me season the world with your goodness*
and shed the light of the gospel in the world's darkness.

Thursday July 23   *Mark 10.32-45*

True greatness defined

James and John tragically misunderstood the nature of the Kingdom of God. They thought it to be like an earthly kingdom in which a supreme ruler hands out favours to his friends. Note that when Matthew tells the same story (Matthew 20.20-21) he is so embarrassed by the behaviour of these two disciples that he blames it on an over-ambitious mother! Similarly embarrassed, Luke camouflages the event totally (Luke 22.24).

Matthew, Mark and Luke, however, each use the incident to reinforce the real nature of Christian leadership. Leadership is servanthood. Greatness is humility. Top dogs are mongrels. No wonder they said that Christianity had 'turned the world upside down'.

We still have not learned to put this into practice. Even the Church is too often run by hierarchies in which the few dominate the many. Local churches can still pay more attention to members' standing in society than to faith commitment. Race, colour, and gender can still dominate. Oscar Romero hit the nail on the head: 'The Church's good name is not a matter of being on good terms with the powerful ... but of knowing that the poor regard the church as their own.'

The man who once demonstrated true leadership by washing his disciples' feet would have gently nodded his approval to that.

✳ *Servant leader, lead us into service.*

Friday July 24   1 Timothy 3.1-13
Leadership with integrity
These verses are a clarion call to a leadership style based on **Christian integrity** – what are the marks of such leadership?
good relationships in the home and amongst friends;
temperate behaviour avoiding quarrels or an excessive life-style;
open-heartedness hospitable in attitude and action;
transparent goodness that commends the faith to non-Christians;
inner contentment based on a well-held faith and a clear conscience.

Timothy might well have asked – if so much is needed then who can be a leader? Paul had already given the answer through his own leadership experience (1.12-14): 'I thank him who has made me equal to the task, Christ Jesus our Lord ... the grace of our Lord was lavished upon me, with the faith and love which are ours in Christ Jesus.'

The Scottish theologian John Baillie gave another clue. He knew his parents' authority over him but he also knew instinctively that his parents lived, spoke and acted in ways which showed that they themselves lived under God's authority. Without that knowledge, he writes, 'their authority over me could not have had the character which I actually felt it to possess'.

✳ *O, lead me Lord, that I may lead.*

Saturday July 25   *Philippians 2.1-11*

The model of leadership

How was it possible? A man with the right to claim equality with God deliberately chose to become a slave. Slaves have no choice; they are owned by others. Having given up choice this man was in the world's hands. The world decided to reject him and, in the end, kill him. He accepted it. This is true leadership because it is based on love.

Survivors of the wartime concentration camps say that the people they remember are those who walked through the camps comforting others and giving away their last pieces of bread. They prove that even when we are robbed of all seeming freedom, one freedom remains – that of choosing how we want to live. Some choose servanthood.

✳ *Servant Lord, a stable marked your entrance and your birth,*
the world took little notice of your life,
a city in despair brought forth your tears.
Your war-horse was a donkey through the streets,
a bowl and towel the sign of kingly reign,
and on a villain's cross you died
before you lay within a borrowed tomb.
When we seek power and influence, status and renown,
remind us, Lord.
Servant Lord, remind us.
From *Seasons & Celebrations* (NCEC)

For further reflection or group discussion and ACTION

● Can you think of occasions in your own experience when the poem by Lao Tzu given in the notes for July 19 was true?
● How is the call of Jesus, 'Follow me' heard in our own time?
● Which of the two symbols for leadership in evangelism is most helpful – that of salt, or light? (See notes for July 22.)

THE POWER OF PRAYER

Notes based on the New Jerusalem Bible by
Sheila Cassidy

Sheila Cassidy is working as a specialist in Psychosocial Oncology – how patients and those related to them are helped to cope with cancer – at Plymouth General Hospital (UK). In her spare time she preaches, lectures, broadcasts and writes books. Her writing is deeply influenced by her involvement with suffering both in cancer wards and in her personal experience of imprisonment, torture and solitary confinement in Chile.

Prayer is pivotal to our lives as Christians because it is how we communicate with God. It is also a subject that can make us feel uneasy, because most 'committed' Christians feel they don't pray very well and that they don't pray enough. In the reflections that follow, I'll be trying to see what guidance the scriptures offer us when, like the apostles, we cry 'Lord, teach us to pray.'

Sunday July 26   *Genesis 18.20-31 *C*

Abraham stays God's hand

Here is a glimpse of Abraham's relationship with God. Abraham is the archetypal man of faith, the man who, believing himself called by God, left his home in Mesopotamia, the fertile land between the rivers Tigris and Euphrates, and set off with his wife and family into the wilderness. God was full of promises, but he didn't give a lot away. Go, he told Abraham, to a place which I will show you. Trust me. It'll all be OK. Your descendants will be as many as the stars of heaven! So Abraham and Sarah journeyed in hope until Sarah, well past the menopause, became cynical.

Then, one day, Abraham and Sarah had some visitors ... but you'll have to read that bit for yourself – it comes just before today's reading (18.1-15).

After being royally entertained by Abraham, God decides to tell his friend his plans to destroy the city of Sodom. Abraham, however, is shocked at such violent retribution and begins to negotiate with God to see if he will spare the Sodomites. It feels a bit like someone negotiating with a terrorist: 'If I can persuade you that there are ten good men here, will you spare the wicked to save the just?' Abraham is wrestling with the 'Shiva' side of God, the just judge, the ruthless destroyer. Is there really a shadow side of God? What are we to make of Isaiah's words:

'I am Yahweh, and there is no other,
I form the light and I create darkness,
I make well-being, and I create disaster,
I, Yahweh, do all things' (Isaiah 45.6a-7).

Does God really 'create' the 'darkness' of cot-death and cancer? Does he tell the volcano to spew its fury over a hapless motley of people, good and bad? I don't know. And you? If you think you understand God, I suspect your God concept is naive, too small. As the Jesuit Tony de Mello once said, 'Empty out your tea-cup God.'

✳ *Mysterious God, holy and strong,*
we bow down in awe before you.
Give us the strength and wisdom
to accept our dependence upon you and the faith to
trust.

Monday July 27   *Isaiah 38.1-20*

The cure of Hezekiah

This passage is magical in both senses of the word. The Canticle of the dying Hezekiah is a lyrical account of what it feels like to be facing death: the sense of one's dwelling place uprooted, of being cut prematurely from the loom. This shining example of Isaiah's poetry is one of my favourites and I have used it often in lectures and sermons about the dying.

The other bit of magic, however, riles me, as do most contemporary accounts of magical healing. It's not that I don't believe that God can heal anyone he chooses – it's just that, generally speaking, he doesn't. My problem with this and similar passages is that it gives the impression that a sick person has only to beg God to heal him or her and, if he or she has sufficient faith then, hey presto, we have a miracle. The problem is, life is just not like that. Cancer and other diseases are no respecters of persons, and thousands of good God-fearing people lay siege to heaven without so much as a postcard in reply. Our God is utterly mysterious. As it says somewhere, 'The Lord does whatever she wills' – sometimes she cures people – but mostly she doesn't. So what is wrong with our prayers?

✳ *Lord our God, please listen!*
Why did you heal Hezekiah?
Was it because you loved him specially?
Why don't you heal people so often these days?
Don't you love us so much? Is our faith not strong
*   enough?*
Have you lost your magic?
Lord, forgive these questions,
but we do not understand your ways.

Tuesday July 28   *Psalm 85 *C*

A prayer to appease an angry God

I can imagine the people of Bosnia praying this Psalm, just as the Hebrew exiles prayed it thousands of years ago. 'Lord, will you be angry with us for ever? When will the fighting stop?' It would be a good prayer in a drought too: 'Lord, so long, so long? When will you send us the rain? Our cattle are dying, the earth is parched, our children starve? When, O Lord, when?'

Perhaps this is the commonest age-old heresy: that God is a sort of Santa Claus who sends the sun and rain, and makes the land fertile if he's in a good mood, but withholds it if he's cross with us or just plain dyspeptic. But the Christian God isn't like that: he doesn't withhold the rain; he dies of thirst at the withered breast along with the rest of us.

I see an important issue here: we have a human need to pray for help in time of trouble: we cry to God as a child cries out to a parent. But here, I believe, the simile breaks down. We need to pray: but God does not need our prayers. I do not believe in a God who will withhold bread or rain from his people until they pray for it. It's making God into a monster, like a parent who won't give his hungry child a biscuit until he says 'please'. That may be the way we train our children, but I don't believe it's the way God trains us!

✳ *Lord our God, help us to understand your ways.*
Did six million Jews die in the gas chamber
because no one prayed hard enough for them?
Were their anguished prayers not good enough
(forgive me God, for speaking so bluntly).
Lord of Hosts, what more do you want?
Or have we got the wrong end of the stick
*   completely ...?*

Jesus experiences his Father's blessing

It's worth comparing this brief account of Jesus' baptism by John the Baptist with the versions in Mark and Matthew. They are very similar in some ways, but quite different in others. Both Matthew and Mark have the skies opening and the dove descending as Jesus comes up out of the water. If we consider this scene in an Ignatian imaginative contemplation, we may 'see' Jesus emerge from being dunked in the Jordan, perhaps gasping and spluttering a bit, and wiping the water from his eyes.

Luke, however, has Jesus experience the presence of his Father after the baptism, while he is at prayer. As far as I can see, there is no significance in the difference between these accounts: what each Evangelist is trying to convey is that Jesus, the man, had a very powerful experience of the presence of God either during or soon after his baptism in the Jordan. This gratuitous gift would have confirmed his growing sense of call and mission, a confirmation of what must have been a very scary choice: to deliberately challenge the religious authority of his day. If you think about it, to challenge the established Church must be one of the hardest callings of any religious person. We all long for the Church to be right, to be a good, solid 'father' to us: to guide and to comfort, to heal and forgive. The difficulty is, the 'church' is a body of believers and the hierarchy is drawn from that same fallible group. Our allegiance is to the one, holy, all-powerful God, not to his human ministers. The difficulty comes when we believe these ministers are wrong and we are right. Should we submit or stand firm? – that is the question.

✷ *Lord, give us the humility to respect our teachers;*
but give us, too, the courage to challenge them
when they are not true to your gospel. Amen

Jesus prays at night

Have you ever spent a night in prayer? I haven't: though I have stayed up late many times for the Easter Vigil, falling asleep on my feet and lurching about in a drunken fashion. I have, however, got up sometimes in the middle of the night to pray: once on retreat, when I was bidden to rise at 2a.m. and contemplate my death, and occasionally when I have woken and felt 'called' to pray. There's something very special about praying in the middle of the night: a curious tension between the longing to go back to bed and the desire to keep vigil, to wait in silence on the Lord. At night, and in the very early morning, there is a stillness, an emptiness which invites prayer. The mind has a quality of virgin snow: an unwalked-over quality, that makes it more receptive than in the heated activity of the day.

Jesus took prayer seriously, as must any man or woman who feels called by God for a special mission. Prayer is about listening to God, listening for those curious insights, movements of the heart which, like a sailor steering by compass, tell a person that he or she is on or a little off course.

Imagine yourself on the mountain with Jesus that night: see the stars, hear the gentle sounds of the night, the movements of birds, of restless animals, of thieves and furtive lovers. Feel your heart expand to encompass the unseen God – and your knees ache, and your weary brain cry out for rest.

✳ *Lord, teach us to listen, teach us to pray.*
Give us the courage and the will power to 'waste time'
each day with you – for how else can we come to know
you,
how else love you as we should?

Friday July 31   *Luke 11.1-4 *C*

Lord, teach us to pray

What was it about Jesus that made the disciples ask him to teach them to pray? My guess is that they realized that he had something that they hadn't got, and they wanted it. I think this because I asked precisely the same question of the Catholic Chaplain when I was a second year undergraduate at Oxford. The priest was what I would call an 'icon' figure: he had a certain something about him that attracted me: it was a kind of joy, a generosity, a depth that I envied, and I knew that it was connected with the fact that he prayed. Jesus, too, was clearly an immensely charismatic figure, for he attracted men and women by the hundred: people who all knew intuitively that here was a man who was special, who was close to God.

Jesus' answer to the disciples is interesting too, for he teaches them a prayer which is short and simple, and yet which contains the essential elements of vocal prayer: praise, petition and a plea for forgiveness. I don't know enough about the Jewish worship of the day to know how different this prayer was from the disciples' previous experience of prayer, but my guess is that it was very different in one feature: the addressing of God as *Abba* – Aramaic for 'Father', 'Daddy'. There had always been this image of God as Father in the Old Testament: we see it clearly in Deuteronomy 1.31 and in Hosea 11.1, but people find it hard to imagine the unseen God as lover or father, and cling on to the fiercer images: the judge and the warrior. The challenge to us is to hold on to the mystery of conflicting images: Father, mother, spouse, judge ... Once more we can only bow our heads in awe and remember the advice: 'empty out your tea-cup God!'

✳ *Lord, be patient with our lack of understanding.*
   We are a simple people, wise in the ways of material
      things
   but foolish in the ways of the spirit.
   Teach us to recognize the things that matter,
   to re-order our priorities, to be your disciples.

Saturday August 1   *Luke 11.5-13 *C*

Perseverance in prayer

I find this passage very difficult because it seems to offer a simplistic formula which I believe to be untrue. We all know that people pray for a loved one's cure, for rain, for peace, and that their prayers are not answered – or they don't get the answer they want. So why should we bother? Why do we pray for what we want? And why does God seem to answer some prayers and not others? Is there something 'wrong' with our prayer? Is our faith not strong enough? Are our hearts not pure enough? What's going on?

I wish I knew. Perhaps I should be honest here and say that personally I hardly ever use petitionary prayer. I know we're told to – but I am also aware of what Jesus says in Matthew 6.7-8. 'In your prayers do not babble as the gentiles do, for they think that by using many words they will make themselves heard. Do not be like them; your Father knows what you need before you ask him.' I am so sure that God knows what I want that it feels inappropriate to ask. I just lay my wants and needs at the throne of mercy and leave it to him. Having said this, I have to admit that I pray like a child if my car won't start, and, if I've lost something, I always turn to St Anthony, patron of lost things!

✳ *Lord, you know what I need better than I do myself.*
   Teach me to trust in you,
   as a child trusts her parents to care for her every need.

For further reflection or group discussion

● Think of other examples of prayers of protest from the Bible, from contemporary prayers, and from your own experience. How have these deepened your understanding of the nature of prayer?

● 'Empty out your tea-cup God.' In what ways is your God 'too small'?

Sunday August 2   *Luke 18.1-8*

The power of prayer

In this chapter, Jesus tells another story about the need for perseverance in prayer. So what's going on? Why does Jesus keep repeating himself and also, why does he compare God to an unjust judge? I don't really understand this teaching and neither, it seems, does the writer of 2 Peter for he tries to give God a sort of escape clause, telling his disciples that they must never forget what it says in the psalm: that in God's sight, 'a thousand years are like a day' (2 Peter 3.8). I find it touching that a first-century Church leader had to cope with tiresome questions like mine and that he too had noticed that some prayers never seem to get answered!

I have my own slightly naive answer to the thorny question of unanswered prayer. I have a theory that our prayers of petition all go like mail to a great heavenly sorting office where they get used for those most in need. Perhaps a family's prayers for a sunny day for their daughter's wedding get diverted to something less frivolous. Who knows! What I do believe, however, is that we need to pray, and that God likes us to pray – after all, he has made us with this need. Just how he answers our prayers is clearly his business. All he asks is that we have faith that he will care for us in his own inimitable way!

✳ *Lord, we ask for health, for love, for success,*
for long life and joy for our loved ones,
but if you have other plans for us,
help us to trust in your love for us.

Monday August 3   *Luke 18.9-14*

God prefers the humble

I love this story. I can see the proud Pharisee in his fine robes telling God what a splendid fellow he is. From time to time, we all meet people who feel they have to tell us how marvellous they are and it's hard to love them. Even as I write this, I know that when I am feeling insecure I often try to impress people by telling them about the work I do, the books I write, etc. Maybe the poor Pharisee didn't know any better: he thought God would be impressed by his status and his good works. We know better, for we have been told from our first days in Sunday School that God's heart went out to the humble tax-collector. It's not always easy to be humble, especially if we are reasonably loving, law-abiding people. Humility is not about dismissing our good qualities and making up sins that we have not committed. If we do that, we fall into the trap of denigrating ourselves which is a form of ingratitude. Humility is about honesty: about acknowledging both our gifts and our faults. I thank God every day (although not always in so many words) for my gifts of intelligence and creativity, and for the fact that I am able to bring comfort to suffering people. I thank him because I know that everything I am and do is pure gift. It is no virtue of mine that I can do this or that: all is gift. In the same way, I give him my sorrow for my endless weaknesses: for acquisitiveness, a sharp tongue, for greed and backbiting and lack of love. One of my favourite positions in prayer is face down on the floor: if you've never tried it, do. It is the ultimate position of trust before our Creator.

✳ *Holy God, holy and strong,*
we bow down before your throne,
confident in your goodness and mercy,
knowing that you love those with a humble and contrite
heart.

Tuesday August 4   *Luke 22.39-46; 23.32-34a, 44-46*

Not my will

Jesus is in Gethsemane, his passion begun. How frightened he must have been. Did he know that he was going to die? I think he did, or rather, he thought it was inevitable, because he knew how deeply he had angered the Pharisees. In this, his last time of private prayer, Jesus wrestles with his fear and his sense of destiny. It is important not to gloss over his fear, because Jesus was human and as such he shared the agony of uncertainty and anticipation of all those who face death. His prayer here is an example for all who are fearful of suffering to come: he prays to be released – 'Father, if you are willing, take this cup away from me.'

When I was a political prisoner in Chile I too, after being tortured, prayed, 'Lord, let me out. Rescue me. Save me. Please!' But then it came to me that there was a better way: the way that Jesus showed us. So I said, haltingly, 'Lord, not my will, but thine be done.' If you don't want to release me, if it's part of your plan that I should remain a prisoner, or even be executed, so be it. I want nothing that you don't want.'

This prayer was very hard to say, but, once said, and meant, it gave me a great sense of peace. It was not that I ceased to be afraid, but that, somehow, I knew that God was with me. Dietrich Bonhoeffer, the Lutheran Pastor executed by the Nazis, wrote, 'I believe that God will give us the strength to face whatever is going to happen: but he doesn't give it in advance, lest we rely on ourselves and not on him.' Jesus in Gethsemane has given us an example of how to face suffering: to admit our fear, to ask for release, but to trust in God. It's easier said than done.

✳ *Lord our God: it seems strange to think of you afraid,*
sweating blood in the garden.
Go for us into the cancer wards, the torture cells,
and comfort those who are beyond our reach.
Take water for their lips, oil for their wounds
and love to fill their hearts.

Wednesday August 5   Acts 4.23-31

Kindle a flame

The next three passages look at the early days of the Church. Were there really miracles and healings? Perhaps there were, although I suspect that the greatest miracle was in the courage and energy of the apostles. The descent of the Holy Spirit at Pentecost had 'informed' them, strengthened them in their conviction that Jesus was God and that they must preach his message. This motley of simple fishermen had been converted to a team of evangelists: men on fire with the love of God, filled with a determination to carry his message to the ends of the earth.

For me, it has always been this holy fire which has led me to God. When I was a novice in an enclosed convent, I had a poster which read something like this – to be a witness does not consist in stirring things up but in living one's life in a way which only makes sense if God exists. That's how it was with the apostles: either they were crazy (which is always a possibility with Zealots) or they had inside information about the meaning of life. Perhaps this is what we should be asking ourselves today: does my way of life only make sense if God exists: or is my faith a kind of optional extra, a cultural accretion inherited from my parents? Only you can answer that question for yourself.

✳ *Lord our God, set fire to our hearts*
that we may burn with love for you.
Let that fire be a light in the darkness
for those who are lost and afraid,
a source of warmth and comfort
for those who feel themselves shut out from God's love.

Thursday August 6   *Acts 12.11-19*

An angel rescues Peter from prison

This is a lovely story: a magical tale of divine intervention, the triumph of good over evil. But what are we to make of it all? Do we take it at face value – did God really send an angel to rescue Peter? There is, of course, no answer to this question, although I think it's important to ask it. 'There are more things in heaven and earth than are contained in your philosophy' (*Hamlet,* William Shakespeare). The fact is, that things do happen which we cannot explain. There is a story called 'The Shepherd' in which a lost pilot is guided to safety by another plane: but when, thankfully, he lands, it turns out that there was no other plane. It seems to me that, to be a Christian, indeed to be a religious person of any faith, requires that we learn to live with mystery. Once we have come to terms with that, we can enjoy the Scriptures much more, and use our intelligence in a more fruitful way. I don't mean that we shouldn't question things we don't understand. Of course we should – but there comes a point when we must choose between saying, 'this is clearly a myth', or accepting that we just do not understand what is going on. After a while, we find that living comfortably with mystery seems quite a logical way to behave.

✳ *Lord of mystery, God of surprises,*
we thank you for the way you tease us.
Teach us to live in faith and wonder,
ever astonished at your love.

Friday August 7   *Acts 14.21-28*

Prayer with fasting?

'With prayer and fasting, they commended them to the Lord in whom they had come to believe.' I'm not quite clear from the grammar of this sentence who 'had come to believe', but I think it must refer to the newly appointed elders who were, themselves, new converts. The important question for us, of course, is – why would Paul and Barnabas feel the need to fast in order to commend their new disciples to the Lord? I don't really know, except that fasting is an ancient spiritual exercise and it is said to sharpen the senses. I have little personal experience of fasting except for when I was in the Convent, and then I became absurdly neurotic about the whole business. At our fasting suppers of dry bread and tea, the bread stuck in my throat and I was thrown into despair by memories of the dry bread which was our staple food when I was in prison. Eventually I was excused fasting and struggled ignominiously through an ever drier plate of over-cooked rice!

But that, of course, is my story. If you've never tried it, I think it's worth seeing whether fasting makes it easier to pray, easier to be more fully present to God. My guess is that the best sort of fasting is that which some people do to be in solidarity with the hungry. 'Fasting', i.e. frugal lunches taken instead of a full meal enable people to find money they thought they didn't have to give to charity. That, surely, can only be good.

✱ *Lord of the harvest, we admit, in shame – we eat too much.*
   Help us to restrain our appetites so that we may act justly and share what we have
   with those who do not have sufficient.

Saturday August 8   *Colossians 1.3-14 *C*

Fruits of prayer

This letter of St Paul to the newly converted Christians of Colossae contains a wonderful description of the power of prayer to change lives: or perhaps it's truer to say the power of God's Spirit to change lives. For when we pray, we invite God into our lives, to live within us, to change us.

God may not answer our pleas for fine weather, success in examinations, or for healing, but if we ask him to stay with us, then he will come, bringing his special gifts: Charity, Joy, Peace, Patience, Wisdom, Understanding and the Fear (awe) of the Lord. Paul describes these gifts more fully: 'through perfect wisdom and spiritual understanding you should reach the fullest knowledge of his will, and so be able to lead a life worthy of the Lord, a life bearing fruit in every kind of good work' (verses 9-11).

If our love of God does not bear fruit in this way: if we have no care for the orphaned, the widowed, the tortured, the handicapped, the abused, then we are fooling ourselves. As St John says, 'How can you say you love God whom you cannot see if you do not love your brother whom you can see?'

This love of neighbour must be cashed out in action: in feeding the hungry, sheltering the homeless and so on. Like love and marriage which in the old song 'go together like a horse and carriage', so prayer and action should be inseparable. It's not that work is prayer (as the Benedictine motto is often misquoted), but that if our work is underpinned by prayer, then it will bear fruit. And, as Jesus said: by their fruits, you shall know them.

✳ *Lord, come live with me and be my love,*
for my heart longs for you like a dried-up land without
  rain.
Come, live with me, for without you I can do nothing.

For further reflection or group discussion

- 'Not my will ...' When have you prayed this prayer? Reflect on the significance of such experience to the development of our faith.
- In the light of these readings, reflect on the meaning of Luke 11.9-13.
- How does daily reflection on the Word of God deepen or direct your prayer? What other resources can you use to achieve this?

FOR ACTION

Make a decision to give more time to prayer, if that is your need, or to try other forms of prayer.

THE KINGDOM IS FOR CHILDREN

Notes based on the New Revised Standard Version by
Rosemary Wass

Rosemary Wass – mother, farmer, local preacher and former President of the Women's Network of the Methodist Church (UK) – has been much involved in campaigning for the rights of children caught up in the trap of sex tourism.

The status of children has changed over the centuries. *The Rights Of The Child* have become widely recognized and debated in the closing stages of the twentieth century. Sadly, even today, there are countries where children's rights are continually abused. Jesus challenged, in his own disciples, attitudes which ignore children, and tried to show them the chasm in their understanding of himself and his purposes by bringing before them the example of a child.

Sunday August 9   *Genesis 21.1-20*

A child is born

A child is born to Sarah and Abraham – a cause for great joy. God has honoured Sarah beyond her wildest dreams. Nothing else matters to her now. Isaac is her most precious and protected possession. But Isaac is not Abraham's only child. Sarah's Egyptian slave had borne him a son – Ishmael, when there seemed no other way for him to have an heir.

Sarah is uneasy and seizes her opportunity to banish Ishmael and his mother, to safeguard her son's rights. What a difficult situation for Abraham, torn between the love of each of his children – but God is present to give assurance that both children are heirs to his promise, and all will be revealed in due course.

In being expelled from Abraham's household, Hagar ceases to be a slave to Sarah. Her status changes: she is the mother of Ishmael.

✳ *Loving Creator, we pray for children who will be born today*
to women who are young, to women who are ageing.
Children born into poverty,

children born into insecurity,
children born into well-organized households,
children born into difficult circumstances,
children whose coming has been long awaited,
children whose coming was not anticipated;
children who have been born today,
defenceless and vulnerable –
children who are your creation,
citizens of your Kingdom. Amen

Monday August 10   *Genesis 22.1-19*

A child asks questions

Abraham has 'lost' one son by obeying his wife Sarah. Now he is required by God to give up his second son and deny Sarah her 'birthed' son. Is there any conversation between father and son as they travel to the land of Moriah? The child must have been quite familiar with the preparation for sacrifice and asks the obvious question: Where is the lamb for a burnt offering? Abraham is put to the ultimate test, and in return the 'specialness' of Isaac is confirmed. Abraham completes the sacrifice in due course, and he and Isaac return home. What do they tell or not tell Sarah? Does Isaac know how near he is was losing his life?

✳ *We pray for all who are going through severe times*
of testing today;
for those who hear questions they prefer not to be asked;
for those who seek answers to difficult questions,
and, where decisions have to be made
regarding the welfare of children,
ask for your presence.
We look for your transforming power
in the lives of those we know who carry burdens. Amen

Tuesday August 11   *1 Samuel 3.1-20*

A child responds

Hannah and Sarah have a lot in common. They both bore longed-for sons in seemingly impossible circumstances. Samuel is seen as a gift from God and, when he is weaned, he is literally given back to God by being left in the temple. When Samuel hears a voice in the night, he assumes naturally that the elderly blind priest is calling for his attention. The message from God becomes clear to Samuel and on invitation he shares his prophetic word with Eli.

Do we encourage people/children to listen for the unexpected messages? How easy is it for children and young people to express their feelings? The beauty of innocent statements made by the very young often gives way to more difficult periods when children and young people feel 'lost' and ignored by parents and elders. Sometimes adults think they can speak on behalf of their offspring, even in their presence. How can we help children to feel free to share their perceptions through different mediums – through people, through music, and through reflection? Perhaps the most critical question of all is to ask ourselves how we respond to comments when they are offered? Eli, blind and woken from his sleep, accepts the difficult message Samuel shares with him, leaving Samuel feeling valued and useful. Would we, or could we, have reacted as graciously?

✳ *Loving God, give us we pray*
   the childhood innocence and openness of Samuel.
   We long for the ability to respond
   without prejudice or suspicion.
   Help us to be alert
   to the ways in which you might speak to us today.

   'Give me the childlike praying love,
       Which longs to build thy house again;
   Thy love, let it my heart o'erpower,
       And all my simple soul devour.'

                                        Charles Wesley (1707-88)

Wednesday August 12   *Luke 2.41-52*

A child of purpose

Jesus, the highly perceptive firstborn son of Mary, assumes it normal to remain in the Temple – his 'Father's house'. His confidence is frustrating to those who have other ideas about family courtesies! Jesus returns to Nazareth, but this is a signal to Mary to begin the process of 'letting go'.

Imagine how we would feel and react in the same situation. Yet we are in possession of the end of the story, and know much more about Jesus' life than his parents, friends or listeners at the time of the Temple incident. How easy is it to recognize that children are growing up and need to be given stepping-stones in new areas of freedom and independence? What qualities does it require of us as parents or other older relatives, teachers, friends or neighbours?

‪✳ *We pray for children and young people*
       who feel misunderstood by their parents;
   for those who continually test the limits
       of parental love and understanding;
   for those who have chosen to leave home and family.
   We think of them in their vulnerability
       and pray for those they have left behind.
   We pray for reconciliation
       and an opportunity to hear one another,
       so that new understanding and relationships may be
       made.

Thursday August 13   *John 6.1-13*

A child gives up his lunch

Imagine this as the headline of a newspaper on the next day.
There are questions I would like to ask around the event. How did
this child get so involved? Was the child unaccompanied? Who
else knew he was there? Where was this child (the Greek text
indicates a boy) in relation to the huge gathering – in the midst, on
the edge of the crowd, with other children? What drew him to the
crowd, and to stay there? Who packed the loaves and fishes in
the first place? How easily was the food offered for the disciple's
use? Whatever the answers, the fact seems to be that the child
offered all and as a consequence everyone was fed! I wonder if
the child knew what a great thing had been wrought, and who
made it possible. There were no 'ifs' and 'buts', no holding back.
If only adults could be like that child, wouldn't the world be a
happier place to live in?

✳ *We thank you for the example of this child.*
   Help us to be more willing to offer
   even what seems small and insignificant
   in the face of great need.
   Increase our trust and faith. Amen

Friday August 14   *Mark 9.33-37 *J*

A child is the answer

Children are symbols of powerlessness and vulnerability. What a
shocking statement Jesus made to the disciples as a result of an
undercurrent among them. 'Whoever welcomes this child, welcomes me.' In this child is the vulnerability and powerlessness of
God made man. In this child is the image of Christ living on the

margins, associating with the downtrodden and undervalued of society. So the question has to be asked: *where do we see ourselves?*

✳ *Forgive us, Christ the child,*
for the 'importance' we give to ourselves
and to what we do;
for the times we discredit others because of comparisons
and measures we make.
We remember your humble birth at Bethlehem
and the vulnerability of your early months and years
after King Herod's decree.
We thank you for the care of Joseph and Mary
who responded to God's word and led you to safety.
Help us to look at the genuine qualities
of children around us and, in seeing them, see you,
and use them as our example. Amen.

Saturday August 15   *1 Timothy 4.6-16*

A child destined as leader

Timothy was a young leader. It is possible that his ideas could be easily dismissed as 'just' enthusiasm, inexperience, too radical or whatever. How do we treat those who are younger than ourselves? Do we listen carefully to them? Do we encourage them? Do we say, 'But we've always done it this way'?

We must be honest about the way we treat one another. Can we make a personal resolve to put age to one side, to treat people equally, and to refuse to think of young people as being the 'future generation', or the 'Church of tomorrow'? Rather, insist that they are the hope for today in order that there can be a tomorrow, and listen carefully to them before sharing any insights or pearls of wisdom we may wish to share ourselves.

✳ *Lord God, help us to value the gifts*
you give to each of us. Let not age
dampen the enthusiasm and vitality of the young.
Save us from being so wise
that we miss the gem which is only partially visible,
because it is still being perfected by you.
I hold before you, Mary, a young person I know,
whose life is full of potential.
I promise to help to nurture and support her
as she continues along the journey of life. Amen.

For further reflection or group discussion

● In what ways do children remind us that life is a gift?
● Are there ways in which children are undervalued in your country?
● Are there actions we could encourage to make children less vulnerable today?

Sunday August 16   *Deuteronomy 11.18-21*

Listen, love and worship

It may help you to read Deuteronomy 6.1-9 which reminds us of the importance of these words within a Jewish household. From a very early age, a child was taught to 'love God with all the heart'. Learning to recite the Law and obey its dictates was part of daily life. It was not challenged or questioned. It was part of parental responsibility – along with all the other tasks of nurturing children – to help their children develop an awareness of the presence and protection of God. The command to love God was tied to the body in the phylactery worn on the forehead and on the arm (next to the heart), and it was reverently touched, in the little box on their door posts, each time they entered their home, and rooms within the home.

In Christian families today, are there similar ways in which we emphasize to children in our midst the importance of loving God and allowing that love to influence the whole of our lives? In so-called 'developed countries' families tend to eat informally and Grace is seldom shared before meals; television and other technologies have replaced story time with parents, and prayers at bedtime. Society has made créches and playgroups the norm, so that often children are separated from Christian worship and seeing parental involvement within it. Extended family support is often not close at hand as our society has become more mobile. Social changes have enticed people from regular attendance at worship. Worship competes with sports activities and open shopping malls on Sundays.

✳ *In an age of changing values,*
help us to find time for children;
help us to find ways to share the stories of Jesus with them;
and may we not compromise the gospel.
In an age of changing values,
help us to live as wholeheartedly for you as Jesus did;
and may we encourage others to develop values that
*   endure.*

Children and household relationships

Paul highlights the importance of good mutually respecting relationships. Wives, husbands and children are brought into focus. From the background of his first century Jewish culture, Paul emphasizes the building of relationships between and across all generations of the family. It requires more skill, tolerance and patience than we realize, but once it is practised, then the same quality of relationships can be encouraged in all areas of life.

How can this be achieved? It means doing things for the good of the whole, moving the focus from personal goals and ambitions. It means taking time to listen and understand, and being willing to reach decisions together. It is not always easy – even within stable relationships; different members work and act at different speeds. Some want to do things instantly, others want to take time to ponder, whilst others find it hard to understand what the time lag is about. It can be frustrating as well as rewarding.

✳ *Loving God, help us to love each other*
  as much as we love ourselves.

Children and sacrifice

It is thought that child sacrifice, which originated in the indigenous worship of Canaan, was practised by some Israelites as late as the sixth century BC, and was challenged by the prophets. To the twentieth century mind, the very thought is abhorrent, and yet there are equally inhuman practices to be challenged today. As of old, it takes a long time to gather evidence and convince governments that such practices must be stopped so that all children are given dignity and respect.

'The abuse of children is a crime against humanity;
it is a crime which can be prevented;
it is a slavery which must be ended.'

Dr. Rita Sussmuth, president of the German Bundestag, was speaking in 1993 at the first End Child Prostitution in Asian Tourism executive meeting to be held in Germany.

Seven countries in south Asia have committed themselves to eliminate child labour from bonded work by the year 2000, and ending child labour by the year 2010. In 1994, the Government of India estimated that 30 percent of all prostitutes in six major cities were below the age of 20, and that almost 40 per cent of these prostitutes entered the profession before the age of 18. In Nepal, the age of girls entering brothels is between 10 and 14 years. Some 5000 to 7000 of them are being trafficked between Nepal and India annually.

✳ *God of love, whose Kingdom is for all people,*
show us the way to treat children with proper respect.
Where children are exploited for their labour,
for their goodwill, for their innocence and trust,
may a way be found to bring about justice
and a proper understanding of the value of human life.
   Amen

Wednesday August 19   *Matthew 2.13-18*

Rescue and delivery

Joseph acts quickly, responding to a message in a dream – not for the first time – and Jesus is saved. He is removed from his birthplace, and taken to a place of safety, away from the power of King Herod. His safety is secured, but he has posed such a threat to Herod, and the innocent lives of all boys under the age of two years are jeopardized. Pause now, to think what that must have meant for the families and communities for a whole lifetime. If the reason for the massacre was spelled out, how would those families feel towards God and the only surviving child, Jesus? Reflect too on the story of the saving of the child Moses.

Are there parallels that you can think of today, where children are moved away from their families for their own protection? We might think of refugees, or abused children, or situations of violence and war, of government policies or environmental hazards. Two million children have died in wars in the last decade. Between four and five million children have been physically disabled. More than five million have been forced into refugee camps, and over twelve million left homeless.

✳ *Suffering God, we pause to hear the grief and wailing*
at the loss of all defenceless children.
We pause to hear the voice of power
making awful demands on the powerless.
We pause to think of the lives of Moses and Jesus
who were allowed to grow by your divine intervention.
We thank you for those who acted
as your instruments on earth
so that your plan might come to fruition.
Teach us also how to intervene in your name. Amen

Children have equal rights into the Kingdom

In today's reading there is a series of sayings which have been gathered together with linking words which carry warnings. The Greek verb 'to cause to stumble' or 'to trip up' is *scandalizo* from which the English 'scandal' is derived. It is indeed a 'scandal' when little ones are tripped up and prevented from entering the Kingdom. Reflect again on Mark 9.37 and Luke 2.41-52.

Think of ways in which children are 'tripped up' and denied the confidence of knowing that they are a vital part of the Kingdom. Think of church services and activities and how relevant they are to life in the latter part of the twentieth century. Think of the language that is used in church. Think of how children are treated in church. What improvements could we make? Do children/young people have the opportunity to share their feelings, or do adults speak on their behalf thinking that they know what is best for them?

Take heed of the consequences of which Jesus warns if we are failing in keeping the way clear for the entry of children into his Kingdom.

✳ *Think of a child you know reasonably well – where and with whom s/he lives. Think of some of the activities that child will share in each day outside the home. Commit the child into God's loving care. Include his/her name in the following blessing:*

**The Lord bless you and keep you,
The Lord make his face to shine upon you and be
    gracious to you,
today and always. Amen**

Before joy – pain

Before a child is born, there is usually a series of signs followed by several stages of advancement which culminate in the birth. There is often apprehension mingled with excitement, pain mixed with anticipation that the end cannot be far away, and soon the baby emerges, leaving the womb of security to enter another world. This kind of language is caught up in today's words of hope, offered by the prophet to the returned, but disillusioned exiles. The new creation here is the new city, Jerusalem, made up of a holy people. This new creation is about the impossible becoming possible. What was once barren has become pregnant with hope. All things are possible when God intervenes as we have already seen through Sarah and Hannah and other Old Testament matriarchs whose lives were changed, whose hopes were realized as a result of divine intervention.

God is portrayed here as a mother, nurturing Zion, and comforter to Israel her son, and the world will see and recognize the transformation that has taken place. Israel is God's child and God will do everything possible for the good of that nation, as indeed he will do for all the nations who are 'children of God' today – each needing to be nurtured and loved; each with different skills, weaknesses and needs; all sharing the same loving God who never tires or gives up loving.

✳ *Praise to the Lord, who doth nourish thy life*
and restore thee,
Fitting thee well for the tasks that are ever before thee,
   Then to thy need
   He like a mother doth speed,
Spreading the wings of grace o'er thee.

Joachim Neander (1650-80)

Saturday August 22   Mark 10.13-16

The Kingdom is for children

How do we make judgements about people of any age? Do we jump to conclusions about them by their clothes, body language, speech or hairstyle? The disciples categorized the sort of people Jesus should be spending his time with (they had become self-appointed managers). Their ideas often clashed with Jesus' intentions. They were mere children and women (two categories regarded as non-people with no legal rights). But Jesus always identified with the marginalized and used the inevitable criticism to his advantage.

Children are often quick to assess the atmosphere accurately. They appeared to feel secure with Jesus and accepted the blessing he offered them, accepting them into the Kingdom, which he very clearly says is specifically for such as them.

✳ *Give us the eyes and mind of a child.*
That we might see Jesus as he truly is.
Give us the acceptance,
the direct questioning and the heart of a child.
That we might learn quickly and clearly from Jesus.
Give us the ears of a child to hear Jesus' words with clarity.
That we might be part of the Kingdom in our midst
and live in peace and joy with all. Amen

For further reflection, group discussion and ACTION

- What sort of a Kingdom would it be without children?
- What are we doing to make the world a better place for children?

MAKING SENSE OF LIFE!
The Book of Proverbs

Notes based on the New Jerusalem Bible by
Joseph G Donders

Joseph Donders, a Dutch priest of the Society of Missionaries of Africa, is Professor of Mission and Cross-cultural Studies at Washington Theological Union. He was formerly Head of the Department of Philosophy and Religious Studies and Chaplain to Catholic students at the State University of Nairobi, Kenya.

One of the ways in which human societies communicate their experience is through their proverbs. This 'popular wisdom' is often no more than common sense, the expression of a sound realism based on the truth about ourselves. 'Dame Wisdom' existed before she was discovered by humanity (Proverbs 8.22). This wisdom is the first and perhaps sole foundation human beings have as a common inheritance.

The Hebrew Book of Proverbs shows this shared heritage by including sayings from non-Hebrew sources like the Egyptian Wisdom of Amenemope (22.17 to 24.34), and the proverbs of Lemuel, the king of Massa, learned from his mother (31.1-9). It contains sayings that assert universal and lasting insights, expressing in a few words a wisdom that will last for ever.

Sunday August 23   *Proverbs 1.1-9*
Family values

Proverbs are not private property. They belong to everyone. They are among the ways communities cherish their experience and express their values. The Book of Proverbs teaches a conduct that secures a long life, health, friends, children, just and fair human relations, family values and all that is needed to overcome difficulties.

Some children were following their parents as they climbed a mountain. They came to a place where the ascent was difficult and dangerous. While their parents paused to consider which way to go, the oldest called out, 'Choose the right path, we are coming right behind you!' That is how proverbs connect one generation with another. The wisdom stored up in proverbs links today's social and ethical problems to the experience of the past. And this experience teaches that the beginning of all wisdom is 'the fear of God'. No one can be called 'wise' without a vital relationship with God. It is what children should be taught by their parents, who in turn should have listened to theirs. Parents who do this will be like 'a crown' to their children's heads, 'a circlet' around their necks.

✷ *You have been generous to your servant, Yahweh ...*
Teach me judgement and knowledge,
for I rely on your commandments.   *Psalm 119.65-66*

Monday August 24   *Proverbs 23.13*

Spare the rod and spoil the child?

A story about William Coleridge tells how that great poet once spoke with a man who did not believe in disciplining children. His theory was that children's minds should not be prejudiced in any direction, so that they would be free to form their own opinions. The great poet said nothing in response but asked if his visitor would like to see his garden. The man agreed, and Coleridge took him to a garden where only weeds were growing. The man looked at him in surprise and said, 'There's nothing but weeds here!'

'Well, you see,' answered Coleridge, 'I didn't want to infringe upon the liberty of the garden in any way. I was giving the garden a chance to express itself!'

Children need discipline. They want it! Do they need to be beaten? The Book of Wisdom is asking for discipline, not for the rod. Paul, writing on this very topic, noted, 'Never drive your children to resentment but bring them up with correction and advice inspired by the Lord' (Ephesians 6.4).

✷ *Loving God, help us neither to abandon our youngsters,*
nor to exasperate them. Help us to find the right balance
and the way to their hearts. Amen

Tuesday August 25   *Proverbs 17.19b; 23.1-8*

'Keeping up with the Joneses'?

'The proud courts ruin'. You could not say it more concisely. A dictionary or thesaurus will tell you that the word 'proud' can be replaced by 'arrogant' which comes from a Latin verb meaning 'to claim for oneself'. In Old Latin, it meant 'overbearing'. When you take a good look at that word, the proverbs referred to above fall into place.

You over-burden a pitchfork when you put too much on it; a car when you overload it; your stomach when you eat too much; your desire when you long for too much; and you bear yourself down when you take those who are more gifted or wealthier than you as your ideal.

'Put a knife to your throat', or in other words curb your appetite, control yourself. Bite your tongue. Learn contentment. Forget what the 'Joneses' have. Let what you have be enough. Be grateful for who you are and for what you have.

✳ *Almighty and loving God, let me never forget*
that without you I can do nothing.
Let me neither boast nor be jealous.
Let me truly be the one you made me! Amen

Wednesday August 26   *Proverbs 15.17*

Vegetarianism

Vegetables are better than beef. The American biblical scholar Walter Brueggemann (*Texts Under Negotiation,* Fortress Press, Minneapolis, 1993) notes that this is not a cholesterol verdict. It is more than that because the saying adds something to both vegetables and beef. Vegetables are where love is; beef goes with hatred.

This saying reflects the world of our economic and social practices that inevitably go with food. To allow yourself to eat beef you have to be rich. It takes more work to produce beef. Not only does a bullock need pounds of vegetables to produce one pound of beef: it takes more human work, most likely two working parents. Each day, they arrive home late and too tired to socialize. Their overworked nerves lead to worry, which in turn leads to tension, and finally tears.

Brueggemann adds that he is 'over-reading' the text. Is he really? Is this interpretation not close to the crisis in many of our families when you take beef as a model for their lifestyle? Would it not be close to the mind of the proverb?

✳ *Loving God,*
who created all of us depending on minerals,
plants and animals,
help us to be good householders
in the world you entrusted to us.

Gambling and lotteries

'What good is money in the hand of a fool?' There is another proverb one could add in this context: 'No one who chases fantasies has any sense' (Proverbs 28.19).

One way of spending your money on your fantasies is spending it on gambling and lotteries. According to *Consumers' Research,* it is eight times more likely that you will be struck by lightning than win a million dollars in sweepstakes (*Bad Odds, Lutheran Witness,* September 1990). Yet, it is something that happens more and more all over the world. American studies show that the amount of money risked on legal gambling in the United States rose by more than 1400% from the mid 1970s to the late 1980s. The same studies showed that people who earn less than $10,000 buy more tickets than any other income group. And the *Wesleyan Advocate* noted, in April 1995, that the annual cost of gambling around the world is estimated at $700,000 million!

The Book of Proverbs has a warning even for the rare winner(!): 'A sudden fortune will dwindle away, accumulation little by little is the way to riches' (13.11).

✳ *Almighty Creator, remind us that it is not*
'the one who has the most toys when he dies' who wins,
but those who end up in your embrace.

Apathy

A preacher, urging his congregation to turn from sinful practices, challenged them to tell him what they promised to give up. They responded promising to quit swearing, lying, gossiping and sins like that. Then a woman came forward, who said: 'I am guilty of not doing anything – and I am going to quit that too!'

She had been doing things. There is no one who has not something to do. Yet, you can do things without doing them really, without paying attention to what you are doing, without putting your heart into your activities. That is what apathy is about. People who put their hearts into what they do are happier and healthier than the lazy and indolent.

The Book of Proverbs asks us to ponder on an ants' nest. If you do, you will not see a single ant on the sideline watching the others. They all contribute to the welfare of their community. What ants do instinctively we should do voluntarily, taking the Lord, his mother and all the saints as our examples.

✱ *Lord Jesus, let me be 'eaten up with zeal for your house';*
Psalm 69.9
and, being in your presence, let my heart 'burn within' me.
Luke 24.32

Amen!

Saturday August 29   *Proverbs 11.20; 16.11; 20.23*
Business integrity

Reading sayings like 'Tortuous hearts are abhorrent to Yahweh', 'The balances and scales belong to Yahweh', and 'False scales are not good', we might be inclined to see them as a condemnation of dishonest business deals.

They do condemn any 'tilting of the scales' during business transactions. There should be no doubt about that. But, not only do they condemn all double dealing; they throw positive light on the world of commerce. They imply that God is the source of honesty and justice in all human business enterprises. Honest scales and balances, righteous and just measures, honest business deals all have their source in God. Consequently, doctored and fraudulent scales and balances, unfair and unjust deals are not from God.

Business relates in this way to either the enabling or the disabling of the Reign of God among us. The health of our society depends on the soundness of its structures; the soundness of its structures depends on the righteousness of its members.

✱ *All-powerful God, through our professional dealings*
we are engaged in the organization of your world,
leading either to a greater justice
or to a further impairing of your Kingdom.
Let us see this, understand it, and take it to heart!

For further reflection or group discussion

● How far is it correct to suggest that while the historical and prophetic books in Holy Scripture represent the insights that various religious leaders wanted to communicate to the people to improve their lives, the Wisdom literature expresses the experience of common people to do the same?
● Recall, and make a list of proverbs from your own culture. How much importance have we attached to them, and is it any more difficult to pass them on to younger generations today?

Speech and gossip

Just as a sponge cannot be blamed for what comes out of it when it is squeezed, the tongue cannot be blamed for what it utters. The sponge produces whatever is in it. The tongue brings forth what is in the heart. It is not the tongue but the heart that counts.

Out of the wise heart wisdom will flow in a gushing stream. The untrustworthy fool will slander and gossip. Those who hate might hide their hatred for a while with their tongue, but in a crisis – in panic – will betray their malevolence, and fall into the pit they have dug for themselves.

A tongue alone can do nothing. A speaker to whom no one listens is like a puff of wind in the air. It is only when others delight in gossip, swallowing the slander like choice delicacies, ever eager for more, that the gossiper has a chance. It is that flaw in our nature that has to be overcome, even when we do not allow ourselves to slander or tittle-tattle like fools.

✳ *Lord, you taught us that those who use their tongue well 'draw from the store of goodness in their hearts'.*

(Luke 6.45)

Help us to open ourselves to your Spirit,
and to have that goodness of heart.

Drug abuse and alcoholism

The effects of alcoholism have remained the same over the ages: raving, bloodshot eyes, picking quarrels, loss of control, mental confusion, hallucinations and insensitivity to danger and pain. Had we lived long ago, we might not have detected that addiction is a medical problem, but we would have recognized it as a moral one, involving choices and endangering other people.

When the one who drinks too much is in authority, laws and decrees are forgotten and the poor suffer – in kingdoms and empires, but even more so in families and households.

The Book of Proverbs is wise enough not to forbid the use of alcohol (and drugs)! In certain circumstances their use is even advisable. 'Procure some strong drink for someone about to die, some wine for them whose hearts are heavy.'

The first miracle Jesus works, according to John's Gospel, is to procure wine for a happy crowd, and the last thing he does – as he is dying – is to suck wine from a sponge (John 19.29-30).

✳ *Lord Jesus, let me be drunk*
not with the old wine of this world,
but with the new one you came to provide for us
as a sign of the wine we will drink with you
in the Kingdom of your Father.   *cf. Matthew 26.29*

Tuesday September 1   *Proverbs 5.11-13*

Sexual education

When someone regrets not having listened to the teaching of his elders on the dangers of promiscuity, and on the need for self-discipline, that teaching is presupposed. In *The Human Cycle,* the anthropologist Colin Turnbull complains that as a Western boy he never received proper information on these matters in contrast to the information given in African and Asian societies. He had to find out by experimenting with his peer group. This lack of adult counsel led him into distress, as it undoubtedly does to many others.

With sexual education, it is often like the story about the lost child Jesus. Mary thought he was with Joseph, and Joseph thought he was with Mary. Parents think the church does it; the church thinks the parents do it; the school thinks the parents and the church do it. And in the end children are often left alone and can't even blame themselves for not having listened.

The blame is on those who did not speak. A child and an adolescent can receive no greater gift than being introduced properly into adult life, spiritually, intellectually and bodily!

✳ *God, sustainer of all life, help those who are responsible*
for teaching children and young people
about the transmitting of life,
to do it in a way that assures total health.

Wednesday September 2   *Proverbs 31.10-31*

What about the single person?

Does Proverbs' picture of 'The Truly Capable Woman' censure the women (and men) in our world who decide to remain single?

In her book *The Joy Luck Club,* Amy Tan tells the story of a Baptist mother whose son drowns. She believes that her faith will be able to bring her son back. When her belief fails to do this, she does away with her Bible, using it as a prop to steady her kitchen table. She does not see in it any purpose for her faith. But every day she carefully dusts that Bible. Rita Nakashima Brock uses this story in *Searching the Scriptures, A Feminist Introduction*

(Ed. Elisabeth Schussler Fiorenza, New York, 1993) to explain her view on Wisdom texts like this one.

We should neither reject nor accept them, but use them as a mirror 'to sharpen our view of what our past has been, of what we believe and do not believe, of what we must transform, and of who we are to become.'

✷ *Lord, who gave us the example*
of someone who remained single, let us not forget
that you also told us that the grain of wheat
cannot bring forth its fruit if does not fall into the ground
and open itself up.   *John 12.24*

Thursday September 3   *Proverbs 16.31*

Old age

She was sitting in the back of the church. The pastor had seen her in the same place many a Sunday. She was elderly, white-haired and of an unusual dignity and charm. That Sunday he walked up to her, looked into her wrinkled, smiling face: 'Believe me', he said, 'you are really wonderful.'

'Well, I ought to be,' she replied somewhat mischievously. 'I have had 82 years to let the Lord work on me!'

He asked her what her secret was. She answered: 'Every day I ask God to guide me and show me something I can do to show my love. And every day God answers my prayer.' She went on to say that it might be a warm smile, a word of encouragement, holding a hand, rendering a service, lending a listening ear, or reading something to someone. 'God has always something more for us to do, and I am listening for what it might be.'

White hairs can, indeed, be a crown of honour, a sign of a long journey with God as companion, in anticipation of lasting fellowship with God in glory.

✷ *My God, let the Psalmist's words be true of my old age:*
'... they will still bear fruit,
will remain fresh and green,
to proclaim Yahweh's integrity.'   *Psalm 92.14-15*

Friday September 4   *Proverbs 25.6-7*

Giving yourself airs

It is not good to praise your own ego, like one who insists on taking the place of honour at table. By quoting this proverb (Luke

14.7-11), Jesus does not intend to offer us table manners, nor warn us to avoid embarrassment.

Jesus wants to teach us that we have to let our ego depend on others. The honour we attribute to ourselves does not only sound false; it is false. The honour others give us makes us know and feel that we are valued and useful – and this feeling gives us confidence and a new impetus to our energies.

What is true of the others is even more true of God, the source of our existence. God, calling every one of us by name, is the one who confers honour and value on us. It is no good to blow your own trumpet. It just sounds hollow. But when God – honouring you – invites you to God's table, 'everyone with you at the table will see you honoured' (Luke 14.11). It is the only honour that counts. It is the honour we are to live for.

✴ *[My God,] you have always been my help;*
in the shadow of your wings I rejoice;
my heart clings to you,
your right hand supports me. Amen　　　　*Psalm 63.7-8*

Saturday September 5　　　　*Proverbs 25.21-22*

Crossing barriers

An old Chinese adage says, 'Meet good with good that good can be maintained; meet evil with good that good may be created.' When you meet evil with evil, you are only increasing what you are trying to fight. Mere complaining about the evil done to you is no help either. Even driving evil away is no good; it only displaces evil to somewhere else. The only way to overcome evil is to get back at one's enemy with kindness. 'If your enemy is hungry, give him something to eat.'

Jesus refers to the same dynamics when he tells us to pray for our enemies and to love them (Matthew 5.44-48). Jesus does not speak about 'heaping red-hot coals' on the heads of those who are mistreating you. Even if this is done to bring our enemies to better thoughts and conversion, it always implies their humiliation. Jesus states simply and unconditionally that you should love your enemies. His reason is simple: God loves them! All those who live are accepted by God as God's children!

✴ *Lord Jesus, before you died on the cross,*
you prayed, 'that they may be one'.
Help us to engage wholeheartedly in that prayer
by doing all we can to overcome the racism and enmity
existing among us. Amen

For further reflection or group discussion

- How far would it be correct to suggest that while the historical and prophetic books in Holy Scripture move 'from above to below' and from 'the outside to the inside', a Wisdom Book like the Book of Proverbs moves 'from below to above' and from 'the inside to the outside?'
- Do you think that the human experience as expressed in the Book of Proverbs can help you in answering questions like

  'How should you live your life?',

  'What must you do to succeed in life?' and

  'How should we behave?'

FOR ACTION

'A glad heart is excellent medicine,
a depressed spirit wastes the bones away' (Proverbs 17.22).

The 'Book of Proverbs' refers to a basic attitude for living life well and acting in a sensible way. It is 'a philosophy of life' (Carlos Mesters, *God Where Are You?* Orbis New York, 1995).

- When you are meeting people of other religious convictions and sense a mutual desire to enter into dialogue with each other, take the Book of Proverbs as a starting point.
- Do the same when you relate to others – young or old – who have difficulties in starting with what 'the Church' wants to teach them.

EXAMINE ME, O GOD

Notes based on the New International Version by
Philip Barker

Having served in Methodist circuits in South Humberside, Kent, Essex and West Sussex, Philip Barker is now the Methodist minister at Fleet and Hartley Wintney in Hampshire (UK).

To open our lives to God's scrutiny is one of those experiences which need time and thought to prepare for and then to build on. This theme starts with some basic convictions of our faith which will stay with us as we invite his 'kind but searching gaze' and then takes us through the experience. In the second week we build positively on its implications for our faith and practice, as we move forward secure in God's amazing grace.

Sunday September 6   *Exodus 32.7-14 *C*

Remember whose you are!

These verses of Exodus reveal the stark contrast between the close, intimate relationship the Lord has with Moses and the fickleness of ordinary people. Moses is talking with the Lord on the mountain 'as a man talks with his friend', while the people are behaving in a way that casts serious doubt even on their right to be called to be God's People! No wonder that in his dialogue with Moses, the Lord describes them as 'your people' (verse 7) and 'these people' (verse 9).

Moses reminds the Lord that he has a special relationship with those he has brought out of Egypt – they are his people (verses 11 and 12) – and pleads for time to allow this relationship to be restored. The Lord has done so much for them in the past that surely it doesn't make sense to abandon them now.

If the idea of allowing God to examine us seems too difficult because of what we have been, or what we have done, then there is comfort here – 'he is our God and we are his people'. He has already done so much for us, especially through Jesus Christ our Saviour and Lord that he won't abandon us now. No one is beyond the grace of God!

✳ *Have mercy on me, O God,*
  according to your unfailing love;
  according to your great compassion
  blot out my transgressions.   *Psalm 51.1*

Monday September 7   *Deuteronomy 30.15-20 *C*

Hold fast!

Yesterday's reading was about Moses talking to the Lord, but today we hear him speaking to the people as they prepare to enter the Promised Land. In the face of new opportunities, what matters is that they 'hold fast to God' (verse 20). Then they will know life at its best!

Etty Hillesum was a young Jewish woman who died in Auschwitz. In her diaries, *An Interrupted Life*, she wrote, 'there is a really deep well inside me, and in it, dwells God. Sometimes, I am there too. But more often stones and grit block the well and God is buried beneath, then He must be dug out again.'

It's a Monday, and the rest of the week lies ahead. For many too, September is a time of new opportunities and fresh challenges. We must make sure that stones and grit are not blocking our relationship with God. If so, we have to work at restoring it and pray that we may hold fast to him through it all. 'For the LORD is your life ...' (verse 20).

✳ *Create in me a pure heart, O God,*
  and renew a steadfast spirit within me.
  Do not cast me from your presence
  or take your Holy Spirit from me.   *Psalm 51.10-11*

Tuesday September 8   *Isaiah 46.1-9*

No comparison!

Advertisements invite us to make comparisons and we are used to choosing between things. The prophet is challenging the people to compare the gods of Babylon with the Lord and make a positive decision for him. Even the gods themselves bow down in disgrace before the Lord who has not only made his people but will carry, sustain and rescue them (verse 4).

We may not join a current trend and make ourselves acceptable to other people, but nothing can take the place of a growing relationship which allows God to examine our lives. He will share the whole of his life with us and, when necessary, will carry us through, or even rescue us. Jesus underlines how special God is by describing this relationship as that of an ideal parent.

What might we put in the place of God? Perhaps a contrary lifestyle or an alternative view to that revealed by Jesus? 'I am God, and there is none like me' (verse 9) has to be taken seriously, but he will be the first to strengthen and support us as we sort out our priorities.

✳ *Restore to me the joy of your salvation*
and grant me a willing spirit, to sustain me.   Psalm 51.12

Wednesday September 9   *Isaiah 59.9-15*

Coming clean

Prophets are not afraid of speaking out and aim to bring God's word into a contemporary situation. Often this means calling people, individuals and nations, to account – they have to face up to the truth about themselves and their situation. Here the prophet includes himself in the condemnation which has resulted in turning their backs on their God (verse 13).

Part of Christian devotion is to accept some responsibility for what is wrong in our society. If we have access to a recent newspaper with national and international news, it will not take us long to realize the need for coming clean and seeking forgiveness for our part in the total picture. What is happening now may not be so different from the situation described by Isaiah – yet there is comfort to be found in verse 1:

'Surely the arm of the LORD is not too short to save,
nor his ear too dull to hear.'

Once more we are thrown back on the grace of God to declare, like the prophet, the need for that change of heart which justice and reconciliation demand.

✳ *O Lord, open my lips,*
and my mouth will declare your praise.   Psalm 51.15

Thursday September 10   *Psalm 51.1-10 *C*

Have mercy

From yesterday's corporate confession, we move to an intensely personal prayer. The traditional title refers to a particular event in David's life when, having given in to temptation, he returns to the Lord to plead for mercy.

As Jesus dies on the cross, we realize that brokenness is a necessary part of following him. It is in moments of brokenness that we come closest to God. We come to the heart of our faith in a way that makes us face reality and throw ourselves on the mercy of our Lord.

As vicar of Calcutta Cathedral, Canon Subir Biswas gave himself totally for deprived people. In a collection of daily meditations following a heart attack in 1976, he wrote: 'Yet sometimes Lord, I am too busy to receive you or distorted by so many cares. Sometimes I have offered myself to others so that there is little left for you. Yet when I am sick and helpless and defenceless, and you come to me in the simplicity of bread and wine, I can only open wide my heart and mouth and receive you. Forgive my tears which well out of the poverty of my offering, yet I know now that you will receive me in my poverty and nakedness and make me whole and beautiful' *(Lord let me share* – CMS 1978).

✷ *Today, let us make this prayer our own.*

Friday September 11   *Psalm 139.1-12 *C*
No hiding place
In his book *Beyond the Mirror,* Henri Nouwen reflects on his life following a serious accident one winter's morning. He speaks about important things in his search for God, such as books and articles that he read, but then he adds that it is the interruptions to daily life which reveal 'the divine mystery of which I am a part'.

How awesome it is to ask God to examine one's life and soul – God who knows every thought, word and deed, and from whom there is no hiding. The writer of the Psalm seems to suggest a whole series of surprises or interruptions which reveal the closeness of God to him whether he expected it or not, and which lead to every aspect of life being put under a microscope!

It is not easy to open our lives to him completely and submit to his close scrutiny, yet we need to remember that he is not trying to catch us out. He is there much more out of a desire to support and strengthen us and, where necessary, will rescue and forgive.

✷ *Almighty God, you have made us for yourself*
   and our hearts are restless
   till they find their rest in you.

Search me, O God

It's not just giving in to the inevitable! The writer of the Psalm makes a positive decision to allow God to clear the path and lead him in the way everlasting (verses 23 and 24).

In an interview in *The Independent* (14 May 1990), the Bishop of Lincoln recalls a service when he was 19 years old: 'I remember ... having an enormous sense of personal fulfilment, and an assurance that God was real, and that He knew me, and that it was possible for me to know Him ... When I came out of the cathedral I was quite clear ... that I had been face to face with God – not that I was a marked man or anything special, but that He knew me and loved me. There was this feeling of security, peace, relationship, well-being, that things were OK.'

To be examined by God is to be known as we are, our vulnerability and our potential. God shares the difficult experiences, and tremendous possibilities are revealed as we allow him to lead us forward.

✳ *Lord, it is so hard to know which way to choose,*
which way to go.
But you know how my life can best be spent.
Lead on then, and I will choose to live in you,
and only walk where you would have me go.

For further reflection or group discussion

● Think of some 'interruptions' that have changed your life.
● How have they deepened your faith and experience of God? How does God comfort us when we are feeling most vulnerable?
● What gives us the confidence to allow him to examine our lives?

Sunday September 13   *Luke 11.37-41*

Inside out

When Jon Sobrino, the one survivor of the massacre of the Jesuit priests in El Salvador in 1990, was to speak, many people came to listen to him. 'This is going to be good,' they said, 'he will say some very hard and critical things about the governments involved.' To their surprise, he talked about forgiveness. People went away angry because he had not addressed their agenda. But he had brought a Christian perspective!

Over the meal, the host Pharisee was surprised that Jesus did not obey their ceremonial law. In God's Kingdom, things are turned inside-out. It is more than just saying the right words and performing religious rituals. Top of Jesus' agenda is giving from the heart. To help the poor shows that one's heart is no longer in the grip of greed and wickedness (verse 39).

It is all too easy for something that starts as an aid to devotion to become an end in itself. At the beginning of another week, we must invite the Lord to examine the rituals of our lives and, if necessary, to turn them inside-out!

✽ *May all our prayer today be genuine –*
the worship offered by mind and heart.

Monday September 14   *Luke 11.42-44*
Both and ...
'Woe to you Pharisees,' says Jesus in a series of challenging statements about balancing different interests. Here the emphasis is on practising the justice and love of God as well as obeying the details of the Law (verse 42). Even ritual can have a place so long as it leads to a clear expression of Christian values. Jesus leaves no room for a heartless and slavish obedience to an outward appearance of religion.

In *So God said to me* (Epworth 1978), Richard Adams includes a dialogue about prayer in which God says, 'It's not a bad habit for setting your thoughts in order and deciding what to do – as long as it's not an excuse for putting off something that badly wants doing, or salving your conscience by thinking you can have a good pray about something and leave the rest to me.'

Our prayers are important, but we must recognize that we are often the means God uses to provide an answer. As we invite God to examine our lives, we can be sure he will be looking for both words and actions that express our faith.

✽ *Father, as we pray for people in need,*
may our prayers become actions to help them.

Tuesday September 15   *Luke 11.45-52*
Saying and doing
Jesus' words are directed not just to the Pharisees, but also to 'experts in the law' (verse 45). This is Luke's way of describing the scribes or 'teachers of the law'. They added more rules and

regulations to the Law of Moses, and invented ways to avoid them themselves while doing nothing to help ordinary people to keep them. Teachers who should have opened people's minds left them ignorant of God's way. A deeper sense of responsibility is expected of experts!

People look up to us in the family, the community, the church. Because we are known as Christ's disciples, they watch to see if our lives are true to our words – that we care for and support those who need it most. The Christian is called to see and feel the sufferings of others and to make that recognition the starting-point of service.

✷ *Father, keep us sensitive to the needs of those around us, and may we be worthy of the name 'Christian'.*

Wednesday September 16   *Luke 12.1-3*

Not two-faced

In a world changed by modern methods of communication, where other people's ideas are beamed straight into our homes through satellite and the Internet, we need to be on our guard against wrong ideas and ways of thinking that creep insidiously into our lives without our realizing. Where once moral decisions were either right or wrong and issues seemed clear-cut, we now look at issues from all points of view (or be thought to be intolerant), so that it is all too easy to appear hypocritical.

Be on your guard against wrong ideas that creep into our thinking and penetrate our lives like yeast, says Jesus, for before you know where you are your faith will be undermined and you will appear two-faced. When God examines our lives, he exposes what is hidden and requires us to be genuine, honest and open about ourselves. Decisions about lifestyle and the principles we accept must be based on the values of God's Kingdom.

✷ *But the fruit of the Spirit is love, joy, peace, patience, kindness, goodness, faithfulness, gentleness and self-control.*   *Galatians 5.22-23a*

Thursday September 17   *Luke 13.1-5*

No special cases

When we are involved in a calamity, it is a frequent reaction to say, 'Why me?' or 'What have I done to deserve this?' We are not the first to think like that, but Christians need to remember that this is not the view of Jesus. Here he recalls two otherwise unknown calamities and emphasizes that there are no special cases. God does not punish some people because they are more sinful than others. All are sinners and need to repent – there are no exceptions.

As we allow God to examine our lives, we may compare ourselves to someone else and decide that, at least, we are not as bad. The danger then is that we fail to respond properly ourselves and do not repent of our sin. In our time of prayer today, let us make no comparisons with others or claim that we are a special case. Rather concentrate on confessing our sin with sincere repentance. We can be sure of God's forgiving grace at work in our lives!

✳ **Father, I repent of my sin and seek your forgiveness.**
May my heart be warmed by your forgiving love
today and every day.

Friday September 18   *Mark 7.1-23*

No excuses

This passage brings together many of the themes we have explored this week. If we make 'Examine me, O God' our prayer, we can make no excuses. Least of all can it be claimed that we are saved by the tradition of the Law. Obeying the letter of the Law is one thing; living by its spirit is quite another.

To illustrate this, Jesus reminds his listeners of the *Corban* formula, a clear example of using the letter of the Law as an excuse to avoid responsibility for their parents. Mark explains the word *Corban* as 'a gift devoted to God'. Jewish people would have known what was meant, so he must have been addressing a significant proportion of Gentile readers. This message is not just for someone else; it is for us. What excuses will we use today for avoiding the spirit of our faith? Will we be too busy, have too little time, or even be too involved in running the Church to accept our responsibilities as disciples of Jesus?

✳ **Father, help me not to try to find excuses**
instead of acting compassionately,
or to replace concern for other people with religious
fervour.

Saturday September 19   *1 Timothy 1.12-17 *C*

The heart of the matter

Paul wrote this letter to Timothy to encourage him in the task of caring for the Church at Ephesus. A personal testimony is an excellent way to do this! If you have any doubt about the grace of God, listen to the story of 'the chief of sinners' told by Paul.

As we have invited God to examine our lives, much of our thinking has inevitably been subjective. Today's passage aims to redress the balance. The focus of attention is the unlimited grace of God.

In an article, 'The Light in my darkness', Terry Waite writes of his experience in the prison cell where he was held hostage and how he felt totally alone. 'Then I see it: a tiny beam of sunlight, pushing through a gap in the shutter and illuminating the corner of my room. I watch the light intently. The rays have travelled millions of miles through space to this corner of the Middle East. They shine with a burning intensity, reminding me that light has overcome darkness. No matter what my captors do to me, I will still be part of this wonderful, complex universe. "You may break my body," I say silently, "but my soul is not yours to possess." The light reminds me that God is at the very heart of life ...' (*Reprinted with permission from the September 1996 Reader's Digest Magazine © Reader's Digest Association Ltd.*).

✳ *Lord, turn our thoughts away from ourselves*
   and enable us to put our trust in your amazing grace.

For further reflection or group discussion

● If it is the religion of the heart that matters most, what value do the rituals of worship have for you?
● Thank God for everyday experiences that turn your thoughts towards his amazing grace.

FOR ACTION

To help you receive God's forgiveness, write down the actions and attitudes in your life for which you need his grace and mercy. Then pray your way through the list and, if you can, share it with a trusted friend.

INTERNATIONAL BIBLE READING ASSOCIATION
1020 Bristol Road, Selly Oak, Birmingham, Great Britain B29 6LB

ORDER FORM – For 1999 Books

Please send me the following books: Office Ref: 99102

Name: _____

Address: _____

_____

_____ Postcode: _____

*To qualify for 1999 books at the prices shown, this order form must be used (photocopies not accepted). Your order will be dispatched when **all** books are available.*

Code	Title of Book	Quantity	Unit Price	Total
ZYW0909	Words For Today 1999		£3.99	
ZYL0908	Light For Our Path 1999		£3.99	
ZYL0912	Large Print Light For Our Path 1999		✳	
ZYF0910	Finding Our Way Together Book 2		✳	
ZYP0911	Preachers' Handbook 1999		£4.99	
ZYI0889	Invitation To Read		£2.99	
ZYE0213	Everyday Prayers		£4.95	
ZYM0325	More Everyday Prayers		£4.95	
ZYL0575	Looking At The Cross		£4.50	
ZYL0684	Looking At Advent		£4.50	
ZYL0781	Looking At Easter & Ascension		£4.50	
ZYL0871	Living Prayers For Today		£11.99	
ZYM0902	More Living Prayers For Today		£11.99	

✳ *Price on application*

I enclose cheque/PO (Payable to IBRA) Please charge my ACCESS/MASTERCARD/VISA Card No:	Total cost of books
	Post – UK free Overseas – add £2.00 per book
	Donation to International Fund
⬜⬜⬜⬜⬜⬜⬜⬜⬜⬜⬜⬜⬜⬜⬜⬜	TOTAL DUE

Expiry Date: _____   *Payments in Pounds Sterling, please*

Signature: _____

The INTERNATIONAL BIBLE READING ASSOCIATION is a Registered Charity

INTERNATIONAL BIBLE READING ASSOCIATION

Help us to continue our work of providing Bible study notes for use by Christians in this country and throughout the world.

The need is as great as it was when IBRA was founded in 1882 by Charles Waters as part of the work of the Sunday School Union.

Please leave a legacy to the International Bible Reading Association.

An easy-to-use leaflet has been prepared to help you provide a legacy. Please write to me at IBRA and I will send you this leaflet – and answer any questions you might have about a legacy or other donations. Please help us to strengthen this and the next generation of Christians.

Thank you very much
Sincerely

Alec Gilmore
Chairman, IBRA

**IBRA, Dept 298, 1020 Bristol Road,
Selly Oak, Birmingham B29 6LB Great Britain**
Tel: 0121 472 4242   Fax: 0121 472 7575

Our solicitors are Pothecary and Barratt, Talbot House, Talbot Court, Gracechurch Street, London EC3V 0BS

Charity No. 211542

BLESSED ARE THE POOR?

Notes based on the Good News Bible by
Magali do Nascimento Cunha

*Magali do Nascimento Cunha is a young Brazilian Methodist
laywoman who works as a journalist with KOINONIA Ecumenical
Presence and Service in Rio de Janeiro.*

The Word of God brings us a promise: 'Happy are you poor; the
Kingdom of God is yours' (Luke 6.20). But if we look at the world,
not with the eyes of faith but with rational human eyes, we see no
sign of its fulfilment. Poverty increases in our world and the poor
suffer more and more. 'Blessed are the poor?' we ask. 'How?
Shall they wait for Jesus' second coming to be finally blessed?'
To believe in the promise of the Word of God, we need to look at
life with the eyes of faith and see behind it how blessed the poor
really are, and how they are a paradigm for all who opt to be
followers of Jesus.

Sunday September 20   *Amos 8.4-7 *C*

Eyes open to see and remember ...

When you live in a country like Brazil, you are permanently struck
by contrasts of poverty and wealth living side by side. If you live in
Rio de Janeiro, a city of eight million inhabitants, of charming
beaches and marvellous mountains but surrounded by large
shanty towns called *favelas*, it is impossible to close your eyes.
They are all just here, living in horrible little houses or simply on
the streets: cleaning cars or selling sweets at traffic lights;
begging or stealing; they are all just here, trying to survive and
see what is good in life. The poor are here and they threaten with
their presence. They threaten the country that needs to achieve
development and avoid poverty; they threaten the local
government that needs tourists in the city; they threaten those
who walk in the streets and do not want to be disturbed or robbed.
Nobody wants to be like them; nobody wants them.

They are here, not only in Rio, not only in Brazil, but all over
the world. Sometimes we close our eyes so that we don't see.
Sometimes we see but try to forget. Yet, there is one whose eyes
are never closed and who never forgets. The Lord Yahweh, The

211

One Who Is, here and there, with eyes and ears open to remember always. God is ready to act with justice for those who suffer and over those who cause their sufferings. 'I will never forget their evil deeds' (Amos 8.7). The poor may have hope.

✳ **Thank you, Lord, for looking after us in this world.**
Forgive us for not following your example
when we close our eyes so as not to see and care for
our brothers and sisters who suffer poverty. Amen

Monday September 21   *Amos 6.1a, 4-7 *C*

Why poverty?

It is part of a competition of sinful human nature: selfishness, greed, trampling on others' feelings and attitudes, and the result is division and exclusion. This exclusion has produced the poor of the earth: those who do not have the means to compete, to occupy the space and share the good things of life that human nature reserves for the few.

But God has a dream: that men and women – God's creation – shall live in peace, with justice, with no suffering, sharing the good things of life in harmony. It was because of this project that God, *Yahweh*, the One Who Is, heard the cry of the slaves in Egypt and helped them to find freedom. Through this project, God sent the Son Jesus Christ to fill 'the hungry with good things' and 'sent the rich away with empty hands' (Luke 1.53).

Sinful human nature has created a division between rich and poor – those who can say that life is good and those who can't; those who are never satisfied with what is enough, and those who learn to live with less than the minimum; those who enjoy the present and plan the future, and those who simply survive and fear what is reserved for tomorrow. No! God's project has nothing to do with this cruel reality. The poor may have hope.

✳ **Dear God, forgive our sin of greed and selfishness.**
Give us the gift of sharing what we have with those in
need.

Tuesday September 22   *Deuteronomy 15.1-11*

Salvation means solidarity and mercy!

Poverty has always existed, and it always makes people uncomfortable. It is not good to know about the poor ... What can be done? For centuries, people have tried to find answers, especially through economic doctrines.

Now, towards the close of the 20th century, someone has said that history has reached an end. The wall that divided the world into two different systems has fallen; it has been proved that capitalism provides salvation for the nations. Market economy is the system that claims to provide everything people need. They just need to have the means to consume. Nothing more is needed. Salvation has come in the form of houses, food, clothes, health, education, transportation, communication, leisure ... Everything is there, available. People just need to pay.

Drawing by Cerezo Barredo
From *El Tayacan,* Nicaragua Libre

So, poverty is over? No, the system says that poverty will always exist because the market just cares for those who consume. If people have no means to consume, they are destined to be excluded from the market – or from salvation. The market says more: there is no need to be worried. Poverty exists because some people are not able to access the market. It is not for all. Those who are 'in' have to look after their own situation to remain in. Few care about the poor – they are destined to die. But God shows us a different way. God cares. Goodness, mercy and solidarity are values to God who does not like to act alone. God invites us all to follow these steps: to act and destroy unjust systems that preach division and exclusion. 'There will always be some who are poor and in need, and so I command you to be generous to them' (Deuteronomy 15.11).

✳ *Give me, Lord, clear eyes to see ways to act with you and make our world a world with a heart. Amen*

Wednesday September 23   Leviticus 19.1-4; 9-10
Searching for a promised land
Land is one of the major struggles of the poor in Brazil. When the Portuguese conquerors arrived in 1500, land was taken from the indigenous population and distributed to a few colonizers, who developed large concentrations of land among the few (4% of Brazilian people own 61% of the land).

Today there are millions of landless people exploited for cheap labour, or scattered because of land disputes – caused by rich landowners or multinational companies. This has even led to the murder of thousands of land workers. Since 1964, with the military dictatorship, more than 1700 people have been killed by gunmen hired by rich landowners in the countryside.

There are, however, signs of hope. Brazilians have a culture which provides them with a courage and resistance that are fed by hope. This resistance has been a means of strength to land workers in their struggle for a piece of land on which to live and plant their crops. They have organized themselves into the *Movimento dos Trabalhadores Rurais sem Terra* (Movement of the Landless Rural Workers). During the last decades, the movement has gone to Court to claim possession of unproductive land, and rights of property for those who have worked unproductive land for more than ten years. Brazilian law guarantees that, but powerless land workers are often not able to pay the costs of the legal process. As a result, thousands of

214

families have settled on abandoned land. The movement has also organized lobbies in Parliament for Land Reform, and campaigns to denounce the murders and put an end to impunity and abuse of power. The struggle continues: there is still a long way ahead, but it continues with joy and hope as the results of all the efforts can be seen. The Lord, God of the poor and sufferers, feeds the people with faith and hope, and these are the last things to die.

✳ *Thank you, God, for giving strength and courage*
   for the poor to struggle for life. Help us to learn
   with those in need how to keep hope alive in our world.

Thursday September 24   *Lamentations 5.1-15, 19-22*

Bring us back to you, Lord!

It is easy to compare and identify many situations of the Bible with situations faced by Latin American peoples. In 1992 the world remembered the 500th anniversary of the arrival of Europeans in these lands. But nothing more has been said since. Peoples in this continent, however, will never cease lamenting and talking about what represented for them the coming of the conquerors. Exploitation and suffering began – with complete disrespect for the sovereignty of indigenous populations – and continue today with total disregard for human rights. The cries of the victims can still be heard in all the countries of Latin America: the indigenous people who survived – descendants of black slaves, men, women, children who have to sell their work for a very cheap price to secure some basic needs. They lack food, land, health, education, respect, dignity. They are the dispossessed, the poor, the sufferers.

Throughout this difficult journey, the Bible story has given strength and courage. How the Bible has illumined the Latin American resistance! Through the Bible we learn that God cares; that God's ears are open to listen to the cries of the poor, and God is ready to deliver them.

We learn to believe that God's action is giving strength and courage to communities and organizations who search for liberation and transformation. We learn to believe that God is using people as prophets and agents for the coming of the Kingdom of justice and peace. All people have the chance to participate, denounce unjust systems and stay alongside the poor. This message is not Latin American property but is a message for all. God spoke in the past and is speaking today. 'Listen, then, if you have ears!'

215

✳ *Help us, Lord, to be prophets and agents for the coming of your Kingdom. Give us strength and courage to stay alongside the poor of the earth and preach your justice. Amen*

Friday September 25   *Psalm 68.4-10*

Praise the One who cares!

The Bible tells of orphans and widows. They were poor as a result of a process of discrimination. Men were 'the head' of the family. When they died, their widows were of even less importance than before they were married; they did not have a 'head' any more. The same happened with orphans. Widows and orphans survived by depending on other people's help. This situation is not confined to the past, or to a different cultural background.

Dona Ester is 65 years old. Like almost everybody who lives in the Baixada Fluminense, an area on the outskirts of Rio de Janeiro City, her family came from the countryside for a better life in the city. Now she is a widow and the pension she receives from the government is very small. She has to work to support her family. She is a housemaid for a family in a wealthy area in Rio. They pay her the minimum salary to clean the house, to cook, and to iron clothes. Every day at 4 a.m., she has to wake up, clean her house and cook before going to work. It takes her two hours to get there and at 8 p.m. she comes home to finish her housework. She never sleeps before 11 p.m. This is the normal life for many Brazilian women. But she says the best thing in her life is to go to church. She is a member of an organized group of women and of a group that visits families in need to show love and solidarity. God deserves our praise because God cares. People like Dona Ester can be forgotten by people of this world but God is ready to give them strength and dignity.

✳ *Praise be to you, O Lord, for your mercy and care for the poor of our world. Thank you for being our God who looks after us all. Amen*

Saturday September 26   *Psalm 113 *C*

God's preference for the poor

Many Christians try to explain that when the Bible refers to 'poor', it means 'poor in spirit' or 'those who are marginalized, excluded in many ways in society'. But the Bible clearly shows the value

216

God gives to the poor. The experience of the Exodus, the struggle for a piece of land in Canaan, the pain and hope at the time of the exile, are strong examples.

Jesus is the supreme example: Jesus, the Word made flesh, was dispossessed, a startling revelation of the heart of God. He was born in a manger among animals, and the first ones to testify to his birth were simple, ordinary shepherds (Luke 2.1-20).

Mary understood God's option for the poor when she sang,

'He has brought down mighty kings from their thrones,
    and lifted up the lowly.
He has filled the hungry with good things,
    and sent the rich away with empty hands'   *(Luke 1.53)*.

Jesus chose as followers and targeted his preaching at fishermen, tax-collectors, nationalist revolutionaries, women, children, the sick, disabled, leprosy victims, land and urban workers, Samaritans. Those who were discriminated against, disregarded, oppressed by a sexist culture and an expensive religious system which benefited the rich and the powerful, were the ones embraced by God through Jesus Christ (e.g. Luke 5.1-11, 27-31; 6.12-17; 8.1-3; 9.46-48; 10.30-37; 18.35-43). The rich and powerful are challenged to respond to the call to be alongside the poor and oppressed – with them! The Kingdom exists when and where the imperative is togetherness and sharing. In this way God is revealed for rich and poor (Luke 24.13-35).

✳ *Dear Lord, help us to learn with the poor*
the values of your Kingdom.
Show us ways of solidarity, togetherness and sharing
through which you may be revealed in our world.

For further reflection or group discussion

● Who are the poor in the area where you live? What signs of God's blessing can you identify in their attitudes and way of life? What can you learn with them? Think of real experiences.
● Is it possible that your attitudes and lifestyle help to sustain or increase poverty? Reflect seriously: do you ignore poor people around you, or vote for a political party which sustains the market system? Do you value accumulation and competition more than sharing and solidarity?

Can the rich be blessed?

Can we say simply what is God's will for the earth? We could say that it is the opposite of the human will which prefers to accumulate instead of sharing; to compete instead of serving; to exclude instead of showing solidarity; to trample down instead of being merciful. God's will is that people may freely love each other without self-interest; that justice may flow like a river and every person be considered and given dignity as a human being.

Unfortunately, those who accumulate riches are articulate. The poor have sinned, but their need to survive, their weakness and fragility, make them humble, simple, available to share, closer to God's will. Yes, blessed are the poor who have the Kingdom of God. The rich have the chance to achieve this blessing too. This does not mean losing money and properties to become poor: it is to follow the way of the Kingdom that means humbleness, simplicity, sharing and solidarity. 'No servant can be the slave of two masters; he will hate one and love the other; he will be loyal to one and despise the other. You cannot serve both God and money' (Luke 16.13). The challenge is to be available to serve God first. Blessed will be the rich who love without expecting interest.

✳ *Forgive us, Lord, when we allow our human will*
to prevail instead of your will. Show us how to serve you
and love those who are around us. In Jesus' love. Amen

The poor show the way to the Kingdom

When we reflect on God's preference for the poor there is a risk of over-simplification: 'the rich are bad and the poor are good'. Reading the Gospels and having our eyes open to see what is going on around us, we are able to understand what Jesus and the Bible are saying to us. God created the world for peace and harmony, not for divisions and for some human beings to claim superiority. We should love the whole creation and look after it. People have sinned and discovered that they can trample on others and take advantage of them. People have learned to accumulate and in doing this have made others destitute.

From God's wisdom and from our own experience, we learn that the more we have, the more we want. It is our sinful human nature which turns away from God's will. That is why Jesus said,

'It is much harder for a rich person to enter the Kingdom of God than for a camel to go through the eye of a needle' (Luke 18.25). The rich are worried about keeping properties, earning more, accumulating for the future. This is contrary to God's project of having enough, sharing and conserving for the future. Poor people take risks; they have nothing to lose. And so it is with the Kingdom of God: to achieve it is to take a risk.

Is it impossible for the rich? Jesus says: 'What is impossible for man is possible for God' (Luke 18.27). God acts through the poor like Lazarus, showing the rich the way of the Kingdom.

✳ *Thank you, our God, because nothing is impossible for you and because the opportunity to embrace the faith and your Kingdom is given to all, with no discrimination. Praise be your name! Amen*

Tuesday September 29   *Luke 12.13-21*

Searching for a true life

Jesus says that 'a person's true life is not made up of the things he owns, no matter how rich he may be' (verse 15), and he tells the parable of a man who piled up riches for himself, thinking that he would have all the good things he needed for many years. But he was interrupted by the Lord: 'You fool! This very night you will have to give up your life; then who will get all these things you have kept for yourself?'(verse 20).

Who is not worried about the future? We are always thinking of the need of guaranteeing a safe future with a house, health, food, and all our needs satisfied. It is normal and understandable. The problem is when we dedicate our life to this project of guaranteeing the future and forget all the rest. We work hard day and night, at weekends, and with no holidays, thinking that it will be good for the future. 'Enough' is a word that we do not know. Is this a true life? Jesus is saying 'No'. Life is short. We never know what is going to happen tomorrow. Of course we need to care about our future, but how about the present? Are we enjoying God's creation? Are we paying attention to our brothers and sisters who are around us? Are we cultivating relationships? Do we set aside time to be quiet? Are we listening to the birds or the wind? Do we know the names of our neighbours? Are we living a true life?

✳ *Lord Jesus, renew our life that we may be really touched by your words of liberation. Help us to be free of everything that enslaves us, especially any kind of greed.*

Learning with the poor

I will never forget Dona Maria. I was part of a group sharing with Catholic Base Communities in Mato Grosso do Sul, a state in the Centre West of Brazil, full of rich farms and poor land workers. The local priest was showing us around and decided to stop at Dona Maria's house. It was lunch-time. I was embarrassed at the thought of four of us going into a poor house unannounced at lunch-time. The family would have just enough for themselves. Dona Maria and her husband received us with a bright smile. 'What a shame!' she said. 'We've already had lunch. I'm sorry you came late!' 'Clever woman!' I thought, 'She's avoiding embarrassment all round.' Then she added, 'But don't worry! I won't leave you hungry. I'll prepare something for you.' She called her little son, and in some minutes he was back with five fish he had caught in a river behind the house. In a short time we were all sitting around the table, eating and talking with a family which was happy to share the table with us. I was able to understand why God has chosen the poor to be an example for us. Humility, simplicity, availability to share – these are the values we discover among the poor, and they are the values of the Kingdom. 'Your heart will always be where your riches are' (Luke 12.34).

✴ *Forgive us, O Lord, when we trust in ourselves*
and our plans, instead of in you. Teach us to learn
with the crows, the wild flowers, and the poor of the
earth,
to have faith and believe the future belongs to you.
Amen

A radical proposal

Christians – there are many in this world, a result of successful missionary enterprise that began with the apostles after the day of Pentecost. Actually, since the church of the apostles, many people have been called Christians but have been reprehended for being false ones. People find it difficult to be Christians because Jesus' proposal is radical. Love God with all our heart, soul and mind – no problem. Love our neighbour as we love ourselves – what a task! It is difficult because it implies giving to others the attention we pay to ourselves, to wish and do our best for them, so that they have their basic needs and are satisfied, happy, and able to overcome prejudices and disputes.

A Brazilian rock singer understood very well Jesus' proposal when he wrote a song that says: 'It is necessary to love all people as if there is no future.' Paul wrote to Timothy to warn him about false 'Christianism' and false teachings. He shared in this letter the challenge of being rich and Christian – to avoid the love of money: it is to strive for righteousness, godliness, faith, love, endurance and gentleness; not to be proud, to place hope – not in riches – but in God; to be rich in good works, to be generous and share with others. In this way, the rich 'will be able to win the life which is true life' (verse 19).

✷ *Our Lord, help us to search for righteousness, godliness, faith, love, endurance, gentleness, and to place our hope – not in riches – but in you. In Jesus' loving name. Amen*

Friday October 2   2 Corinthians 8.1-9

Paul's update letter

Today's reading reminds me of Christians in Piabet – a district in the outskirts of Rio de Janeiro City. They are descendants of former slaves and peasants escaping from the hard life of the countryside. There is a small Methodist congregation of about one hundred people. They are poor but try to respond to all the challenges we are facing.

As part of their commitment, Dona Eulina, who is 54 years old, offered her house to the church to start missionary work in one of the poorest areas. The place is called *Novo Horizonte* – 'New Horizon' and as usual in Piabet, it lacks adequate housing, a water supply, or paved streets, and so violence has increased. The church used to meet in Dona Eulina's house on Sunday afternoons and Tuesday mornings, to celebrate, pray and share their needs – food, clothes, health – and to learn more about their rights. Their offerings have now made it possible to buy a small plot with a little house where, during the week, there is a space for teaching children and organizing women's groups. The group used to say that they all are poor but they share what they have. It is possible to imagine the words of Paul referring to that community in Piabet: 'They have been severely tested by the troubles they went through; but their joy was so great that they were extremely generous in their giving, even though they are very poor' (2 Corinthians 8.2).

✷ *Praise be to you, loving God, for putting joy in the hearts of those who suffer poverty and find ways of being generous to others in need. May the same feeling and attitude be part of our lives every day. Amen*

Prosperity *vis-à-vis* poverty

Some Christian groups have developed the so-called 'Theology of Prosperity'. They preach that all those who are faithful to God will prosper – that God transforms what is received from believers in properties and gives back for them to enjoy. They say we must give our life to God, pray, read the Bible, do what is right, help the poor, contribute to the church with our money, and all our problems will be solved: and children of God cannot be poor or ill. The poor and the ill are those who do not have enough faith to have a better life.

This idea has met with 'success' in countries like Brazil where poverty has increased, unemployment is a sad reality and public health is abandoned. Hearing this message, people have searched for God in order to get rid of illness and to have a house to live in, a car, money, jobs or even an industry. There is nothing more neo-liberal. This reasoning is the same as the logic of market economy which says: 'the poor are poor because they are not able to earn money and consume'; the theology of prosperity says: 'the poor are poor because they do not have enough faith'. Nothing could be farther from the gospel. The words of Paul are clear when he reminds us from the Book of Exodus: 'The one who gathered much did not have too much, and the one who gathered little did not have too little.' The logic of the gospel is completely different from the logic of the world. The last will be the first; to serve is better than to be served; to share is more important than to gather; the future belongs to God; poverty is a value.

Wealth, in God's dictionary, does not mean the accumulation of money, properties and goods but to have access to the fruits of labour, to live well and with justice. The example of Jesus, the Son of Man, who did not have a place to lay his head, is God's clearest demonstration of what it means to be rich in the Kingdom of God.

✳ ***Dear Lord, may the example of Jesus be an instrument to bring humbleness, mercy and solidarity to this world, especially among groups called Christians. Amen.***

For personal reflection or group discussion

Think of the radical nature of Jesus' proposal and how difficult it is to be a Christian. Do you think that it is impossible to accept the challenge of being a Christian as Jesus called us to be? Why? Think about your life and try to discover what you have to continue to do, what you have to abandon and what you need to change in order to follow in Jesus' steps.

FOR ACTION

Neo-liberal ideology has a strong appeal especially through the mass media, making people believe that to consume more is the solution for humanity. This is making people forget solidarity. It is making them more individualistic and strengthening their prejudice against the poor. Read about it and the criticisms of this system. Talk about this to your family, friends and church and try to find ways together to organize small and simple actions in the area where you live to help to overcome this situation and strengthen the values of the Kingdom of God.

Reserve every day some minutes to pray for the poor of the earth, that governments and all those who have the means may have mercy on them as God has.

HUMAN RIGHTS

Notes based on the Revised Standard Version by
Keith Johnson

Keith Johnson, a Methodist minister, is now pastor of Newport United Reformed Church (Shropshire, UK). He has been a member of Amnesty International since 1963, has served on the UK Council for six years, and currently chairs its Religious Bodies Liaison Panel and the East Shropshire Group.

The phrase 'Human Rights' has been well used this century, not that previous centuries have been more just, but today there is a deepening awareness of the issues. The brutality and bloodiness of two World Wars, and more sophisticated media informing us of the violation of human rights in other parts of the world, have challenged more people to engage in concerted action. Not all human rights' activists are Christians, by any means, but Christians cannot stay silent in the face of evil.

Sunday October 4   *Jeremiah 37.11-21*
Wrongful imprisonment

Unlawful imprisonment for nothing more than a non-violent expression of one's religious or political views existed before the time of Jeremiah, or Jesus – another innocent victim.

Jeremiah was lucky: he was given better than usual treatment. As the king's 'ear', he was assured he would not be executed. Vast numbers of prisoners today are less fortunate. They too are imprisoned for no crime. They are tortured repeatedly and brutally with no access to doctors or lawyers, and they usually need both. They do not know the outcome of their detention. It may well be execution. In January 1996, for example, nine Buddhist monks from a monastery in Tashilhunpo, Tibet, were reported to have been detained by Chinese authorities because they burned the pictures of Gyaltsen Norbu, the boy the Chinese wanted to set up as a rival Buddhist leader to the Dalai Lama.

Another example is Nguyen Ngoc Tan, a 75-year-old Vietnamese journalist and former MP, who was sentenced in 1994 to eleven years' imprisonment because he helped to form an opposition political party – nothing more. At the time of writing

(November 1996), he has already been imprisoned for 15 years: his trial appears to have been unfair.

There is no excuse for ignoring these as unpleasant examples. Awareness needs to grow, for how can evil be fought if it is not clearly exposed?

✳ *Good Lord, may we let our eyes and ears be opened*
to injustice in your world: remove our complacency
and make us eager, in your power, to fight against evil
wherever we come across it.
Give strength to all who are wrongfully imprisoned, we
pray.

Monday October 5   *Lamentations 1.1-6 *C*
Exile
The writer of Lamentations may be right in seeing God's hand in the punishment meted out to Judah (exiled in Babylon in the sixth century BC), but it was hard on those, possibly the majority, 'ordinary folk' who lived 'decent lives'. Was all Judah exceptionally wicked, or only her leaders?

Deserved or not, exile is a terrible experience for most, little understood especially by those who live in a peaceful land which has not suffered recent invasion. It means being uprooted, often suddenly and violently, from possessions, home, community, a familiar and happy way of life, and being harassed, shunted on in great discomfort to a place where one may be kept under hostile guard in the midst of enemies or, at best, people who do not want to receive refugees.

In recent years, we have seen seemingly endless TV pictures of refugees, masses of them in Iraq, Central Africa ... There is a danger that such familiarity may numb our feelings and lead us to un-concern, if not contempt. But the fact remains that millions of refugees move slowly and painfully across the world. Those countries which have room, economic prosperity and internal peace should welcome them, particularly when returning home would mean facing injury or death. Jesus was a refugee (Matthew 2.13-14).

✳ *Christ the refugee,*
may we live and work to encourage our nation
to welcome all who seek safety from persecution.
May we not succumb to self-protectiveness
or fear of financial burden, but live and pray
that the persecuted may be truly blessed
as you receive them through our caring.

Violence

'Destruction and violence are before us' as much as, if not more than, in Habakkuk's day. Many more people can be destroyed by one weapon. So what do the Churches say to the arms industry? Over the centuries, the Church has not only overlooked mass violence in wartime; it has supported and encouraged violence between nations and engaged in it in Christ's name. Think of examples. It is, however, a good sign that today the Church is openly opposed to many forms of violence.

Jesus warned against the ultimate self-destructiveness of the violent, but in the short-term they cause immeasurable pain to countless people: the Argentinian mothers who paraded every day in silent protest that their loved ones had 'disappeared', most apparently killed by government violence.

If there is more violence in the world today, it is largely because it even pervades parts of life which should be marked by tenderness and love. In Britain, for example, we hear more about rape than ever before. Is it surprising that 'having sex' so often replaces 'making love'?

What then do we do about violence? Simply deplore it, and wait until it exhausts itself? Habakkuk 2.4 may speak to us if we are victims of violence, but when we see others suffer from it, we must combat it and oppose the perpetrators. We may sign petitions for the abolition of torture, but is that enough?

✷ *O Lord, remember not only the men and women of goodwill but also those of evil will. But do not remember all the suffering they have inflicted upon us; remember the fruits we have borne thanks to this suffering – our comradeship, our loyalty, our humility, our courage, our generosity, the greatness of heart which has grown out of all this; and when they come to judgement, let all the fruits that we have borne be their forgiveness.*

This prayer was found scribbled on a piece of wrapping paper near the body of a dead child at a Ravensbruck Concentration Camp.

Wednesday October 7   *Luke 4.16-21*

Liberty

Fine words, great rhetoric, making us glad to follow such a 'redeemer'. Was it only proclamation, or the work of Jesus? Is he just describing his role, or should these words inspire us to live likewise?

'Liberty' is a good slogan, but it may not be a clear ideal. Liberty for some can mean the deprivation, loss or reduction of liberty for others. Think of examples. Some Christians tend to think that Jesus was here talking about internal, spiritual liberty, freedom from neuroses: that the deepest liberty is in the heart, regardless of external circumstances – men and women who are not defeated, like those whose faith and integrity endured Auschwitz.

But slavery – the oppression of the weak by the strong – is an evil. In his youth, Abraham Lincoln is said to have seen a slave market in New Orleans and vowed that if ever he could hit the slave trade, he would hit it hard. We have not the political power Lincoln gained, but does that excuse us from all action that helps to liberate the oppressed? All that is needed for the triumph of evil is that good people do nothing.

✴ *God who has given us grace*
to be instruments of love in its work
of healing and judgement,
who has commissioned us to proclaim ...
deliverance to the captive ...
give us the impatience of those who love;
that the might of your gentleness may work through us.
                              Tonga - From Oceans of Prayer (NCEC)

Thursday October 8   Acts 25.6-12

Justice

Life isn't fair, but the Christian, if no other, must work to make it fairer. Justice, which might be called the social, institutional form of love, is not sought uniquely by Christians. It is a major theme in the Old Testament (e.g. Proverbs 21.3; Micah 6.8). God is often portrayed as judge. The Gospels, though appearing to be more concerned with individuals than social development, do not contradict this concern.

Paul's trial, like that of Jesus, was a travesty of justice, including false charges. One of the most significant fields in the work of Amnesty International is to expose and draw attention to situations of injustice: civilians brought before military tribunals without adequate or legal advice. Sometimes, Amnesty International helps to prepare a defence when someone is tried in criminal courts for non-criminal offences, after making 'confessions' extracted through torture. In some countries, we

227

complain about 'rough' justice, while in others thousands would rejoice if they could be heard with a small measure of impartiality, or to have had Paul's chance of a second or fairer trial.

✳ *'... As long as there's injustice*
in any of God's lands,
I am my brother's keeper,
I dare not wash my hands.'   *John Ferguson*

Lord, save us from Pilate's sin.
Lord, let justice roll down like rivers.

Friday October 9   *2 Timothy 1.1-14 *C*

The cost of true witness

Paul Schneider was a German pastor, imprisoned in Buchenwald before the 1939 War. Despite repeated and excruciating torture, he refused to stop speaking out against the evils of Nazism until he died at the hands of his tormentors.

Paul, writing from prison, urges Timothy to continue 'testifying to our Lord' (verse 8), though he may suffer from doing so: easy words if they did not come from one who knew in his own experience what it was to suffer persecution for witnessing to his faith (2 Corinthians 11.23-27).

What does discipleship cost us? Most, if not all of us will never suffer in this way, at the hands of enemies. Might we testify more about our faith – what it means to us – if we did? If we are silent about it, why are we? There is a cost to true discipleship; the blood of the martyrs is claimed as the 'seed' of the Church. Do we enjoy the 'comfort' of faith too easily? Would it be deeper if we had to suffer for it?

✳ *We pray for those whose faith is tested by others' cruelty*
that they may endure and triumph.
When our beliefs are also challenged,
let our faith not be a veneer, but make it strong and deep.

Saturday October 10   *Revelation 1.9-20*

Victory

Sadly, movements like Amnesty International will be needed for a long time yet. It can well be argued that the history of the world is one of war and violence, broken occasionally by short spells of peace and tranquillity.

'God made a hopeful beginning,
but we've gone and spoiled it by sinning.
We hope that the story will end in God's glory,
but at present the other side's winning.'   *Source unknown*

John's vision is of a world in which God and goodness do triumph: we must, if we are to have hope, believe that ultimately good, justice and love will win. If we believe that God is in control and that love cannot be defeated, then we will become, in the power of the Spirit, co-workers with God to bring this about. This conviction is echoed in Martin Luther King's vision of that time when 'the lion and the lamb shall lie down together, and everyone shall sit under their own vine and fig tree and none shall be afraid. We shall overcome ...'

✷ *Take away from us, Lord, all despondency*
as we look at the misery, sin and evil in your world.
May our hope in you and your triumph grow in us
as we work with you to build hope for those in despair
that your Kingdom may come on earth.

For further reflection or group discussion

● How central are 'human rights' to the gospel?
● What makes the gospel 'good news to the poor'?
● To what extent is the faith of the individual intertwined with seeking the rights of others?

FOR ACTION

Find out more about human rights' issues in your country – and how you can become involved in working on behalf of those who are discriminated against or persecuted. There are Amnesty International Sections in most countries of the world. If you cannot find out the headquarters of the section in your country, or do not know if there is one, the International Secretariat (1 Easton Street, London WC1X 8DJ, UK) can help you.

GOD'S SHALOM –
Healing minds and bodies

Notes based on the New Revised Standard Version Bible by
Helen Richmond

Helen Richmond, a Minister of the Uniting Church in Australia, spent two years studying theology in Indonesia. She went on to serve as a parish minister in Sydney and later as Consultant for World Mission and Social Responsibility and Justice in the Synod of Western Australia. Helen is presently working as Tutor in Mission Studies at the United College of the Ascension, Selly Oak, Birmingham (UK).

The rich meaning of *shalom* is not easy to translate into English. It embraces an understanding of peace and wholeness in the fullest possible sense. *Shalom* is the vision of well-being for the individual as well as for communities. In the coming week we will focus on *shalom* as God's gift of healing to bodies and minds. The Scriptures attest to the power of God's grace to transform peoples' lives. Jesus' ministry embodied this: those who are tortured in mind or body find release; the sinful are forgiven; the outcasts are included. Living by this vision of *shalom* means being committed to a vision of wholeness of life as God intends it for all God's children.

Sunday October 11   *Luke 7.36-50*
A costly gift

A woman's desire for forgiveness was so great that she risked harsh reproach. An uninvited guest, compelled by some strange impulse, came to the house of Simon the Pharisee. She broke her alabaster jar of costly perfume and at Jesus' feet offered her gift of love. There were those quick to point out that this woman was not the kind of person Jesus should be associating with. In their eyes this woman of disrepute should be excluded. But Jesus saw things differently. He saw her tears and love, her faith and her desire for forgiveness.

At Jesus' feet we too can find forgiveness and healing. If we come to him, he will not send us away. What would it mean if we were willing to take up Jesus' model of ministry in our own lives?

Are we building congregations and communities where there is a place for all, especially those who see themselves as outsiders, or who feel unworthy?

✳ *At your feet we discover that we are forgiven.*
As we have experienced your loving acceptance
may we grow in what it means to share your loving
embrace with others.
Help your Church to model the ministry of Jesus.

Monday October 12   *2 Kings 5.1-3, 7-15 *C*

Wash and be clean

Naaman expected to be treated with the respect he felt his status and position surely deserved. He was a powerful man, accustomed to giving orders. Following instructions was difficult, particularly ones that sounded to him unintelligible and ridiculous. Why should he, a commander of a great army from Syria, and a servant of the great king of Aram, 'wash in the Jordan seven times'? Weren't the rivers of Damascus better than the rivers of Israel?

Perhaps we can identify with Naaman. We too want others to see us for the real value we like to think we have. We do not want to risk doing something which seems 'below us', or makes us appear foolish. Naaman's desire for healing had to overcome his doubts, prejudice, disbelief, and scorn. As he stepped into this unfamiliar river, Naaman not only received healing of his skin disease but his life was transformed and he met the living God.

✳ *Save us from being conformed to this age*
that we may dare to be irrelevant and foolish
as measured by the world's standards.
Help us to risk the way of Jesus, a foolish endeavour,
but which has changed the world more than any other.

Tuesday October 13   *John 5.1-18*

Take up your mat and walk

What kind of mission is this? It is certainly a subversive one. Jesus' healing of a paralytic on the Sabbath caused great offence. In his social world, illness was associated with sin and impurity. Jesus violated this code of exclusion, and reversed it. He was concerned to bring healing and liberation to those who were the most marginal in Palestinian society.

There were those who disapproved of Jesus putting the well-being of this man before their religious and social conventions. Jesus' social interaction with the paralytic broke all the rules and expectations of social order and propriety. There will always be those who resist change which sets people free. Ultimately Jesus' solidarity with the poor and despised would bring him into conflict with the religious and political authorities. The final way to deal with this disturber of the peace was to make him a despised criminal.

✳ *Give us the courage to take up our mat.*
When we prefer the safety of following the status quo,
give us a vision of Jesus' radically different Kingdom.
Help us to be part of your healing work
that invites others in the world to stand up.

Wednesday October 14   *Colossians 3.12-17*

Clothe yourselves with love

The Gentile congregation at Colossae, a cosmopolitan city with religious and cultural diversity, was engulfed in a major crisis. Paul's letter was a defence of the apostolic faith as he sought to distinguish true teaching from false doctrine. The congregation was accommodating Greek Hellenistic thought and in the process Paul believed they had developed a deficient understanding of who Christ is and an over-emphasis on asceticism (2.16). Such teaching led to an arrogant attitude that was far removed from the spirit of Jesus. Paul offered a different vision of what is distinctive about the Christian way of life. He emphasized in a practical way the attitudes and lifestyle that are to be cultivated.

Paul, despite his differences with the congregation, continued to see them as 'God's chosen ones'. Forbearing one another and forgiveness are the hallmarks of Christ's body. Paul's words of peace, love, humility, compassion and patience are needed as much now, in our divided Church, as they were in the first century.

✳ *God, heal your broken body.*
Where your Church falters, lift us up.
When we assume we are right, give us humility.
Where we are confused, give us wisdom.

Thursday October 15   *Romans 12.14-20*

Overcome evil with good

God never gives up on this world and never gives up on a dream to see creation as it was intended to be. God says it is still my world and evil can be overcome with good. The crucified and risen Jesus shows us his hands and side and whispers, 'Yes, these are the marks of true followers of mine.' It is the way of weakness and vulnerability. It requires grace rather than punishment. We are to do good to those who have wronged us rather than seek revenge.

And God our Maker beckons us to join in the dance with the Spirit as our partner. We are slow to catch on. It seems an impossible rhythm, with music composed of wondrous but infuriating harmonies, and depths and heights that we can never reach. We begin to hear the melody of God's grace and peace, reconciling love and forgiveness and learn different steps. It is a dance of hope and resistance; a dance that continues the steps and the moves of Jesus; the dance of *shalom*.

✴ *It is difficult to forgive those who have wronged us.*
  We ask that you would work in our lives –
  healing the places of pain
  and enabling us to let go of our desire for pay back.

Friday October 16   *James 3.13-18*

Who is wise among you?

The writer poses a question – 'Who is wise and understanding among you?' – and then goes on to contrast true wisdom that comes 'from above' with the wisdom 'of this world'. The commonly accepted Greek view of wisdom was of a more abstract, intellectual and philosophical knowledge rather than concern for an ethical and moral life. But James writes that true wisdom that comes 'from above' does not puff up or create boastfulness and envy. Instead it produces 'good fruits'. It is seen in those who are gentle and merciful, who are peacemakers and who do not show partiality or hypocrisy. We return to a key theme in the book of James: true faith must be seen in action, and be visible in the quality of our lives.

✴ *Jesus, you are the one who models for us true wisdom.*
  Save us from selfish ambition and jealousy.
  Give us your gift of wisdom.
  Touch us with your Spirit
  and awaken in us the qualities of wisdom.
  May we be those who plant seeds – sowing in peace,
  and harvesting with you and each other the fruits of
    shalom –
  a healing of bodies and minds, justice and peace.

233

Jesus, a cause of division

We can find it difficult to let those who are members of our family change. We fail to expect much of them because we think we know them. But God's style of loving is not smothering or restrictive; it is liberating. Our loving of others too must let them grow and change, and become all that God has called them to be.

Jesus' mission was not about keeping his family happy at any cost, never rocking the boat. Jesus found a home among strangers and his mission established a new community. Making choices is part of what is involved in bringing in the Kingdom. Ultimately our allegiance must first be to Christ and his Kingdom.

This passage can also be heard as a warning and a challenge to the Church. When Jesus went home to his own people, they did not receive him (Luke 4.16-30). We are Christ's 'family', the ones who claim to know and love him. Are we the ones who restrict the working of the Spirit?

✳ *Forgive us for wanting harmony at the expense of*
justice;
for avoiding conflict. Help us to care enough
to risk disagreeing passionately with one another
for the sake of your Kingdom. Amen

For further reflection or group discussion

● How is God's gift of *shalom* that brings healing and wholeness experienced in your life, in the life of your congregation and in your local community?

● The vision of *shalom* invites us to share God's dream; to contemplate that things could be different and believe that change is possible.

● How do you understand God's 'impossible dream' of *shalom* becoming possible? What part can you play?

FOR ACTION

Find a symbol that represents something of your vision of *shalom*.

GOD'S SHALOM –
Healing communities

Notes based on the Good News Bible by
Stewart Morris

*Stewart Morris, originally from Dublin, is an Irish Methodist
minister who has served in circuits in South Belfast, and rural and
urban communities in the Republic of Ireland. In 1984-90 he was
World Affairs Youth Secretary for the British Methodist Church,
with involvement ecumenically and internationally.*

From pastoral, cross-cultural, international and personal perspectives, we will explore what is community and what makes for
healing within the communities of which each one of us is part.
We must also examine ourselves to see whether what we do as
Christians is resulting in God's love and power being proclaimed.
The way this week's theme is explored may stimulate you to
prayer and action.

Sunday October 18   *Genesis 32.22-31 *C*

First the struggle

Jacob's struggle with God in the context of family estrangement
(typifying a nation's history of communal conflict), reminds me of
a very significant period of my life. Having finished training for the
ministry and started married life, the next eighteen months saw
ministry in the context of life in Belfast. Hunger strikes raged;
former Methodist minister and MP Robert Bradford was
assassinated (his foster parents lived on the housing estate
where I was minister); Bobby Sands, the hunger striker, died and
residents from our estate attacked the coffin as it passed from the
hospital in the hearse; police and prison officers living on the
estate were having £2000 spent on their houses to make them
bullet proof; my wife and I were under suspicion within the
community because we came from the South; when we
befriended someone from Andersontown who had just moved in,
I was accused of 'bringing Catholics in' to the estate.

Out of such life-experience, I can understand Jacob saying, 'I
won't (let you go), unless you bless me'. I sought to name the

name of Jesus Christ, especially when someone offered me words from the Bible – 'an eye for an eye and a tooth for a tooth' – as an appropriate response to the murder of Robert Bradford.

✳ ***Through the struggle of community life,***
may your love and acceptance never fail. Amen

Monday October 19 *Psalm 121 *C*

Then the help

Accompanying trade unionists and African National Congress (ANC) personnel to the scene of a bomb outrage, the wrecked offices of two black trade union organizations in West Transvaal, international church peace monitors noticed an interesting encounter. The local co-ordinator of their team, a minister of the black African Methodist Episcopal Church, had been animatedly talking with the white police captain who was acting as the public relations liaison officer. Later, the minister explained, 'Oh, he's the man that arrested me and then lied in court to get the 30-year sentence that was handed down to me.'

Previously, the police officer, troubled by his conscience, had gone to the cells to ask the man's forgiveness. 'I only did it,' said the policeman, 'because I was ordered to by my superior officers.' The prisoner willingly granted forgiveness before he went off to Robbin Island, where he served three years of his sentence, before political negotiations led to the freeing of prisoners.

The warm and friendly encounter with the arresting officer was the first time the two had met since their conversation in the police cell. Forgiveness had been sought and granted, so maintaining the possibility of relationship. The protection from hurt, the Lord's help, the individual not being allowed to fall are evident both in psalm and story.

✳ ***May your protection empower me to forgive. Amen***

Tuesday October 20 *Luke 9.51-56*

Receiving Jesus

Are you facing some opposition today? It seems to be a professional hazard that clergy and lay leaders have when working in some places. We are very like the Lord in that regard. Times of change, being alongside people who are hurting, facing difficult situations, working with people who are different from church people – all combine at times to create an atmosphere of conflict and tension in church life. What was in the minds of the disciples when they wanted to call down fire on those who would not receive Jesus? Was it the sentiment that here were those Samaritans up to their old tricks? We would describe such attitudes as sectarian or racist today. Yet those attitudes were coming from the companions of our Lord. Some manuscripts give Jesus' rebuke as: 'You don't know what kind of Spirit you belong to; for the Son of Man did not come to destroy people's lives, but to save them.'

In encouraging the work of healing in our communities, we, as Christians, need new attitudes when faced with old enmities. By our openness, love and understanding, we enable people to receive Jesus, so leading to wholesome relationships and not community divisions.

✳ *When we receive you, we receive the right Spirit.*
May our openness lead to understanding and wholeness.
Amen

Wednesday October 21   *Luke 17.11-19 *C*

Giving thanks

There are people in our communities today who are treated as were those with leprosy in the past – those with Alzheimer's Disease, for example. For what can *we* give thanks in a situation of such agonizing illness? A Scottish hospital chaplain came across a woman who did not recognize him. She was rocking backwards and forwards and was very restless. He indicated to the charge nurse that he thought the visit a waste of time. The nurse challenged him just to hold her hand and time himself for ten minutes (the nurses no longer had time to do that). The chaplain held out his hand and she held it. He spoke quite softly about things that had been going on in the church – the well-attended Saturday coffee morning where there had been a stall of fresh, home-baked goods; the lovely Sunday service with the lighting of the Advent candle; the Boys' Brigade parade service. She talked while her hand was being stroked, and it did soothe her. The unconnected words did not make sense, and the last five minutes were just silence. The charge nurse let the chaplain out and said, 'She'll be different tonight because you have given her time.'

✳ *In the task of healing in our communities,*
let us give thanks for those who have time. Amen

Receiving the Holy Spirit

After all the bad press for Samaria, it is really encouraging to see Philip's ministry having such an effect on the people in the principal city. The Holy Spirit was received when ordinary disciples placed their hands on disreputable people who had come through to belief.

We so easily label people. Do we have a 'hands-on' approach towards 'the unemployed', 'the marginalized', 'the problem people' and all those who feel at a distance from Christian people? Usually, we don't get close enough to see such categories as real people needing love and acceptance. For many such vulnerable people, their 'Simon magic-man' is unfortunately an acquaintance with drugs, alcohol, violence or debt. The quick fix does not help them rise above their low self-esteem, their sense of worthlessness, and their inability to find a fulfilling job. The deeply satisfying experience of knowing the Wonderful Counsellor through the work of the Holy Spirit *is* lasting, and results in God's *shalom*, if we as Christians dare to get that close in Christ's name.

✳ *Come, Holy Spirit, and charge us with power to serve,*
   so that you may be received in the hurting place. Amen

Repenting fully

Our churches and communities harbour people who want control. Their love and healing needs are overshadowed by their craving for power – as Simon demonstrates. And he offered money to Peter and John.

The call to repent is one that we are embarrassed to hear within the church, let alone in the community. Peter's words, however, come loudly and clearly – 'You have no part or share in our work, because your heart is not right in God's sight. Repent, then, of this evil plan of yours' (verses 21-22). Can we identify circumstances today that need such thorough repentance? 'Bitter envy' and the characteristics of sin-dominated lives must be purged from our communities and church groups.

Fully changing direction to what is positive at the heart of the good news of Jesus Christ demands our commitment in meaningful prayer and action. The hell we live in when we are motivated by such power-mongering is radically transformed.

We, as humble servants of the Lord say, 'Not my will, but yours be done.'

✳ *May your shalom get to the root of my disease*
and change my characteristic greed into love.

United Nations Day, October 24   John 20.19-23

Peaceful encounters

Fear and peace can be very close to one another, even though we may not realize it. Jesus came into a fearful situation and offered peace. Displaying wounds, his presence evoked joy.

A group of Christians – the Cornerstone Community – live and work together on the Springfield Road in Belfast. They provide a network of support and witness in an area which has seen much violence and tension over the years. The Revd Sam Burch, retired Director, tells of an incident from their life story:

'Some years ago, a neighbour of ours was shot dead by Loyalist gunmen. After visiting the family, some members of our inter-church group asked if they would like us to pray with them in the home at the 'month's mind' (a remembrance one month after the death). A Presbyterian minister who heard of this asked if he might come with some of his congregation and share in this. When we met, there were so many that we had to move out into the front garden to hold the little service. Many neighbours then joined with us and the 'family prayer' became a powerful act of witness for peace and love, not only comforting the bereaved family, but strengthening all who shared, and reinforcing the will of all in the neighbourhood to live together in peace.'

✳ *Lead me, Lord, by your example.*

For further reflection or group discussion

● What is the hurting point in your church or community life that could do with appropriate repentance and forgiveness?
● In what ways do we limit God's *shalom* in our lives?
● In what ways does your church need to risk getting close to vulnerable people?

FOR ACTION

Find out more about what the Christian Church is doing round the world in Christ's name to bring about reconciliation and healing.

GOD'S SHALOM – Healing nations

Notes based on the Jerusalem Bible by
Marcella Althaus-Reid

Dr Marcella Althaus-Reid, an Argentinian theologian, is a lecturer in the Department of Christian Ethics and Practical Theology in New College, the University of Edinburgh, Scotland. Marcella is a Quaker and belongs to the Britain Yearly Meeting.

At national and international levels, God's *shalom* is concerned with justice for all – making sure that everyone has enough to eat, and that every community has freedom to live according to its own God-given culture. As people of *shalom*, we are to live in solidarity with the poor; to pray for the healing of the nations; and we are called to a prophetic ministry.

Sunday October 25   *Leviticus 26.6-10*
'You shall sleep with none to frighten you'
'We give sleeping pills to the children.' This comment was made to me by a Baptist woman from Nicaragua during the war in her country. She told me how mothers wanted to protect their children from the terrors of being bombarded: the noise, the shouting and the spectacle of death. In difficult times, such as war between countries, or in personal troubles (our 'everyday wars') we read the Scriptures in a different way, perhaps searching the Word of God for a very concrete answer for our situation. How could the people who were trying to protect their children from death in Nicaragua, or any other country at war, have reacted to the passage we are reading now? This is a text where God promises to establish peace and prosperity; a sign of it, maybe the possibility to sleep at night without fear. But, how is God going to do this? The answer lies in verses 3-5: the people are asked to follow God's commands, and to put them into practice. God is calling nations to practise justice, because the blessings of God's commands are always seen in the practical way of living in community. Nations following the path of justice become precious in the eyes of God, who then promises to establish true peace.

The ways of God, however, are not the ways of the world, and history tells us that many nations searching for justice have sometimes suffered isolation, economic deprivation and war. The peace of the nations that God provides is of a different kind. It is a costly peace. As countries have been devastated by bombs and destruction, we as individuals also carry with us the demolishing of dreams, hopes and the craters left by suffering in our lives. Yet God promises us peace in our countries and families where children can sleep without fear, as long as we work in Christian solidarity for justice – not only at national levels, but also the small everyday level of action in our neighbourhoods and communities.

✳ *For all the anonymous women and men who work for peace in our nations, let us pray to God.*

Monday October 26   *Joel 2.23-32 *C*

'You will eat to your heart's content'

A man from Buenos Aires, Argentina, tells us his story: It was the end of the month, and his salary was already gone with the payment of rent, bills, transport and food. He did not have any money left, and there was no food in his house. What was he to do then? He said to himself, 'If I don't have any food to eat, I will offer this situation as a fasting to my Lord.' He decided to go to his church, walking, since he couldn't afford a bus ticket, and when he arrived, he sat there to pray and offer his fasting to God. Suddenly, he saw a plastic bag near one of the walls. After some consideration he decided to open it: it was full of bread. He said, 'God heard my prayers and did not allow me to fast. He fulfilled my needs. Praised be God's Name.' This is a true story, and it reflects the strong faith of many poor people in my country. He ate the bread that a charitable person left in church, and he was satisfied to 'his heart's content'.

Yesterday, we were reflecting on costly peace – the peace with justice of the Reign of God. There is no peace in a nation where a man who works eight hours a day cannot afford to eat. There cannot be peace in nations of the world where as a result of injustice these things are allowed to happen. There is a lesson here from Christians of the poor nations to their brothers and sisters of the 'First World': Are you satisfied? Can you 'eat to your heart's content' as this poor man did? The satisfaction in itself seems to be a very significant blessing of the Lord. How often affluent people seem unsatisfied with everything, and unable to enjoy the simple things of life! At another level, the sin of greed in affluent countries condemns many in the Two-thirds World to poverty and suffering.

✴ **God, give us the gift of gratitude, and the blessing**
  of being satisfied as individuals and nations.

Tuesday October 27   Psalm 65 *C
'The valleys are clothed in wheat'
The *Aymara* people of Latin America are very religious: they see
the presence of God in the mountains where they keep their
animals, in the earth's harvests, in their communal meals and in
the elements – the sun, the moon, the winds and the rain – which
are God's blessings. For the *Aymaras*, God's *shalom,* as
manifested in the prosperous harvests of this Psalm, continues
even after death. For them, life after death consists in families
working the land together, with the eternal blessing of God's
presence in good weather, fertile soil and the rich fruits obtained
through their work. What a lesson for us lies in these beliefs!

The *Aymaras* see their life with God in the midst of their work
as a community, and in the relationship between their efforts and
God's blessings. The key element of their spirituality is
reciprocity. God and God's children work together in permanent
gratitude for what each other gives: children looking after the
goats, the mother blessing the harvest, the father ploughing the
land and God manifesting divine grace and love with good
weather and abundant wheat. This is the precious belief of an
indigenous Latin American people, and the source of the
community's solidarity and mutual responsibility. Blessed is the
nation where people live this way! If we could become more open
to learn from the spirituality of other cultures, we – the nations of
the world – will rediscover the gift of living in harmony with our
neighbours, nature and God.

✴ **God, open our eyes**
  that we may rediscover your will for our nations
  through the spirituality of indigenous peoples.

Wednesday October 28   Ezekiel 13.1-16
'They have misled my people by saying: Peace! when there is no peace'
Religious authorities in Brazil often declare that as a Christian
country, Brazil stands against abortion. Brazilian theologian
Ivonne Gebara, however, has said that 'Brazil is an abortive
society'. She considers the thousands of so-called 'street

children' who die every day through hunger, crime or illness, as children 'aborted' from a society which does not care about them. She speaks with a prophetic voice, denouncing a situation that cannot be silenced any longer.

The true prophets of Israel were what we might call 'ordinary believers', called by God to speak the truth to those in power, even if it was dangerous to do so. Like Dr Gebara and ourselves, they were committed to obeying God as they denounced injustices in their nation and announced a way forward. Meanwhile, other prophets, 'the prophets of the court', constantly compromised with the *status quo*, assuring people with promises of peace which were not real. We, as Christians, are called to exercise a prophetic ministry in our countries without which true peace cannot come. Can a nation be prosperous with all the material and spiritual blessings of God's *Shalom* if it pretends there are no signs of injustice in its midst? Is it possible to exercise Christian ministry without a true report of what is happening in our society?

✳ *If the situation arises, help us, God,*
to speak the truth with power today.

Thursday October 29   *Isaiah 45.1-4*

'I will go before you'

Some years ago, when a delegation of European ministers came to visit a Christian community in Buenos Aires, they found that a group of poor people received them with hospitality (which is characteristic of my people). They offered them *mate* (a traditional tea) and biscuits. One of the ministers asked: 'Which theology do you use in this community?' The people looked puzzled so the minister added, 'I mean, how do you use the Scriptures?' 'Ah', replied the woman, 'First of all, we make a circle while one of us reads the text for the day. After that we ask each other "How do you understand this passage?" and then we go to our work. At night, when we return home, we do the same. We make a circle and read the passage again to see how God guided us through the day. You see, before we start our day, we send God before us, and later we reflect on the way God opened doors for us.'

In the countries of Latin America, people organize themselves in 'Basic Christian Communities' in their neighbourhood, sharing a common life of prayer, Bible study and action. They are an example to the world of how, sending God before us, a nation can start to work together for peace and prosperity.

✻ Pray that we may grow closer to one another as united communities as we work together for peace and justice in our nations.

Friday October 30   *Sirach (Ecclesiasticus) 35.12-20 *C*

Today's text:

'Offer him no bribe, he will not accept it,
    do not put your faith in an unvirtuous sacrifice;
since the Lord is a judge
    who is no respecter of personages.
He shows no respect of personages to the detriment
        of a poor man,
    he listens to the plea of the injured party.
He does not ignore the orphan's supplication,
    nor the widow's as she pours out her story.
Do the widow's tears not run down her cheeks,
    as she cries out against the man who caused them?
The man who with his whole heart serves God
        will be accepted,
    his petitions will carry to the clouds,
The humble man's prayer pierces the clouds,
    until it arrives he is inconsolable,
nor will he desist until the Most High takes notice of him,
    acquits the virtuous and delivers judgement.'

Jerusalem Bible

The prayer of the humble 'pierces the clouds'

She says she came from Huancayo to Lima (Peru). She has three children, but she needed to leave the mountains where money is not necessary (animals and a small farm provide what is needed), because in the confrontation between the army and the guerrillas her husband was killed and she feared for the children. With the frankness and simplicity of many indigenous women she confessed that in her desperation, she considered suicide. She ended up in a small slum in Lima, without money or food and without a single friend or relative to ask for help, but the people of the slum although she did not know it, were part of a Basic Christian Community. The day after her arrival, some neighbours knocked at her door and told her: '*Señora*, without offence, but we gather that you have problems and we would like to help you and your children.' They offered her a small job in the community and in time she became a biblical teacher. The people said that because she had suffered so much, she could interpret

God's word for others who suffer. She says, 'See how things are in my life. The one who suffers understands suffering. Jesus suffered too, and perhaps this is the reason why he is always listening to the cries of suffering people. God never abandons us, but helps us through our brothers and sisters. Even when you are alone, away from your land, God never abandons you' (story from *Paginas 100, December 1989*).

In a nation divided by violence, God listened to the prayer of this widow, through the compassion and resolution of other Christians. The wounds inflicted by political violence are healed by people who, oppressed and poor as the widow, do not hesitate to show their faith in action. Their prayers together with a small job to give her some earnings restored her self-confidence.

✴ *For the whole Church which is experiencing this renewal, and for the renewal of our nation, let us pray to God.*

Saturday October 31   *Revelation 22.1-5*

'The Lord God will be shining on them'

The people who live in Paraguay, the *Guaranies,* have the legend of the *Tierra sin Males* – 'Land without Evil'. The word *males* can be translated as 'evil', 'illness', or any kind of suffering, physical or emotional. When the Spaniards came to the continent, they heard about the legend and decided to explore the area searching for that land of gold and treasures. They were wrong. The 'Land without Evil' of the *Guaranies* was not a city of gold, but a place where God was present and people lived and worked in harmony, praising and blessing God day and night. It was the concept of a land without fear, without hunger, without illness or suffering. Every several years, the *Guaranies* undertook pilgrimages guided by their priests in search of such a land, which they believe was located in their region. These were spiritual pilgrimages and nowadays Christian *Guaranies* have related this legend to the text from Revelation.

Christians in Latin America, therefore, celebrate the liturgy of the Mass of the 'Land without Evil', praying and singing for the presence of God among them now, and in the promised future. For them, this is a journey in which they must remain faithful and hopeful, working in solidarity with each other for the coming of the Reign of God. They believe that the healing of the nations depends on that. The wounds of violence, poverty, oppression and despair require the faith-in-action of Christian people who know that *La Tierra sin Males* awaits us, but we must look for it every day.

245

✳ *That we may not lack courage and hope on our journey, let us pray to the Lord.*

For further reflection or group discussion
- What challenge comes to you from this week's readings, and from the Latin American experience?
- Read again the notes for Thursday and Friday. What is the value of reading the Bible together in community?
- From the last three weeks' study, write your own definition of the Hebrew word, *shalom.*

FOR ACTION
Encourage some of your neighbours and friends to read the Bible with you, and reflect together on its challenges.

ONENESS IN CHRIST
Letter to the Ephesians

Notes based on the Revised English Bible by
Salvador T Martinez

Salvador T Martinez teaches theology and Christian ethics at the McGilvary Faculty of Theology, Payap University in Chiang Mai, Thailand. He was formerly the secretary for theological concerns of the Christian Conference of Asia. He is an ordained minister of the United Church of Christ in the Philippines, sent to the Church of Christ in Thailand as an international associate under the auspices of the Common Global Ministries Board [United Church of Christ (USA) and Disciples of Christ (Christian Church)].

The Epistle to the Ephesians is one of the greatest books of the New Testament. Whether the Apostle Paul wrote it or not, it was written at the author's best. There is a knowledge of God's design and a longing to convey this to his readers. It was God's purpose, he says, from the very beginning of creation to bring all humanity together as one. In Christ, this is brought into fulfilment, and the Church – the one body of Christ – lives the experience of that unity, and is called upon to proclaim it to all humanity. As the instrument of reconciliation, the Church must embody the love and forgiveness of God in Christ in its daily life. It must live in Christ who walked and lived among the people and gave himself on their behalf.

Sunday November 1   *Ephesians 1.1-14*
For God's glory

'Grace' and 'peace' are two words that summarize the message of this epistle. Through God's unmerited love and mercy (grace), he liberates us to a life of fullness (peace) in Christ who is 'himself our peace' (2.14). In the original Greek, verses 3-14 form a single sentence. It is a doxology reciting the mighty acts of God in Christ.

> Blessed be God, who before creation chose us to be
>   God's people and adopted children,
> who liberated us, forgave us and gave us
>   wisdom and insight,

who brings all things into harmony with Christ and
who guarantees our final redemption with the seal
   of the Holy Spirit.

God's great act of salvation spans the past, present and future. It is an act of the triune God: God the Creator, the source of all blessings; Christ Jesus the Son, our liberator and the mediator of God's blessings and the Holy Spirit of promise, the seal and the guarantee of our inheritance and final redemption. Our liberation begins from the gracious will of God and ends in his glory and praise. Everything begins with God and ends in God. To God be the glory and praise.

✳ *To you alone, our God, belongs the glory and the praise.*
   May your name be blessed for ever. Amen

Monday November 2   *Ephesians 1.15-23 *C*

Loving God's people

In a remote village in Thailand lives a woman who lost all members of her family to AIDS. Her first husband, her son-in-law, her son and daughter died in quick succession. As a Christian, she asked the elders of her local church to come and give her daughter a Christian funeral. She waited for more than a day, but the elders did not come. In desperation, she went to the Buddhist monks in her village. They asked no questions, but willingly and gladly performed the last rites for her daughter.

Why do you think the elders refused this young woman a Christian burial? What would you have done in their place? What can we learn from the action of the Buddhist monks?

The writer of today's reading thanked God for the faith of his readers, and the love they bear for all God's people. Would he have said this of the church in that village? Could he say the same of us?

✳ *Lord God, forgive us for failing so often to live up*
   to our faith and the hope that is within us.
   Help us to be worthy of Christ, our Lord. Amen

Tuesday November 3   *Ephesians 2.1-10*

A life of good deeds

Somsri is a very devout religious person. Each morning, at five o'clock, she sits at a street corner with a basket of fresh vegetables and fruits that she carefully picked from her little garden. She waits for the monks to come with their begging bowls and she offers her gifts. The monks pray for her and she goes away contented as she faces a new day. She has fulfilled her daily obligation to 'make merit', an essential part of her religion. Making merit could be a simple act of offering food to the monks or paying for the building of a new temple, all in hope of a better life after death.

Today's passage plainly says that it is by grace through faith that God enters our lives. Salvation is God's gift, not a reward for good deeds. Good deeds, however, are the evidence of the new life God gives us in love, for we are 'created in Christ Jesus for the life of good deeds which God designed for us.'

✳ *Gracious God, help us to show, by our acts*
of love and justice to our fellow human beings,
how grateful we are for your gift of reconciliation. Amen

Wednesday November 4   *Ephesians 2.11-22*

A new community

The apostle begins this section with a description of the former condition of the Gentiles. They were separated from God and from the community of Israel. Their world was without hope and without God. Change came with the coming of the Lord Jesus in their lives. Through their faith in the crucified Christ, they have become united with God and God's people. A new humanity has been created, united in God and with each other.

This new human community is what the Church ought to be. The Church is unity. Unfortunately, despite our Councils of Churches and other attempts to come together, the Church is as divided as ever over many issues. Christ destroyed the barriers of disunity, but we erected new walls of separation based on doctrine, polity, race, caste, nationality, politics and gender. Only when the church can break down these barriers will it be worthy of its name and bring honour to Christ, our mediator and peacemaker.

✳ *God of peace, you have rent the veil that separated*
your people. Do it once more in our midst. Amen

Thursday November 5   *Ephesians 3.1-13*

Joint heirs in Christ

The writer speaks of God's unmerited gift of grace that allowed him to receive God's revelation and the privilege to proclaim it. The word 'secret' is a translation of the Greek word *mysterion* which refers to a truth that was formerly hidden from human understanding but is now revealed. What is the secret? Gentiles are joint heirs with the Jews. They are part of the same body and share the promise made in Christ Jesus. This is the good news! Christ died and rose again so that the whole human family may become one. This was incredible to first-century orthodox Jews who found it difficult to cross racial barriers and get to know people of other cultures.

The inclusion of all people in the love and mercy of God did not happen because the Jews rejected Christ (as some itinerant evangelists would have it). It was always part of God's design. Now it is the Church's responsibility to proclaim the grace of God in its 'infinite variety'. So multicoloured is God's grace, it can take care of any and every situation.

✳ *Confident that Christ has given us access to you,*
O God, we offer ourselves that you may proclaim
through us
the good news of your eternal love for all peoples.
Amen

Friday November 6   *Ephesians 3.14-21*

Rooted in love

A young couple was visited by a team of committed Christians who have dedicated their lives to helping persons living with AIDS in northern Thailand. The team not only helped the couple to cope with their situation, they also helped their family to understand their predicament and to accept and care for them. After the husband died, the team continued to visit the young widow. During one of the visits, she said that she had never known such happiness as she had experienced in their love and concern for herself and her late husband. 'In the midst of this personal and family disaster, I have discovered the meaning of love ... I think it is worth it, don't you?'

When Christ dwells in the hearts of Christians and their lives are rooted and grounded in his love, others will only have praise for God 'who is able through the power which is at work among us to do immeasurably more than all we can ask or conceive' (verse 20).

✳ *O God, help us to be rooted in love*
that we may grasp 'the breadth and length
and height and depth of Christ's love'. Amen

Call for unity

As Jesus earnestly prayed, 'that they may be one, even as we are one' (John 17.11), the writer urgently begs his readers to live in unity and peace. To demonstrate and maintain that unity, they are 'to live up to their calling' by living a life of humility, gentleness, patience and tolerance. Humility springs out of our dependence on God's mercy and grace. Gentleness develops from our kind consideration of the need of others. Patience grows out of supporting and strengthening those who are weak. And tolerance is 'putting up with one another's failings in the spirit of love' (verse 2).

We must relentlessly direct our effort towards unity for there is one body, one spirit, one Lord, one faith, one baptism and one God! Peace and unity are so elusive. Is there anything we can do, however insignificant, to attain it?

'How good and pleasant it is
to live together as brothers (and sisters) in unity!'

Psalm 133.1

✳ *O God, as Christ our Lord prayed, 'that they may be one, as we are one', may that unity come in our time. Amen*

For further reflection or group discussion

- How did we become God's people and for what reason did God make us his people?
- How do you envision a church that is 'worthy of its calling?'
- Identify some problems or needs in your community. Is there anything to which your church can respond?

Full humanity

Christian unity is also a colourful diversity. The members of the one body have differing gifts distributed to them by Christ who 'ascended on high'. This is an apparent reference to Psalm 68.18. There, however, the triumphant conqueror receives the gifts from his subjects. Here, our Lord, the triumphant conqueror, gives the gifts. What a difference!

Christ is said also to have descended 'to the very earth', undoubtedly a reference to his incarnation and humiliation on the cross for the sake of suffering and struggling humanity. It is this

Christ who gives gifts that we may be apostles, prophets, evangelists, pastors and teachers – all for one purpose: 'equip God's people for work in his service, for the building up of the body of Christ' (verse 12). The goal is to attain our full humanity, measured by the standard set by Christ himself. This means that we are called to place ourselves in the very place where Jesus Christ was – in the midst of injustice and suffering and do something to change the situation.

✳ *O God, let your mission fill your children's vision,*
to heal the suffering and help the struggling. Amen

From the hymn 'In the lands of Asia' by Salvador Martinez
(Christian Conference of Asia Hymnal 1990)

In the Lands of Asia

1. In the lands of A – sia, peo – ple are op – pressed;
   man – y cry for jus – tice, beg – ging for some so – lace.
2. In the global village, tears fall on dry fa – ces;
   chil – dren, men and wo – men, hun – gry, dy – ing, hope – less.
3. Everywhere around us fear and ter – ror reign
   peo – ple long for true peace in the light of your face.

Refrain Faster (♩ = c 100)

O God, let your mis – sion fill your chil – dren's vi – sion,
to heal the suff – 'ring and help the strug – gling.

Exodus 6:6-7
Psalm 80:4-7

Words: Salvador T. Martinez, Philippines
Music: CIPANAS; Salvador T. Martinez, Philippines

A new humanity

The members of a united church should live differently. In verses 17-24, the writer lays down the theological basis for this change: the truth of Christ has liberated believers from the power of ignorance and the bondage of falsehood. They have 'learned Christ'. They must now put off the old humanity and, renewed in mind and spirit, put on a new humanity. How should the Christians demonstrate this new nature created in God's likeness?

The writer lists six dos and don'ts to guide us in our new lifestyle: Don't lie, tell the truth; don't let your anger turn bitter, be ready to forgive; don't steal, work hard and give to the needy; don't mouth evil, but use your lips to edify and bless; don't grieve the Holy Spirit of God, don't be spiteful or lose your temper, but be generous and tender-hearted. In short, as God's children, be as God. 'Live in love as Christ loved you, and gave himself up on your behalf' (verse 2).

✶ *Loving God, help us to become like you*
in loving and forgiving. May our daily life
demonstrate the greatness of your love. Amen

Children of light

Most religions use light to symbolize the nature and presence of God and devotion to God: the Jews in the celebration of *Hanukkah*, and Hindus in *Diwali*. In northern Thailand, especially in Chiang Mai and Sukothai, a very festive celebration known as *Loy Krathong* is held during the full moon in November. For days the devotees make floats of various shapes and sizes, decorated with flowers, joss sticks and candles or lanterns. These are floated on the lakes and rivers. Thai Buddhists light the joss sticks and candles and pray for forgiveness of sins. Others pray for love and blessings. During the festival, houses and public buildings are also decorated with candles and tiny lanterns, and fireworks and hot air balloons are set off.

In the Old Testament 'light' is also used to celebrate God's nature and presence. The Gospels refer to our Lord as 'light' (John 1.9) and the Nicene Creed calls Christ the 'light of light'.

How does the writer use the symbol of light in this passage? Why are Christians called 'light'? As children of light we are known by our moral fruit. By our acts of kindness, justice and truth we expose the works of darkness.

* *O God, light of light, help us*
  to live in such a way that we may shed your light
  on our fellow human beings. Amen

Blessed be God

'Speak to one another in psalms, hymns and songs; sing and make music from your heart to the Lord ...'

Blest be God who forever lives,
whose reign lasts through eternity;
God the Lord, merciful and just,
loves and heals those who repent.

The oppressed, God lifts, salves their hurts;
pays them heed, strength'ning bodies and hearts;
calling humankind out of fear;
God is Lord for evermore.

O eternal God, be with us,
lift the poor from their misery;
give back dignity to all who trust
in the words and deeds of Christ.
Salvador T Martinez – From Sound the Bamboo, CCA Hymnal
1990 (Christian Conference of Asia, Hong Kong)

* *In the name of our Lord Jesus Christ, we give you thanks*
  every day for everything, O God our Creator. Amen

Created equal

These passages have been used to justify the exploitation and subjugation of women, children and slaves. Liberation movements in our time have opposed the dehumanizing treatment of some sectors of our society, and rightly so. Any form of human oppression and exploitation is contrary to the will and purpose of God. We are all created in the image of God. We are equal before God. Moreover, as believers in Christ, we are united as one body in Christ.

How do we interpret these passages on submission today? It must be emphasized that authority is ordained by God, hence those who exercise it must do so responsibly. Unity in the church must be reflected in unity at home. Where unity in the church is based on the principle of self-giving love and respect, the harmonious relationship between husband and wife needs also to be established on mutual love and honour. We submit to God's ordained authority in reverence to Christ who humbled himself and became a servant.

✳ *O Creator God, may we learn to respect one another and to discern authority that comes from you. Amen*

Mutual respect

Continuing his exhortation regarding human relationships, the writer focuses attention on the relationships between parents and children, and between employers and employees. These relationships are based on the principle of mutual respect and equal responsibilities to each other, for all belong to God. In the awareness of God, there must be love and respect for each other.

Children are to obey and honour their parents; parents are to love their children and bring them up in the awareness of God. Employees are to be responsible to their employers with humility; employers must show the same honour towards their employees. Today, with so many reported cases of child abuse, child labour, sex tourism and child prostitution, discrimination in the workplace and other indignities, the words of the apostle are ever more pertinent.

✳ *God of justice and mercy, help us to have a clear understanding of our relationship with one another. Amen*

Armour of God

Dr Pisut Pornsumrichok, named in 1992 as 'Outstanding Rural Doctor of Thailand', resigned rather than be a 'dead hero'. The conscientious young doctor worked among poor Thai farmers and ethnic hill-tribespeople. He went beyond just healing sick bodies and led the villagers in their protests against the use of chemical pesticides, distribution of illegal drugs among the young people, hazardous lignite mining, illegal logging and general corruption. Those influential people whose vested interests were affected by his community involvement threatened Dr Pisut and his family with death. It is always risky to do what is right.

The forces of evil that led our Lord to the cross are still at work and will be against us. If we walk in the steps of our Lord, we should not expect anything less than the treatment he received. They will not stop until we are silenced. The apostle, therefore, enjoins us to put on the full armour of God. Only then can we stand our ground against the powers of evil.

✳ *O God, help us to speak boldly as it is our duty*
   and may 'God's grace be with all who love
   our Lord Jesus Christ with undying love.' Amen

For further reflection or group discussion

● What attitudes and actions characterize the work of your church in your community?
● Is there unity in your church? If not, what are the reasons for its disunity? How do you think your church can overcome them?

FOR ACTION

There are organizations like the World Council of Churches, the Christian Conference of Asia and other regional church organizations that are trying to promote unity among the churches and peace with justice in the world. Study their aims and purposes. Is your church related to them? What can your church do to support them?

CHRIST COMES IN THE FLESH
1, 2 & 3 John

Notes based on the Revised English Bible by
Jan Sutch Pickard

Jan Sutch Pickard is a writer and Editor of Connect, a Methodist magazine linking faith and action, and has lived in Nigeria, Notting Hill in London and New Mills in Derbyshire. She is a Methodist local preacher and a member of the ecumenical Iona Community.

These three 'letters' are not the most familiar part of the New Testament to most of us! Probably the strongest association is between 1 John 4.7-21, and the beginning of John's Gospel. They are often read together. Although the letters are attributed to the Gospel writer, and so linked with 'the beloved disciple', there are many reasons why this could be questioned. The author, if it is indeed a single person, does not give the autobiographical detail that Paul does. He is identified as an 'Elder', a leader of the Early Church but, if he was a local leader, it is not clear why he writes authoritatively to congregations elsewhere.

The purpose of these texts is to keep young Christians on the right path. They offer a mixture of encouragement, warnings and a style of argument which is repetitive and rhetorical rather than reasoned. Sometimes what is said seems contradictory. Sometimes we are more aware of power struggles in the church than the word of God. And yet they contain some powerful images (e.g. 'walking in the light', 'crossing over from death to life') which still have relevance to us today.

Useful reading *The Johannine Epistles* by Ruth B Edwards (New Testament Guides, Sheffield Academic Press)

Sunday November 15   1 John 1.1-4
Seeing with our own eyes
How do we know when a message is urgent? It may be the way that people speak ... 'Listen!' ... their tone of voice or their body language, the way they come into a room, or do not waste time on conventional greetings. If the message is in a letter we may

guess from the kind of envelope, the handwriting, a first-class stamp, or the word 'URGENT'.

These few verses convey such urgency. Although this is called a 'letter' of John it does not begin like one. Compare Paul's epistles, which begin with greetings and are addressed to specific people or groups. Scholars have various theories about why 1 John is this way: it may be a different kind of document, maybe a tract sent round like a circular letter. Or we could compare it to a sermon or a handbook.

That doesn't take away the tremendous urgency of these first few verses, the sense of a group of people who have experienced something they must share, a first-hand, eye-witness, hands-on experience. It is as though they have come into the room where we are, saying 'Listen!'

The theme of 'the Word which gives life' links this letter with John's Gospel. Here it means both the Word made flesh – Jesus – and the life-bringing message about Jesus.

✳ *Life-giving Word, at work in our lives,*
help us to find the words to share with others –
what we have heard and seen,
what we have touched
and what touches us most deeply. Amen

Monday November 16   *1 John 1.5-10*

Doing the truth

The urgent message continues: 'God is light, and in him there is no darkness at all.' Light has many meanings – glory, guidance, revelation. Here it is used to mean primarily 'goodness'. God's entire goodness is contrasted with our sinfulness, the shadow side of human nature.

'In him is no darkness at all' is not about black as a colour, particularly not a skin colour. Sometimes we do use a primitive symbolism linking colour and moral qualities, e.g. when the villain in a cowboy film is the one with a black hat, or when we use a phrase like 'black-list'. This may reinforce racism, without our being fully aware of it. But the darkness here is something different: total absence of light, the places where light cannot penetrate and so bring change and hope.

At this point the text becomes like a sermon. It emphasizes the contrast between God and ourselves: it repeats the warning against self-deception and hypocrisy (verses 6, 8, 10). But it also repeats the promise of forgiveness through Jesus (verses 7, 9) and of hope for those who 'do the truth'. The Greek word for 'truth', *aletheia,* in this context describes genuineness, reliability, integrity. John's Gospel often associates this word with those qualities in Jesus. Here they relate to members of the Christian community, and are reminiscent of a similar Hebrew phrase which means 'to act loyally'.

Do we 'do the truth'?

✳ *Pray for the wisdom and integrity to do so.*

Tuesday November 17　　　　　　　　　　　　　　*1 John 2.1-8*

Seeing the light

Outside a college in Birmingham the first snowflakes of winter floated down. Some of the students rushed to gaze in wonder, to try to catch and even taste them. Coming from Africa, they knew about snow from textbooks, but had never experienced its icy beauty at first-hand.

Have you had a similar experience? We may know in theory that the earth is round but can still be amazed by pictures of the earth from space. We may have been told that moisture in the air causes refraction of sunlight, so that the different colours of the prism appear together, but that is not the same as the wonder, after a thunderstorm, of seeing a rainbow appear in the sky.

As 1 John, sounding more and more like a sermon, contrasts sinfulness and forgiveness, obedience and disobedience, there is a reminder that much older traditions and rules for life took on the force of fresh commands and overwhelming insights, when revealed through the teaching and life of Jesus.

✳ *God, we see you in a new light, and are filled with wonder.*
Theory is less challenging than reality:
it was easier to keep our eyes closed,
without risking being amazed by your love.
But we have seen you in Jesus.
The darkness is passing away;
the true light is already shining. Amen

Wednesday November 18　　　　　　　　　　　　　*1 John 2.9-17*

Walking in the light

The house was in darkness. The light switch was on the far side of the kitchen. The householder crossed the room cautiously. But her guest bumped into the table and fell over a stool before the room was flooded with light. The darkness created problems for both of them – for a few moments they were virtually blind. But one of them knew the layout of the room.

The contrast between darkness and light – a major theme in 1 John – is part of the mystery of God's nature: 'There is in God (some say) A deep but dazzling darkness' wrote Henry Vaughan, in his powerful poem 'The Night'. Our trusting sense of God's presence, even in darkness, can enable us to 'walk in the light'.

The idea of knowing God comes over strongly in the next few verses addressed to three groups within the Christian community ('children', 'fathers' and 'young men'), and repeated for emphasis. The letter reflects the Jewish tradition of a religious community with a male leadership. For us today, the 'children' who need to hear the message must mean the whole people of God: women, men, old and young.

What is also relevant for us today is the strong message that knowing, and loving God and walking in God's way, are much harder when we 'trip over' material things. And we cannot claim to be 'doing the truth' if we hate our fellow Christians.

✳ *Pray for grace to see God in darkness and light –*
and in other people.

Thursday November 19   *1 John 2.18-29*
Lies and truth
What does the phrase 'the common life' mean to you?

Earlier in this letter (1.3, 7) is a description of the community of those who believe in God, revealed in Jesus, and who live in God's way. But by the time this letter was written, some had already left that community, because of disagreements. They were now denying that Jesus was the Christ. The writer condemns them as 'the antichrist', enemies of the truth.

Some religious groups still do this today – judging and condemning those with whom they disagree. The strength of the condemnation here probably reflects the precarious existence of the early Christian community.

By contrast, those who believe are seen as blessed by God with understanding. Anointing with oil is one sign of blessing and the word for such oil, *chrism,* comes from the same root as 'Christ'. In Old Testament times, oil was used for consecrating kings, priests, prophets. The Early Church used it in the rite of baptism. It is a metaphor for the work of the Holy Spirit, flowing into our lives, transforming us.

✳ *Spirit of Truth, touch our lives,*
bless us with understanding of all God's ways.
May we be a sign to others,
unashamed of our faith, confident in Christ. Amen

Friday November 20   *1 John 3.1-8*

God's children

'She looks just like her mother.'

'Ah, but look, that's her father's nose!'

The admiring friends and family round a new-born baby look for and find inherited likenesses. As the child grows, they will see the parent not only in features but in smile, voice, behaviour.

The first letter of John constantly addresses its readers and hearers as 'children'. This not only gives the tone of a teacher or pastor but also is a reminder that all the faithful are God's children – not recognized as such by society at large, because its members have no picture of God in their minds. Christians may feel they have not earned the privilege of being called God's children. But that in itself is a sign to us of God's love. In turn, we can be signs of that love to each other by 'dwelling in him' and by doing what is right.

This message was sent to a community living in daily expectation of the Second Coming, the *parousia*. The same Greek word (meaning 'to be made clear') is used for that looked-for event when Christ will appear again; for the discovery of our family likeness, as we grow in stature in Christ; and for that revelation which has already happened – of God's love in the earthly life of Jesus.

✳ *Loving God, you call us your children.*
Help us to understand the privilege,
live up to the responsibility and grow into your likeness,
through the example of Jesus Christ,
our Brother and Saviour. Amen

Saturday November 21   *1 John 3.9-17*

Crossing over from death to life

Have you listened to a news broadcast or looked at newspaper headlines today? How preoccupied we are with death – violent, accidental, tragic. The fear and fascination and threat of death has been a constant theme since the dawn of history, since people began to tell stories about human passions and actions, and to ask: where is God in all this? Read Genesis 4.1-12.

The story of Cain and Abel takes us through jealousy, anger, treachery, violence, guilt, punishment. At what point could it have had a different outcome? What difference would love have made? At what points in our own lives would love make a difference?

✳ *Meditation on an open newspaper*
Maker of the world, what a mess we have made of it!
I look into the abyss. Where is the hope?
What are human beings doing to each other –
Christians even – killing each other, condemning, asking
'Am I my brother's keeper?'
Am I?
I can't cope with these crises,
though I am fascinated by their horror,
and sometimes I am part of the problem.
But how can I bear the pain of other people?
How can you?
You did.
Bearer of the world's pain, Christ,
you gave your life for us: building a bridge over the abyss.
Help me to cross over from death to life.

For further reflection or group discussion
● At what points has this text from the Early Church felt most relevant to your struggle to be a better Christian today?
● Which phrases have stayed with you? Why?

Sunday November 22   *1 John 3.18-24*
Beyond words
Say the word 'love', in more than one language if you can – it's easy to say. Write the word 'love' – it doesn't take long. Think of the kind of greetings' card that has the word 'love' on it. What kind(s) of love do such cards celebrate?

Now think of a hymn with the word in. What does 'love' mean here? How often are we likely to use the word in a church service?

How many times does it appear in 1 John 3? Count, in your own version.

When we repeat a word often it can become meaningless!

Now think of an **action** which for you would express one meaning of love, maybe the central meaning. It could be: *gazing into the eyes of someone special, without words; choosing a special gift; giving food to a starving child; opening a door to welcome a stranger; offering the Peace in worship to someone with whom you have disagreed; embracing someone in distress.*

Sometimes **words** can run away with a preacher. Here verses 19, 20 and 21 appear to contradict themselves, in what they say about conscience. Working out what these particular words are about may be less useful than holding on to 'our certainty that God dwells in us' – summed up in a picture of love in action.

Actions can speak more clearly than words.

✱ *Recall* one of the actions that you thought of earlier between the two asterisks* above, and *reflect* on it.

Monday November 23   1 John 4.1-6

Testing the spirits

Yesterday's passage, about God's love, said 'our certainty ... comes from the Spirit he has given us'.

But in the next breath we are told 'do not trust every spirit'. This reminds us that this very young church was already experiencing divisions. Both Old and New Testaments have plenty of references to 'false prophets'. There is nothing new here. Leadership, lifestyle, teaching can still be sources of conflict among Christians today.

We cannot be sure what these particular divisions were about. The writer of this letter, however, is clear about the best way of testing for truth (4.2-3). The true spirit will acknowledge Jesus, that in him God came to share our human lives.

So is this about more words, statements of faith, formulas that clarify our position on one side or the other?

Or is it about love in action: the kind of picture on which we reflected yesterday, but this time focused in the person of Jesus Christ? (See also 4.14-16.)

✱ *Reflect* on your picture of Jesus, a human being,
   'the Word made flesh'.

No room for fear or hate

These are well-loved words, and they speak for themselves, about God's love, shown in Christ, witnessed and reflected in the life of the Christian community: 'everyone who loves is a child of God and knows God'. When we read on, that 'the unloving know nothing of God', it is easy to think of groups of people – like the Roman occupying forces when this was written, like war criminals in our own century – whose actions seem to put them far outside this circle of love.

But there are challenges to the Church, to us. Read verse 18. Are you afraid? Of what? Are there ways that we, as a Christian community, do not help each other with such fears – for instance the fear that many feel about failure, or death? How could we face these fears together, in faith? 'Perfect love banishes fear'. What does this say to you?

Read verse 20. Do you think it is possible that someone could do this? Has it ever been true of you? What can we do about it? How can we help each other? How can God help us?

✷ *In your prayers give thanks for God's love,*
shown in Jesus, who shared our human lives;
ask for help in overcoming
fear and hatred, part of the human condition.

The testimony in our heart

Have you ever had to testify for legal reasons? It is a serious business, making a statement and swearing that you are telling 'the truth, the whole truth and nothing but the truth.' This text tackles the question, 'How do we know this is the truth?'

The answer comes in several parts: through our experience – of God's love, as God's children; through our faith – believing that Jesus is the Son of God; and through God's evidence. Verse 9 says, 'We accept human testimony, but surely the testimony of God is stronger.'

God's threefold evidence is given in verse 8: 'The Spirit, the water and the blood'. What aspects of the Gospel story do these words evoke? Think of the annunciation, the birth of Jesus, his baptism, ministry ('The Spirit of the Lord is upon me'), his death and resurrection and the events of Pentecost: you will find the water and blood of both birth and death, and the Spirit at work throughout.

Because there are three aspects, some scholars read into this an early reference to the Trinity. Possibly more important for us now is that, while God's evidence is seen to be overwhelming, we are reminded that we have 'the testimony in our own heart'. We have heard and seen the evidence. Do we believe it?

✳ *God of love, may we believe the evidence of that love*
which surrounds us on every side.
Lord of life, may our lives bear witness to your love
that the world may believe. Amen

Thursday November 26   *1 John 5.13-21*

God listens to us

We have come to the end of this first 'letter' of John. It does not end with the kind of 'signing off', commendations, personal greetings and blessings which we find in Paul's letters. More like a sermon, it ends with exhortations, statements of faith and reassurance. Finally, there is a verse which almost sounds like an afterthought!

As we noticed on 15 November, a sense of urgency comes through strongly, as does a pessimistic belief in the power and extent of evil in the world (verse 19) – which is balanced by the presence of 'God's family'. Several points are repeated from earlier in the letter, but there is a new theme: the value of prayer (verses 14-16).

Two kinds of prayer are mentioned: petition and intercession. The first introduced with the helpful statement 'we can approach God with this confidence'. The second, though, raises a question: what do we do if someone is committing a deadly sin – should we still pray for them? Is that still a real question for us today? And what if someone has sinned? Are they beyond prayer? Have you ever argued with fellow Christians about whether we should pray for those who commit crimes as well as for their victims? What arguments were put forward on each side? What do you think? What would – or do – you do?

✳ *Pray for someone you know who is involved in, or*
    tempted to, wrong-doing.
Put him or her, and yourself, with your sinfulness,
    in God's hands.

Living by the truth

This second letter raises many questions. It seems much more personal, opening with what seems to be a greeting to a specific (unnamed?) person. The warmth with which it begins is tempered by formality and then by warnings. Maybe this letter is not quite what it seems.

Some scholars have questioned whether it is in fact a 'Lady chosen by God' who is being addressed, or whether she stands for the Church (just as we talk about 'Mother Church'). Since greetings are included from her 'sister', this would suggest two local churches, rather than the Church as a whole. Other scholars have suggested that both the Greek words translated as 'Lady' and 'Chosen by God' could in fact be proper names. So a lot is unclear. But it is quite possible that a woman (like her sister elsewhere) was the leader of a house church. We have examples of such women leaders from the letters of Paul, and Acts.

Her 'children' would have been the congregation, rather than her family. The writer of the letter is concerned about these 'children'. Some are taking initiatives he considers unsafe (verse 9). They need to be warned not to welcome people whose teaching is not sound. The letter reads like a struggle to impose control and orthodoxy. This is emphasized by the formality of verse 3, which adds to a straightforward Christian greeting a weighty 'church-leader-ish' statement. This feels a long way from the Gospel of John, wrestling with the reality of God's love and its relevance to everyone.

But maybe there are echoes here of the way that Christians today communicate: how some are within the fold and others excluded; where power is felt to lie in the Church; and whether we can control the Spirit!

✳ ***Dear God, give us the grace to listen to good advice
and to take instruction from our elders; but above all,
help us to hear what you are saying to our hearts.
Amen***

Peace be with you

The shortest of the 'letters' of John, this is easiest to read as a real communication. It is to a named person, Gaius, and commends another, Demetrius. In the same community is a troublemaker, Diotrephes. The problem seems to be a pastoral one, rather than an issue of doctrine. Most of the Christians are practising hospitality in a way that has greatly helped other Christians passing through. Diotrephes refuses to do so, discourages others and is generally sowing discord. It is a clear case for action. Meanwhile the message is 'follow good examples not bad ones'.

The style is similar to many short personal letters written in Greek at this time. But where they would have ended with a phrase meaning 'keep well', this uses the word 'peace' (verse 14) – the Hebrew equivalent of course would be *Shalom*. And that is what the writer of the letter desires for the congregation to which he is writing: God's just peace, and wholeness of life.

✳ *Jesus, risen from the dead, you greeted the disciples:*
'Peace be with you, Shalom.'
When we gather as your disciples today
may we offer each other
the shalom of hospitality,
the shalom of hope,
the shalom of acceptance,
the shalom of fear overcome,
the shalom of challenge to change,
the shalom of living the truth. Amen

For further reflection or group discussion

What does *Shalom* mean to you, in your personal life? In the life of your Church community? In the life of your nation? You may like to refer back to the notes and readings for October 11-31.

ADVENT 1 –
Awake! Christ comes to judge

Notes based on the Revised English Bible by
Edmund Banyard

Edmund Banyard is a minister and former Moderator of the General Assembly of the United Reformed Church (UK). He is a committed ecumenist and currently edits All Year Round for the Council of Churches for Britain and Ireland.

With the season of Advent we are once again reminded, not only that the God who came in Jesus will come again at the end of all things, but that he is ever coming and may indeed come this very day. So amid all the other preparations of these busy weeks, we take time to ask ourselves afresh how ready we are to receive this God who can break in so unexpectedly, and what such coming may mean for our daily living.

1st Sunday in Advent, November 29   *Isaiah 2.1-5 *C*

Grounds for hope in evil days

This is a glorious vision, but one far removed from the reality of the world we know. Isaiah's world, however, was no better and he condemns the very people who bring expensive offerings to the Temple for their greed and the trickery, bribery and strong-arm tactics through which they oppress the weak and leave the poor ever poorer.

Isaiah warned of judgement and retribution, but even as he did so he saw this vision of a different quality of living and foretold a day when all peoples would be drawn to God's house, longing to learn God's ways and to accept his justice.

No doubt there were those then, as now, who would think of this as unattainable 'pie in the sky', but Isaiah has no doubt that this is the goal God has set for humanity. He calls his people not only to grasp the vision and make it their own, but also (verse 5) actively to collaborate with God in bringing that day into being, in working to turn the vision into reality. Are we not in our own age called to do the same?

✳ *Lord, give us grace*
to make the Advent hope our own,
and to play our part
in transforming vision
into reality.

Beware the voice of the godless

For the benefit of readers who do not have access to the Apocrypha, here is today's text:

'Come then, let us enjoy the good things while we can, and make full use of the creation, with all the eagerness of youth. Let us have costly wines and perfumes to our heart's content, and let no flower of spring escape us. Let us crown ourselves with rosebuds before they can wither. Let none of us miss his share of good things that are ours; who cares what traces our revelry leaves behind? This is the life for us; it is our birthright.

'Down with the poor and honest man! Let us tread him under foot; let us show no mercy to the widow and no reverence to the grey hairs of old age. For us let might be right! Weakness is proved to be good for nothing. Let us lay a trap for the just man; he stands in our way, a check to us at every turn; he girds at us as law-breakers, and calls us traitors to our upbringing. He knows God, so he says; he styles himself "the servant of the Lord". He is a living condemnation of all our ideas. The very sight of him is an affliction to us, because his life is not like other people's, and his ways are different. He rejects us like a base coin, and avoids us and our ways as if we were filth; he says the just die happy, and boasts that God is his father' (NEB).

This is the voice of those who have no faith in God, acknowledge no moral law, and see nothing in life but grabbing, whilst they have opportunity, all that can be grabbed. In contrast we may read in verse 23, 'But God created man imperishable, and made him the image of his own eternal self' (REB).

How little in some essential respects has the world changed. This could be a voice from our own time. 'Let us take and enjoy all the good things we can; might is right.' Few would say it quite so blatantly of course, but it is the philosophy by which many shape their lives and it lies behind much that we read in our papers, or view on our television screens.

An essential part of the Advent message is 'Be alert, be on your guard.' What have we to be most on guard against? The temptation to do things which are obviously wrong, or the creeping evil of this way of thinking, hardly noticed at the time, working its way in through tiny chinks in our defences, undermining our moral standards, dulling our own ability to distinguish between right and wrong?

✳ *Lord, whenever we are in danger of being possessed*
  by the selfish materialism of our time,
  remind us again
  that your way
  is a way of loving self-giving.

Tuesday December 1   *Matthew 24.36-44 *C*

The Lord may come today

You surely will have had the experience of feverishly preparing for an examination or an inspection, pulling out every stop to make the best impression and then relaxing when it is all over. The coming of the Son of Man, however, will not be like that; it will happen without any advance warning.

Nevertheless we shall still miss the immediacy of the message if we project our expectation of Christ's coming on to some future event and fail to consider its implications for our present living. The essential message is that the Lord may come today!

Whilst it is an article of our faith that Jesus is ever present through the Holy Spirit, are there not times when he confronts us with a particular challenge? In a hot, dry land Jesus spoke of giving a refreshing drink in his name. What might be the parallel challenge which could confront us? And if we are suddenly faced with a need we can do something about, is that not a coming of the Son of Man?

✳ *Lord, if you confront me today*
  in one of your needy ones,
  let me not be blind to your coming
  or unwilling to respond.

Wednesday December 2   *1 Peter 4.7-11*

Above all, love!

The Church of the first century had a sense of urgency. Christians were called to live each moment as fully as it could be lived to the glory of God, but what did this mean in practice?

The foundation of Christian living, writes Peter, is controlled and sober lives. Taken by itself this might suggest rather 'buttoned-up' personalities; but in the next sentence we are urged above all else to maintain the fervour of loving behaviour.

At first sight the loving behaviour encouraged here is centred on a small community – 'your love for one another'; but if we are going to love in the wider world, our loving relationships have to be rooted in the family and the church we know. It is all too easy to take those closest to us for granted, or even give them a wide berth if relationships have for any reason become soured. Love which starts in our own family, our own church; love that is ready to work away at difficult situations and goes on caring for those close at hand even when they hurt us, is much more likely to be able to reach across barriers to embrace some of Christ's other needy ones.

✳ *Lord, help me to love as you loved,*
 and if ever I am tempted
 to say I've had enough of someone,
 remind me that you have never said that about me.

Thursday December 3   Luke 12.4-8

In the hands of a caring God

Live fearlessly, says Jesus, but that is easier said than done; what is more, those who manage to go through life without apparently worrying about anything can be pretty heartless people. But look a little closer at this short passage, and surely what we are being urged to do is to face our fears and realize there is a limit to the worst that evil can do to us.

These few verses are particularly addressed to people who are facing, or likely to be facing, persecution; and verse 8 affirms that Jesus will stand by those who remain faithful, come what may.

There is also a message for those of us who are free from persecution but troubled in other ways. There are other fears which can threaten our loyalty to Christ, which may eat away at and undermine our faith. So for all of us, here is encouragement to face whatever it is that we fear most, in the confidence that we are held in the strong grasp of a loving God.

✳ *You know my fears, Lord,*
 big or small,
 real or imagined,
 you know the harm they can do to me.

Help me to hold to you in the midst of them,
to trust your love
and to face them in your strength.

Friday December 4   Romans 13.11-14 *C

A time of crisis

Paul is here writing about how Christians should live each and every day, yet 'crisis' implies a time when hard facts have to be faced and hard choices made. It can suggest considerable tension. Are we then to live under constant strain? How could we hope to keep it up? Sooner or later it would surely become too much for us and we would snap, fall apart.

For Jesus, most of the days of his earthly ministry must have been critical days, yet he never comes over as tense or strained. His strength was in the quiet times he managed to win out of a tremendously demanding schedule, as when he slipped away from Simon Peter's house in the early morning before anybody else was stirring (Mark 1.35).

Because each day will bring its own particular challenge we need to be prepared, not by being all tensed up, but by being properly relaxed; relaxed because we have committed ourselves afresh into the hands of the Almighty, thought quietly about what God may want of us and sought in advance the strength to meet whatever challenge the day may bring.

✳ *Lord, help me to be quietly alert,*
ready to meet whatever the coming hours may hold,
but let me also be at peace with myself
in the confidence that you will be with me in all things.

Saturday December 5   Matthew 25.31-46

The ultimate test

This story was already well-known long before Jesus used it. Those who kept the many regulations of the religious law were sheep, the rest were goats. If you were sure that you were a sheep it was a very comforting story, spiced by the knowledge that something nasty was likely to happen to folks you didn't much fancy.

Jesus, however, turned the story on its head. In his version those who thought they were safe are rejected, whilst those who were sure they were going to be rejected find they are accepted after all. Everybody is surprised; why should this be? The answer is simple and devastating. In the end it is not the outward forms of religion that matter; it is the way we have behaved towards other human beings and especially the most needy.

During this first week in Advent we have been reminded that we are in the hands of a loving God who wants us to live lovingly. There is a judgement, but there isn't a built-in pass and failure rate. Indeed, God's will as seen in our reading on Advent Sunday is that all should ultimately come to be at home in his Kingdom, a Kingdom of love.

✳ *Loving Lord,*
blow upon the sparks of love
in my own heart
and kindle a flame
in which others may see you
and be glad.

For further reflection, group discussion and ACTION

Looking back over your life, do you identify any specific occasions when the Lord may have come and you failed to recognize him? Are there any steps you might take which would help to increase future awareness?

ADVENT 2 –
What will endure?

Notes based on the Good News Bible by
Desmond Gilliland

Desmond Gilliland is an Irish Methodist minister, now retired. He served formerly as a missionary in China and Hong Kong. In Ireland, as well as pastoral ministry, he has been chaplain to college students, secretary of committees on Social Responsibility and World Development, and has been active in ecumenical concerns.

In 1921, in his poem 'The Second Coming', W B Yeats wrote of things falling apart, and of a centre which would not hold secure. T S Eliot, likewise, in 1922, asked what roots would clutch in the stony rubbish of the waste lands. After almost three-quarters of a troubled century since then, questions have multiplied: old structures of society have been swept away, and old certainties deeply doubted. In these readings, we are at one with Eliot in his poem 'Journey of the Magi' as we seek for enduring guidelines on the wise men's troubled road.

---

*Bible Sunday (2nd in Advent), December 6   Isaiah 11.1-10 *C*
What will endure? – Faith, hope and love

As we search for enduring values in this week's readings, we need to remind ourselves on this Bible Sunday that no passage is complete in itself, but is a facet of truth supported by the authority of Bible teaching as a whole.

Isaiah's wonderful, beautiful song was sung in the face of the overwhelming force of the besieging Assyrian army. Can we, besieged by secular forces contemptuous of the defences of the City of God, find in his song sure guidelines to make our own answer? First, as St Paul says, there *are* three things that last for ever – faith, hope and love. With Isaiah's love for his people, and his faith and shining hope in God, we cannot merely endure, but sing!

Secondly, we can look like Isaiah for a *leader* inspired by God. In the Old Testament, and in Christian history, God is continually raising up leaders who, like Isaiah himself, give enduring strength to God's people. At the centre of all is Jesus our Lord, the author and perfector of our faith. Thirdly, the song enshrines the Bible's enduring vision of a *community* of justice, love and peace.

✴ *Lord, I have made thy word my choice,*
  My lasting heritage.   *Isaac Watts (1674-1748)*

Monday December 7   *Isaiah 35.1-10 *C*
What will endure? – Vision
One thing which has endured is on my desk before me: my father's copy of George Adam Smith's great commentary on Isaiah, dated 1911, the year he entered the ministry. Still more lasting is the authority of its wise scholarship and matchless prose, but even that cannot compete with this enduring testimony from Isaiah himself, 2500 years ago!

Twenty years on from yesterday's reading, the situation had got far worse. The new king had not lived up to Isaiah's hope. In Jerusalem people were starving. The enemy was overwhelming. National hopes were shattered. Only God himself could bring a new age. And what a vision Isaiah has of a universal age of peace. How does this relate to further invasive erosion of our own society? In the UK recently, the Archbishop of Canterbury said that we are living in a post-modernist world of black and depressing relativism, and in a survey of 14-15 year olds 60% said that no one had any right to tell them what was right or wrong. Isaiah records even more desperate times, but sprinkled through the darkness are shining verses of faith. In today's passage, the glimpses come together in a poet's vision of essential reality.

✴ *All work and wisdom begins in dreams. We must see our*
  Utopias before we build our cities.   *George Adam Smith*

Tuesday December 8   *Proverbs 1.20-33; 2.20-22*
What will endure? – Wisdom
Despite the prophet's legitimate exaggeration in Isaiah 11, lions, leopards, bears and wolves do not forsake their instincts and coexist with calves, goats, cows and lambs in a vegetarian society! Their *instincts* decide their behaviour. It is human beings who have to make moral and rational choices. Wisdom is about having the insight to make such choices and having the character and will to implement them. We can give *enduring* quality to such decisions only if we stay close to God whose wisdom is infinite and whose nature and will are perfect and good.

The seven deadly sins – pride, anger, envy, lust, gluttony, greed and sloth – invade our area of wise choices. They act like *pseudo instincts* causing us to act on unwise and evil impulses. Other pseudo-instinctive impulses – like tribalism, sectarianism or nationalism – invade our society, as in Northern Ireland, the Balkans or Israel, creating irrational and sub-human division and strife. For enduring wisdom we must turn to God.

✷ *My mind I give thee – a farthing candle only*
By which to read the thousand books of God.
Before I read but one, it flickers, and the dark is lonely
Thou art the light to read by; Thou the truth I sought.

Wednesday December 9   *Malachi 3.1-5*

What will endure? – Justice and mercy

We might wonder, at first, what facet of enduring reality may be found in this three-page broadsheet by 'The Messenger', an anonymous writer of long ago. In fact, it is exceedingly relevant to religious churchgoers like ourselves! It is written *from* a settled religious community about the danger of confining religion to a churchly context. The Jews had been passionately committed to restoring the Temple but, when it was rebuilt, the prophetic passion for a just society began to be replaced by the comfortable rhythm of their worship. Lacking the old ethical dynamic, worship itself tended to become slack and formal. The Messenger – the *Malachi* – calls on his readers and on ourselves both to improve the quality of worship and to restore the vision of justice and mercy for which the church and its people exist.

This book is full of references and phrases which have been incorporated into hymns and religious oratorios. But its special importance is in foretelling the ministry of another 'messenger'. Tradition has linked these words with John the Baptist who, in his preparation for Jesus, challenged the religious formalism of his day and pointed to standards of morality which endure.

✷ *I am the Lord, and I do not change. And so you, the descendants of Jacob, are not yet completely lost.*

Malachi 3.6

Thursday December 10   *Matthew 3.1-12 *C*

What will endure? – Basic religion

St Matthew's Gospel is just overleaf in the Bible from the book of Malachi, and here we see Malachi's prophecy fulfilled in the person of John the Baptist, the Messenger, the 'Elijah' who prepares the way of the Lord. Indeed John fulfils the vision of all the prophets in his call to righteousness. Verse 3 of today's reading explicitly says, 'John was the man the prophet Isaiah was talking about.'

It is hard to think of any Old Testament prophets save as people of simple or austere lives. The same pattern appears in Christian saints like St Francis, or in the Desert Fathers. John is back to simple, enduring, basic religion, without the false props of the Pharisees' religiosity, the comfortable priestliness of the Sadducees, the violent nationalism of the Zealots, the plain badness of tax collectors and soldiers, or the softness of our own consumer society.

Jesus' message was more rounded, but he endorses the enduring **rightness** of John's message by being himself baptized by John in the Jordan (verses 13-17; see also Luke 7.24-28).

✶ *Reflect – John stands at the gateway to Christmas, pointing not to a shopping spree, but to a new commitment to what is real.*

Friday December 11   *Hebrews 12.18-29*

What will endure? – Judgement

Judgement is an enduring reality. It may be a judgement of approval or of condemnation. A judged society would be one in which the good but unjustly despised people, like Isaiah's Suffering Servant, would find their true place, while the evil, however powerful, would be removed. This dual nature of judgment runs like a thread through all Bible teaching. We are all under judgement – I, as I write; you, as you read. The Ten Commandments of Mount Sinai were a real test of personal and social morality, focused in a covenant with a holy God. Yet it was possible to regard them as **laws** to be outwardly **obeyed**, rather than an **inner** quality of life outwardly **expressed**.

The writer to the Hebrews, however, is intensely personal. Judgement is in a sense self-judgement: it is coming to the great joyful gathering of heavenly spirits centred on Jesus, and finding that we do or do not **belong**. Jesus more simply had said – You did not see me on earth among the poor and needy. You cannot belong to me now.

✶ *Let us be thankful, then, because we receive a kingdom that cannot be shaken. Let us be grateful and worship God in a way that will please him, with reverence and awe; because our God is indeed a destroying fire.*

Hebrews 12.28-29

What will endure? A gospel summary

On our road to what endures, we find Paul building on many of the enduring things which we have noted.

'Paul ... chosen and called by God' (verse 1). Paul is another of those *leaders* on whom God's enduring mission rests.

'Promised long ago by God through his *prophets* (verse 2a). See 2 Corinthians 1.20 – 'He (Jesus) who is the 'yes' to all God's promises.' 'Written in the *Holy Scriptures*' (verse 2b) – the Old Testament is still true for Paul.

'Our Lord Jesus Christ: as to his *humanity* ... (verse 3). See Ezekiel 3.15: 'I came to them of captivity ... and I sat where they sat' (AV). Jesus comes to us as one of ourselves.

'To lead people of *all nations*' (verse 5) – see Isaiah 49.6 '... not only the people of Israel ... but I will also make you a light to the nations'. The enduring line has come to its *fulfilment*. Paul concludes: 'I have complete confidence in the gospel; it is God's power to save all who believe, first the Jews and also the Gentiles' (verse 16).

✳ *In the past, God spoke to our ancestors many times and in many ways through the prophets, but in these last days he has spoken to us through his Son. He is the one through whom God created the universe, the one whom God has chosen to possess all things at the end. He reflects the brightness of God's glory and is the exact likeness of God's own being, sustaining the universe with his powerful word. After achieving forgiveness for the sins of mankind, he sat down in heaven at the right-hand side of God, the Supreme Power.* Hebrews 1.1-3

For further reflection or group discussion

Contemporary society tends to regard what we have called enduring qualities merely as pious, wishful thinking. How do we come to terms with this? Are we 'conformed to this world'?

FOR ACTION

Harness the belief in faith, hope and love to real involvement with people.

ADVENT 3 – The way of obedience

Notes based on the New Revised Standard Version by
Jane Ella Montenegro

Jane Montenegro, pastor of a mountain church in the Philippines, now engaged in the study of Asian feminist theology, was gripped by Christ's liberating gospel in the Martial Law period. She moved into Christian Education within and outside the Church, working in both urban and rural areas. She facilitates workshops on liturgical renewal, children's work, and the empowerment of women.

God's call to obedience is simple, but it is hard. It asks for fidelity. It can mean dying for the sake of God's justice and righteousness. The interplay of total obedience without questioning and the need for questioning before obeying is complex. This is the freedom God has given us. For Jesus obedience meant blessing the needy, and it led him to the cross. You and I have choices too: to obey Jesus which is costly but life-giving; or not to obey which means perpetuating the death-dealing forces of the world.

3rd Sunday in Advent, December 13   *Amos 7.10-17*
Disobedience angers God
These horrifying texts of doom were prophesied as a consequence of Israel's disobedience to God, and they are still relevant.

Let us look at affluent countries today initiating economic global development and its effects on their most vulnerable citizens. In the USA, thousands shiver in winter for lack of food, clothing and heat. In Japan, hundreds of employees sleep on rented bed space by shifting hours. In Europe, millions are unemployed. And yet these are countries which control the world's economy. In the developing world, peasants cannot afford to eat three times a day, their children are unschooled, young girls are forced into prostitution. Yet their national Church leaders live in affluence.

Would that we become modern Amoses, wherever we are! For the rising and falling of civilizations reveal this tragic truth: every nation that forgets the God of its ancestors, that pursues power and gold, that exploits people who are poor, people with disabilities, children, young people and women, have always fallen to destruction.

✳ *Forgive us, O God, for our infidelity,*
   complacency and indifference.
   Shake us, this Advent time, that we may live justly
   and in righteousness with and among our neighbours.

Monday December 14   *2 Chronicles 24.17-22*

Obedience is costly

Today's reading highlights a lesser-known prophet in the days of King Joash, in the eighth century BC. Biblical history is replete with suffering and violence. Almost always it is connected with the people's forgetfulness of God.

Last century, three Filipino priests were executed for speaking against the corruption of the Spanish Church leaders. In 1980, Archbishop Romero of El Salvador was assassinated for championing the cause of the poor. Thousands of obscure priests, monks, nuns and lay people in Christian history have met violent deaths at the hands of rulers who acted like gods.

The Spirit of God enables ordinary men and women to endure, despite their natural fear; the Spirit gives them courage as they confront evil. No threat, harassment or bribery can shut their mouths, or stop them in their tracks. On their knees, they cry out to God. Lying prostrate, they sob before God. In front of Jesus' cross, they lift their hands, 'Be with us even today as we march in the rally.'

At this Advent time, we are reminded of God's demands for justice and righteousness. Zechariah's obedience to God and subsequent violent death haunts us once again.

✳ *O Spirit of God, forgive ...*
   When I fear that your call is not an easy one,
   fill me with courage and the spirit of obedience
   as I seek to tread dangerous paths
   toward justice, peace and righteousness. Amen

Tuesday December 15   *Luke 3.10-14*

Obedience is straightening

John the Baptist is scathing as he calls his nation to repentance. His personal and concrete approaches towards justice and mercy were very clear even to the common people.

Alas, in my country, where over 90% of the population is supposedly Christian, thousands in the cities remain hungry while

McDonalds and other restaurants throw away tons of left-over food; bundles of used clothing from rich countries are a source of brisk business, tax collectors receive 'under the counter' dealings and not a few military men are linked with kidnappings, drug syndicates and extortion. And now that consumerism and materialism have swallowed up the Christmas celebration with exchanging gifts, paid carolling, deducted salaries for Christmas parties, John's call to obedience means a complete change of our lifestyle.

While on field education from the Seminary some years ago, I remember going to a poor sector of the city bringing 'white gifts' of canned sardines and noodles. I was shocked then to see houses bare without Christmas trees or lanterns. I felt ashamed of the unnecessary extravagance of Christmas at the University Church where I worshipped.

✳ *Come, Spirit of God,*
come, spirit of John the Baptist,
that we may see your light.
In the darkness of our lives,
come, 'straighten' our crooked ways. Amen

Wednesday December 16   *Matthew 11.2-15 *C*

Obedience is to serve

John the Baptist's call for national repentance and his outspoken attack on immorality in the royal court resulted in imprisonment. Like countless 'prisoners of conscience', enduring isolation and brutality, he must have begun to question the underlying reasons for his ministry. Was he deluded? Was Jesus really the Christ? And so he sent his disciples to ask Jesus.

Jesus pointed to the unmistakable signs of the Kingdom in their midst. For Jesus, obedience to God's will did not mean acquiring an opulent residence or force of arms, but bringing healing and wholeness to people in need.

Jesus then challenged the crowd who followed. How did they respond to prophets like John? Did they think they could make him conform to their cosy lifestyle as a reed bends in the wind?

And what about ourselves? Do we also – when today's 'prophets' make uncomfortable challenges – try to justify our well-established ways?

✳ *Lord, give us churches that will not merely comfort*
the afflicted,
But afflict the comfortable;

Churches that will not only love the world,
But will judge the world;
Churches that will not only pursue peace,
But will also demand justice;
Churches that will not pass by on the other side,
When wounded humanity is waiting to be healed;
Churches that will not only call us to worship,
But also send us out to witness;
Churches who will follow Christ,
Even when the way points to a cross.
　　　From Your Will Be Done (Christian Conference of Asia)

Thursday December 17　　　　　　　　　　*Matthew 1.18-25 *C*

Obedience may mean 'no questions asked'

She was gentle, firm and aglow with life. The second time he met her, he decided he would ask her to be his wife. His parents would be happy. He was already thirty; it was time he raised his own family. But the neighbours warned him. 'She is pregnant. Can't you see? She went around with another man before you came. And he just left her!'

He could not be moved. 'It doesn't matter. I love her and will marry her!' So his parents brought the dowry and blessed the marriage. Four years later, they have another child. He has not doubted his choice, and they are happy.

In a Filipino community, marriages are not unusual in these circumstances. The bridegroom becomes an *el salvador*, the saviour of a woman's humiliating predicament. Initially, many eyebrows are raised. But the community soon forgets and accepts.

Reflect on this story together with the example of Joseph.

✳ *Forgive me, O God,*
when my judgements are more harsh than your love.
Grant me the gift of discernment
that I may know the difference
between the pettiness of local attitudes and custom
and the quality of love.
So help me, like Joseph, to make your love known.

Friday December 18　　　　　　　　　　　*Luke 1.26-38*

Questions before obedience

Christian tradition has regarded Mary as the model woman: dutiful, submissive and obedient to the Lord. But Mary had a critical mind. Being a young woman and engaged to be married, she must have grown sensitive to the teasing of men-folk. Her face must have betrayed a negative reaction to what the angel Gabriel said. She must have raised questions: 'Who are you? I do not know you and you do not even know me. How can you say that?'

So Gabriel assured her of the purpose of his visit. Again Mary's mind was active. She was not naive. She did not obey blindly. She questioned more: 'How can this be, since I am a virgin? What will my parents – my male relatives say? What will I tell my women friends? I am engaged already. How can I bring shame on Joseph, to his family? Will I still have the face to remain a part of my own community? Won't I be stoned by the male elders?'

The angel Gabriel convinced her that God's Spirit was at work in her life, that her child would be 'holy', no less than the Son of God. Only then did Mary obey.

✳ *O God, grant me the courage*
to be critical of things that I cannot understand.
Help me to become like Mary – questioning if need be –
then obeying according to your will. Amen

Saturday December 19   *Luke 14.25-33*

Obedience is giving up

She left Manila, her home city, family and native language to embrace the ministry of Jesus. She taught Christian Education in the Seminary, facilitated liturgical renewal workshops in all age-groups and empowered ministers in continuing theological education. She hiked mountains, reaching out to nurture lay preachers in their village settings. She inspired women to think out their own theology. Upon retirement, her family gave her a beautiful house in a pleasant, middle-class residential area. They thought she would stay there.

Yet today she is back in the province, accepting a small rural church assignment with a meagre honorarium. She lives in a small room devoid of her precious books and treasures of a lifetime. Her heart bleeds for a poor child who could not go to nursery school, a domestic servant who is overworked and paid a pittance, a university she loves threatened by a Faculty strike. This Advent she struggled not to visit her well-to-do sisters and brothers, fearing the temptations of their gifts. How her heart is torn apart!

❋ *Thank you, God, that in my life and this Christmas*
you lead me to encounter people
who try to follow the way of Jesus.
For honestly, these hard words of Jesus are not easy to
live by.

For further reflection or group discussion
- Where do we find the forces of evil working most strongly in our society today?
- Where do we find life-giving forces at work?
- How are we nurturing children, young people and families to follow the way of Jesus?

FOR ACTION
Pack a parcel of food and give it to a destitute person or family.

CHRISTMAS –
Christ comes to save

Notes based on the Good News Bible by
Peter W Millar

*Peter Millar, minister of the Church of Scotland and member of
the Iona Community, is Warden of Iona Abbey. He and his wife
Dorothy served for many years with the Church of South India,
and together have written on a wide variety of subjects.*

It was a special honour to reflect on these Advent and post-
Christmas readings, many of which are so familiar. Yet every time
we read them, new insights reveal themselves.

The Iona Community, through its ministry at Iona Abbey, is
welcoming each year many thousands of people from every part
of the world. Some come as committed Christians, while others
are seekers. Surely we are all pilgrims – whether to Iona or in our
own situations. And perhaps these Christmas readings illumine in
a particular way some dimensions of our contemporary so-
journing. I certainly think so, and I hope you do too.

4th Sunday in Advent, December 20   *Luke 2.1-7 *C*
God beside us
The coming of Jesus into our world is an overwhelming mystery,
yet so firmly a part of human experience and history. On the one
hand, we are amazed by the sheer ordinariness of the event: this
small, unknown family going about their business, like millions
upon millions of other hidden families down through the centuries.
And on the other, and with the eyes of faith, we can truly say,
without exaggeration, that this is the greatest story ever told: God
revealing himself to human experience in the least expected way.

Nicholas Zernov wrote: 'God always approaches us beneath
and we must stoop to meet him.' Stooping to meet Jesus is a
wonderfully life-giving image. And for me it raises the question –
Can we enter into this mystery in any meaningful way without first
offering to him our own fragmentation and vulnerability? Laying
before him our broken lives and myriad hopes; discovering again,
or perhaps for the first time, that we have to bend low, get down
on our knees, to see this infant lying in an obscure manger. To

experience in our hearts and minds God alive at the hidden centre of human burden.

＊ *Lord, you came into our world in such an ordinary place. May we discover you, each day, in the ordinary events of life.*

Monday December 21   *Luke 2.8-20 *C*

God of surprises

I have always been enthused and challenged by the idea of an 'upside-down Kingdom' – a place where the powerless and forgotten are given front seats. And here in this passage we have a glorious illustration of God's surprising moves.

It was the shepherds, we are told, who glimpsed the angel. Yes, the shepherds, a group of folk who were on the margins of local society. They were in some ways a despised group who, because of their work with the flocks, were often unable to keep their ceremonial commitments in the Temple. They would never have been among Bethlehem's movers and shakers. Yet it was to them – folk right out on the edge – that this extraordinary reality was revealed. At first, they were absolutely terrified, as we would have been, but they listened and understood. And they journeyed to Bethlehem full of wonder. On meeting with Mary and Joseph, they reported that astonishing message and then moved back into obscurity.

This encounter has much to say to us today as we seek to discern God's presence in our divided and violent world. Is it not through the lives of those we so easily label as 'poor' or 'marginalized' that God is working his contemporary miracles?

God is always a God of surprises, and his light is shining forth from countless places marked by poverty. An upside-down Kingdom in our midst. Have we eyes to see it?

＊ *God of surprises, you appear to those we imagined were on the margins, and we ask for humility and insight to see your Kingdom in the hidden places of our world.*

Tuesday December 22   *Luke 2.21-24*

Life as an offering to God

When we lived in South India, my wife and I often had the privilege of being in Hindu temples. The great religions of the world have much to learn from each other, and one thing that always struck me powerfully in these ancient, vast, crowded and prayer-filled temples was the unchanging nature of the rituals. Through the generations minor details had altered, but the essential structures remained intact through countless centuries.

In this part of Luke's Gospel, we stand alongside Mary and Joseph in a timeless Jewish ritual – glimpsing, even momentarily, the faith which moulded and nurtured them – presenting their child to the Lord. We see them moving through the three ancient ceremonies which every Jewish male underwent: circumcision, the redemption of the first-born, and the purification of the mother.

We may not fully identify with such particular Jewish traditions, but as we think of Mary and Joseph and their child in the Temple, let us revisit the truth behind the ceremonies – that every child is a gift from the hand of the Lord. And if that is true, then let us also struggle and fight for global justice in a world where so many of God's children are dying of starvation. Every child, in every place, is truly a gift from God.

✷ *Lord, help me today to revisit*
that ancient and enduring truth
that life on earth is an offering to you.

Wednesday December 23   *Luke 2.25-35*

An expectant heart

Many years ago, before leaving Scotland for India, a wise friend reminded me that God had been in India for thousands of years. How true. The profound and engaged faith of Indian families is something which makes a westerner like myself very humble. It's not a superficial faith in God, or a disconnected 'Sunday religion', but rather a knowledge that all of life, and indeed all of the created order, is enfolded in God's purpose and light. As one Hindu Scripture puts it, 'The very twinkling of eyes are counted by God.' What a marvellous insight into God's nature!

And in the same way, Simeon knew God, not just at an intellectual level, but in a way which possessed his soul and set it ablaze. Who would not be moved by this account of the old man of faith taking the infant in his arms and giving thanks to God? His eyes, his heart, his mind – everything in Simeon – had, in that moment of illumination, experienced God's saving love in Christ.

Annie Dillard in her book *Pilgrim at Tinker's Creek* (© Bantam Books, 1975), captured this reality brilliantly when she wrote:

'You don't pursue grace with baited hooks and nets. You wait for it, empty-handed, and you are filled ... you catch grace as a person fills their cup under a waterfall.'

✳ *God of the ages and of today,*
help us to wait with patient hearts as Simeon did,
before he held you in his arms.

Christmas Eve, December 24   Luke 2.36-40

A prophetic word

In a truly wonderful and beautiful way, both Simeon and Anna open up for us new dimensions of the Gospel story. And on this Christmas Eve, let us pause to think about folk like them – women and men of deep faith – within our local communities; witnesses for the gospel in our own time; people of profound faith, engaged spirituality, wide vision, deep prayer and basic loving kindness – the pilgrims, prophets and visionaries whom we need more than ever in our often self-absorbed societies.

George MacLeod, who in 1938 founded the modern Iona Community was, like Columba before him, both a visionary and a prophet whose ministry touched literally thousands of lives. He saw clearly that in the twentieth century, the message of the gospel must continually permeate and revitalize everyday experience, if Christianity is to be a living, energizing force. That means that our work and our worship are inseparable: that prayer and the commitment to justice are interconnected, and that all creation reflects the glory of God.

All over the world, people are now searching for a faith which can relate to the multiple voices of our time with meaning, hope and authenticity. There is no place in the modern world for 'cheap grace'. Anna and Simeon remind us of the ancient, yet still relevant, disciplines of fasting and prayer: of self-denial and of costly obedience to the divine will.

On Christmas Eve, as we await the coming of the Saviour, we recommit ourselves to this pilgrim path which is marked by self-surrender and mutual accountability. As Ed de la Torre from the Philippines said, 'If we are to be lights for Christ in the world, then we must be prepared to endure the burning.'

✳ *Lord, on this Christmas Eve,*
give your Church on earth the courage to walk your
*   path*
in obedience and costly service.

The morning of joy

✳ *Don't hide;*
Don't run,
But rather
Discover in the midst of life
A new way forward;
A Christmas journey
Sometimes marked by
Fragility and tears.
And on that road
To hold these hands
That even in their brokenness
Create a new tomorrow.
To dance at the margins,
And to see
The face of Christ
Within the beauty
and complexity
of our time.
To be touched anew
by this miracle
of Christmas;
God with us –
enfolding our journeys
on this morning of joy.
Transforming our vision,
healing our pain,
and
renewing, in love,
the slender, yet vibrant threads
of our devotion.

Saturday December 26   *Galatians 4.1-11*

The word of acceptance

Post-modern society in the western world is characterized by a search for personal freedom, as the many movements for liberation testify. Some of Paul's words here remind us of the faith which can move into freedom – a liberation that comes from our knowledge that we are accepted and made whole in the Father's love.

My pastoral work at Iona Abbey has made me acutely aware of the difficulties we all face as we seek to 'let go and let God'.

Within our technological societies, there are enormous pressures to be 'in control' of life. Indirectly and directly the message comes over that there must be something wrong with us if we need to turn to God for 'help'. We find it a hard task to admit our own vulnerability.

The late Henri Nouwen, whose writings have challenged so many hearts and minds, once wrote, 'My only real temptation is to doubt in God's love; to think of myself as beyond that love; to remove myself from the healing radiance of Christ's presence. To do these things is eventually to move into the darkness of despair' (*Seeds of Hope,* © Darton, Longman and Todd Ltd., 1989).

Each new day, Christ offers us this amazing word of acceptance, if only we can take time to hear his still small voice amid the frenetic busyness of our lives. The understanding that we are truly and utterly 'free in Christ' comes through our listening, through our prayers, through our meditation.

The inner journey into freedom demands much of us, and it can be an uncomfortable path. Yet as Paul wrote in his letter to the church in Rome, 'The Spirit comes to help us in our weakness.' It does, and through its guiding we move into a new freedom.

✳ ***Thank you, Lord, that your Spirit is in my heart.***

For further reflection or group discussion

In this week's readings, with whose circumstances can you identify most – with Mary, Joseph, the shepherds, Anna, or Simeon? Reflect again on the story of the person or group you have chosen. What challenge does this make to your life now?

1st Sunday after Christmas, December 27   *John 1.29-34*

The Lamb of God

Here is John the visionary, seeing ahead, preparing the way and speaking from the heart, and in these words, moving far beyond the popular ideas of Jesus into an inner, and spiritual understanding of his forthcoming ministry. He witnesses to Jesus as the 'Eternal Word of God' – the bearer of life upon whom the Spirit has come down – the Light of the world: the sun behind all suns. John points us to a vast canvas and we can scarcely take it in.

For several years I have had the privilege of living on the sacred island of Iona. It is one of the great places of Christian prayer in our world. Geologists tell me that the rock formations on the island are probably around 2700 million years old. They are among the oldest in Europe.

As I read this passage, the thought comes to me that it may take that amount of time to understand the mystery of Christ. The Church believes that ultimately all things will come together in Christ, and I too firmly believe that deeply. Yet that moving into Christ may take millions of years. We may just be at the start of the Christian experience – even after 2000 years.

John the visionary glimpsed something of this greatness of Jesus. 2000 years is but the twinkling of an eye against the back-cloth of creation. The rocks of Iona remind us of this, but they also tell us, as does John, that we are encountering a truly great God who revealed himself, so amazingly, in Christ.

✱ *Set our hearts on fire with love to you, O Christ,*
despite our limited understanding of your eternal purpose.

Monday December 28   *John 1.35-51*

The moment of calling

Writers and poets tell us that Jesus called 'ordinary' people to be his disciples. As we read the Gospels that fact comes over again and again. Andrew, Simon and the others were ordinary folk – individuals just trying to get on with their lives, like the rest of us. They were addressed by Jesus where they were, and as they were. This in itself is comforting and healing for it indicates, in a particular and prophetic way, that the message of the gospel is directly connected to the often mundane routines of each day.

I have always liked these words of Mother Teresa of Calcutta: 'God does not call us to be extraordinary people, but ordinary people with an extraordinary love in our hearts.' And it is exactly this kind of 'extraordinary love' radiating from the lives of 'ordinary' people that is such an authentic and powerful witness to the gospel in our time.

Jean Vanier, co-founder of the international L'Arche communities, has experienced this in his daily work of standing in solidarity with intellectually handicapped women and men. He says, 'The weak ones of our society have taught me so much. They have shown me what it is to live simply, to love tenderly, to speak in truth, to pardon, to receive openly, to be humble in weakness, to be confident in difficulties and to accept handicaps and hardships with love' (*Community and Growth* – Darton, Longman and Todd Ltd. and used by permission).

Our calling is to be a witness for Christ where we are, not where we may like to be, or where we sometimes think we should be, but right on our doorstep in the midst of many contradictions and many false starts.

✳ *Lord, can I be ready in your moment of calling?*

Tuesday December 29   *John 6.60-71*

On the pilgrim way

As she lay dying of cancer, a Christian woman wrote: 'Lord, let my last act be a willed acceptance of Thy will for me.' At many levels, this is a remarkable prayer and was clearly composed by a person who, as they say in my native Scotland, was 'far ben' in the faith. A 'willed acceptance' of Christ's purpose for my life – however hard the road – is truly a gift of the Holy Spirit. It is an intentional act of the mind as we seek to move closer to the one who is always calling us 'home'.

In the Abbey of Iona, we sing these lines:

'Take my talents, take my skills,
Take what's yet to be;
Let my life be yours, and yet
Let it still be me.'

Realizing our full (if often hidden) potential in Christ, while remaining sensitive to our own unique talents and insights, is a challenge. It is hardly surprising that the first disciples found it difficult to keep on the pilgrim way. I find it often overwhelming!

Like the disciples, we need one another on this path – sometimes stumbling, often falling down, invariably uncertain and questioning. One sign of our times is that many are interested in exploring the whole idea of 'Christian community' – its meaning and its direction.

Within the Iona Community, we account to one another for the use of our money and our time. We are also committed to each other through a spiritual discipline and through our belief that worship and life are inseparable. I do not think it is possible to be a 'solitary Christian'. We need not be members in a formal sense of a body like the Iona Community, but God does call us to mutual accountability. The pilgrim path is always a shared journey.

✳ *Lord, in our churches and communities*
 reveal to us new ways of discipleship
 and of living together.

Christ within

'The law on our hearts' – deep within: Chandran Devanesan was a close Indian friend for whom I had immense respect. He carried within himself that radiant serenity which marks much of Eastern spirituality. Chandran's prayer – expressed in words of great beauty – underlined an aspect of the New Covenant mentioned here in the letter to Hebrews:

'O Thou
who hast given me eyes
to see the light
that fills my room,
give me the inward vision
to behold Thee in this place.'

Inward vision is that reality of Christ's Spirit etched in our hearts, the image of God touching into every part of our being.

I think I am not alone in being tempted to see Christ apart from our liturgies and traditions, some of which are increasingly and tragically a source of division rather than of healing and renewal. Yet in the silence of our hearts, we are drawn back, time after time, to this inner light.

Brother Roger of Taizé put it so engagingly when he said, 'Nothing can be built up within you without this adventure – finding Christ in the intimacy of a personal encounter. No one can do that for you.'

✳ ***Lord, how glad we are that we don't hold you,***
   but that you hold us.   *Prayer from Haiti*

Renewing strength

These are magnificent words of hope as we come – as sojourners in Christ – to the year's ending. In the Good News Bible, the heading for this particular passage is 'The Lord's good-ness to Israel'.

This theme of God's constant love and mercy, his protecting power and presence, are threads which run deep within our Celtic inheritance. The encircling grace of the Lord surrounding every moment and every action, and a God of infinite compassion bring to mind this prayer from the Iona Community whose words can give fresh strength as we move into another year and reflect upon an old one.

✴ *Come Lord Jesus, be our guest,*
stay with us for another year is ending.
With friend, with stranger,
With young and with old,
Be among us tonight.
Come close to us that we may come close to you.
Forgive us that we may forgive one another.
Renew us, through your life-giving Spirit
So that where we have failed
We may begin again.   © *Iona Community*

Renewed in love, moving forward into light, our God is with us. We are never alone. We grasp again that outstretched hand and, not for the first time, know that we are held.

For further reflection or group discussion

Reflect on the symbolism of the drawing below, of the way in which you are held within the love of God the Father, Son and Holy Spirit, and of our dependence upon one another in the world and within the local community and church.

FOR ACTION

How are you challenged by Mother Teresa's words quoted in Monday's notes? How will you try to make them a reality in 1999?

MORE
LIVING PRAYERS
FOR TODAY
Compiled by Maureen Edwards

This anthology, a companion volume to *Living Prayers for Today*, focuses on the Christian festivals and includes some prayers for everyday use. The collection reflects the rich variety of insights so characteristic of IBRA's annual publications. It expresses a strong sense of God's love for the world and each person in it. Through many of the prayers, God, ever-present, suffering and celebrating with all peoples, challenges us to translate our concern into action.

'A prayer from Sri Lanka speaks of water falling on dry tea-leaves and bringing out their flavour – many of the prayers in this book did that for me!'
Revd Dr Kathleen Richardson OBE, Moderator, Free Church Federal Council

UK price £11.99

Order through your IBRA representative or from the appropriate address on the front cover.

LIVING PRAYERS
FOR TODAY
Compiled by Maureen Edwards

Living Prayers for Today is the first in a new series of prayer anthologies from the International Bible Reading Association. It gathers together well-known prayers from the past with prayers of today from different parts of the world.

These prayers for all occasions are 'user friendly' to individuals, groups and churches. The prayers reflect insights that are both refreshing and challenging to our own spiritual development. They articulate feelings and longings we often find hard to express.

Includes suggestions of 'something to do and think about' at the beginning of each section of the book.

UK price £11.99

IBRA

Order through your IBRA representative or from the appropriate address on the front cover.

For House Groups
Four Studies on
THE OPEN BOOK

Notes by
ROSEMARY WASS

These studies are based on the notes on *The Open Book* (pages 9 – 35). They are an example of other studies for house groups in IBRA's book *Finding Our Way Together*. Do try it with your group.

Study 1 Celebrate the stories

AIM

To explore, enjoy and celebrate the richness of narrative in the Bible.

Preparation

1. *It will be helpful for the leader to prepare a comfortable atmosphere; lighting, hospitality, and the placing of chairs so that every member of the group can have mutual eye contact, are important for this to happen.*
2. *Please have a supply of paper and pens available.*
3. *Before the meeting, the leader will need to think of a well-known Bible story and think carefully of the details that will remind others of it.*

Way in

Encourage members to think back to their childhood and focus on one incident, perhaps related to family life, or church life, or education, or even a dream, and then share it with another member of the group.

- Could we each relate to the other stories?
- Did it remind us of something else in our own lives?

Telling a story

1. Tell the group that you are going to begin to tell a well-known Bible story, and invite others to continue its telling. You will need to sense when it will be appropriate to invite the group to reveal which story it is. The actual story may be discovered quickly, but continue the telling for the whole of it with as many participating as possible.

297

When the story has been told, invite members to locate (from memory) the narrative in the Bible, insisting on the precise location! Encourage everyone to sit and read the story quietly.

- How accurately was the story told?
- Do different versions of the Bible portray a variety of emphases to the same narrative?
- Are there contemporary stories from our own culture which might complement the shared story? Do not be afraid to take time to think carefully about this and then have a time of sharing.

2. Supply people with a sheet of paper and a pen, and invite them to make a list of their favourite biblical stories. Share the lists by having one contribution per person and keep going round the group until all have been named.

- Was there a clear favourite?
- Why would that particular story have that honour?
- What are the special elements of this/these stories.
- What purposes do you think the writers of the stories had in telling them? E.g. to make a point, a surprise element, to help people relate, to make people think and come to decisions themselves, to disclose a truth, as a protest to what was happening ...

3. People may like to work in pairs and think of examples of specific categories of the narratives set for the week.

- What does this tell us about communication?
- Do you think that these forms of communication will continue to be as relevant for the next millennium?

PRAYER/REFLECTION

To close the session, the leader may invite another member of the group to read again the story they began with, then have a time of quiet followed by open prayer to celebrate the gift of vivid and helpful narrative that has stood the test of time.

Study 2 Celebrate poetry

AIM

To celebrate the beauty of poetry through psalms and poems.

Preparation

Invite members to select a piece of poetry which is special to them, and a favourite psalm to share with the group.

The leader will chair this session to weave together the readings and thoughts of members, remembering that poetry is about concentrated word pictures and expression.

Introductory exercise

Encourage each group member to share an item of celebration during this past week, e.g. a birth, an award, a birthday, an anniversary, good news of some sort, even life itself.

The appeal and challenge of poetry

1. Agree an appropriate procedure for the meeting, e.g. to listen to one another's favourite poem or hymn, and reasons the members wish to share.

2. You may choose to have a short break then, and/or a drink.

3. Then share your favourite psalms and poetry of the Bible, reading to one another the verses which mean most to you.

4. Finally read one of the passages of the week which has not already been chosen, and reflect on the insights which touch your experience.

ACTION

Choose one psalm to share within an act of worship the following Sunday and read it chorally with the congregation.

Conclude your meeting with the following poem:

The Sharing

We told our stories
That's all
We sat and listened to each other
And heard the journeys of each soul.
We sat in silence
Entering each one's pain and sharing each one's joy.
We heard love's longing and the lonely reaching-out
For love and affirmation.
We heard of dreams shattered. And visions fled.
Of hopes and laughter turned stale and dark.
We felt the pain of isolation and the bitterness of death.

But in each brave and lonely story
God's gentle life broke through ...
And we heard music in the darkness
And smelled flowers in the void.

We felt the budding of creation
In the searchings of each soul
And discerned the beauty of God's hand in
Each muddy, twisted path.

And God sang in each story.
God's life sprang from each death.
Our sharing became one story of a simple lonely search
For life and hope and oneness
In a world which sobs for love.
And we knew that in our sharing
God's voice with mighty breath
Was saying ...
Love each other and take each other's hand.

For you are one though many
And in each of you I live.
So listen to my story and share my pain and death
Oh, listen to my story
And rise and live with me.

From Psalms of a Laywoman by Edwina Gateley
(published by Source Books, California, USA)

Study 3 Celebrate history

AIM

To celebrate our Christian history and history within our own lifetime.

Preparation

Encourage group members to spend some time looking at old diaries and/or photographs that they may have, or to reflect on significant points of history in their own lives. Some members may have family trees or family Bibles which they might like to bring and share with the group.

Changes all around us

In pairs,

- reflect on important personal historical events, sharing from the diaries and family albums you have brought;
- think of important advances which are now history, even within our lifetime, e.g. computer technology and the impact on communications, transport, household aids, electrical equipment and forms of heating in our homes, medicine and longer life expectancy in many parts of the world, space travel and environmental implications ...

Biblical reflection

Divide into pairs and ask each pair to read one of the passages of the week. Together as a group share with one another the changes which would have come about as a result of each of the significant moments in history which is described.

- How important is it to understand our history?
- How far is it 'our story'?

Changes in the life of the Church

Encourage members to think of the historical advances of the Church within our respective denominations and ecumenically, trying to keep the emphasis on celebration. E.g. the place of women in the Church (1998 marks the close of *The Decade of Churches In Solidarity With Women*), social outreach, the missionary movement, the understanding of ministry within the Church and the relationship of lay and Presbyteral ministries ...

- Has the Church kept pace with the world's changes, e.g. in music, liturgy, participation, etc?
- What are the most exciting and important pieces of history so far for the members of the group?
- How significant will the dawning of the Millennium be to us all?

301

- How should the Church mark its coming?
- Will this be written into the history books for future generations?

PRAYER/REFLECTION

To bring the session to a close, light a candle as a focus and encourage members to think of individuals who have been a source of encouragement/introduction/nurture to them in their Christian pilgrimage. Following the opportunity for sharing, move into a time of open prayer celebrating the lives of those whose names are part of members' personal histories.

Close with the sharing of the Peace, reminding each other of the historical context in which Jesus promised Peace to his friends and disciples.

Study 4 Celebrate God's love

AIM

To take more time to think of and celebrate God's love for each one of us.

Preparation

You will need a Love-feast cup (or suitable alternative) and a jug of water.

Begin the session with an informal arrangement of chairs, and then for the Agape, move the chairs into a circle, with the jug and loving cup on a table in the centre.

Begin the session by inviting reflection on the 'celebrations' so far. Think of shared stories, poetry and history. Read together Hosea 11.1-4, 8-9; Isaiah 49.13-16; and John 3.1-17 and reflect on the meaning of these words in your lives.

- Do we take God's love for granted?
- Have the keynote readings this week heightened our awareness?
- Invite members to share the reading of Psalm 139 and to think of the assurance of God's love within it.

Agape - Love-feast

Now issue an invitation for members to participate in an *Agape*, a Love-feast, celebrating God's love for each of us. It is important to assure people that this is neither Holy Communion nor a substitute for it. It is a reflection of God's love for us, and thus our love for God and other people. The *Agape* stems from Jesus' summary of the law and the prophets by the double commandment: 'Love the Lord your God with all your heart, with all your soul, and with all your mind', and 'Love your neighbour as yourself'.

Arrange the chairs in a circle with the water and container in the centre. If possible play some reflective music, or have a time of quietness.

The cup of water is passed from one person to the other. A Love-feast cup usually has a handle on each side, so that the cup can be passed easily from one hand to another. As the person holds the cup, s/he takes time to share his/her experience of God's love (*this should be unhurried with room for silence between each contribution*).

You may like to suggest a phrase with which the contribution can be brought to a close, such as 'For the gift of this love to me', so that all can respond with 'Thanks be to God'. When the person has spoken, s/he takes a drink of the water, and then passes the cup to the next person, and so on around the circle.

PRAYER

To bring this celebration to a close:
The cup of water given for thee
   Still holds the freshness of thy grace;
Yet long these multitudes to see
   The strong compassion of thy face.

Frank Mason North (1850-1935)

BLESSING

Go in peace, go in love, finding joy in each other.
Go in peace, go in love, in Christ we're sister and
   brother.
Led by His Spirit, there's strength each day.
Light for the way. Together go in love, go in peace.
And may God be with us forever. Amen   *Anonymous*
From Celebrating Together (Corrymeela Press)

ACTION

This section of four studies on *The Open Book* reminds us of the wealth of insights and the relevance of the Bible to our lives. How will we share this with others? We hope you will continue as a group to use our book *Finding Our Way Together*. Copies can be ordered from your local bookseller, or direct from IBRA (price £4.99).

● It can be used alongside the themes in *Words for Today* and *Light For Our Path*, and by groups who may not use either.
● It provides a variety of material from which to select what is appropriate to meet the needs of your group.
● We believe it is an excellent way to encourage groups and fellowships to study the Bible together.
● It is enjoyable and challenging!